DANGEROUS ENTHUSIASM

£ 30

TH COLLEGE OF HIGHER EDUCATION
(S n Hill)

DANGEROUS ENTHUSIASM

William Blake and the
Culture of Radicalism
in the 1790s

JON MEE

CLARENDON PRESS · OXFORD

1992

Oxford University Press, Walton Street, Oxford OX2 6DP
Oxford New York Toronto
Delhi Bombay Calcutta Madras Karachi
Petaling Jaya Singapore Hong Kong Tokyo
Nairobi Dar es Salaam Cape Town
Melbourne Auckland
and associated companies in
Berlin Ibadan

Oxford is a trade mark of Oxford University Press

Published in the United States
by Oxford University Press, New York

British Library Cataloguing in Publication Data
Data available

Library of Congress Cataloging in Publication Data
Mee, Jon.
Dangerous enthusiasm : William Blake and the culture of radicalism
in the 1790s / Jon Mee.
Includes bibliographical references and index.
1. Blake, William, 1757–1827—Political and social views.
2. Politics and literature—Great Britain—History—18th century.
3. Revolutionary literature, English—History and criticism.
4. France—History—Revolution, 1789–1799—Influence.
5. Radicalism—Great Britain—History—17th century.   6. Radicalism
in literature.   7. Prophecies in literature.   I. Title.
PR4148.P6M44   1992
821'.7—dc20   92–11156
ISBN 0–19–812226–8

Typeset by Cambridge Composing (UK) Ltd.,
Printed and bound in
Great Britain by Biddles Ltd.,
Guildford and King's Lynn.

To my parents
and Michelle

Nothing can be more contemptible than to suppose
Public RECORDS to be True   Read them & Judge. if
you are not a Fool.

William Blake

Preface

THE 1790s of the title refers both to the radical context and the texts produced by Blake discussed in that context. The majority of references will be to works completed by Blake in the 1790s (though they continued to be reissued by him afterwards) together with some reference to the unfinished *The Four Zoas*, begun around 1796, the annotations from the later part of the decade, and some of the commercial engraving work undertaken by Blake at the same time. It is widely assumed that the nature of Blake's poetic enterprise changed around 1800. My decision to stop at that year does not reflect any belief on my part that his poetry and designs reneged on their radical commitment thereafter; rather I am seeking to offer a fuller understanding of Blake's most explicitly radical period which can form a firmer basis for judgements about the politics of Blake's works after 1800. Some critics even offer *The Book of Urizen*, first published in 1794, as the site of such a retreat; as my penultimate chapter makes clear, I strongly disagree with this reading.

I am deeply indebted to the universities at which I have studied: Newcastle upon Tyne, Cambridge, and Oxford. No less to a series of searching and generous teachers at both secondary and tertiary level. These include Graeme Balham, Linda Standen, Bob White, Claire Lamont, Graham McGregor, Heather Glen, and Marilyn Butler. John Kerrigan together with John and Mary Ann Hughes, Nick Merriman, and Soran Reader helped me enormously while I was at Cambridge. I should also thank the Principal and Fellows of Jesus College, Oxford, who elected me to the Junior Research Fellowship which I used to write the book. John Walsh and David Womersley directly contributed advice and ideas. I have been fortunate to encounter the encouragement and patience of a series of very generous people at Oxford, especially Becky Abrams, David Eastwood, Suzanne Farrell, Denis Flanery, David Goldie, Debbie Goldie, Phillip Gorski, Paul Hamilton,

Jerry Johnson, Menno Lievers, Suzanne Matheson, David Nor-
brook, Paul O'Flynn, Simon Palfrey, Roy Park, Ann Ross,
Sarah Squire, Marcus Wood, and Chris Wright. Mark Philp
and Sarah Turvey have frequently provided food for both body
and mind, though Mark inflicted some terrible damage on the
squash courts. In addition, I owe thanks to Steve Clarke, Robert
Essick, and David Worrall. The librarians at the Cambridge
University Library, the Bodleian, and the English Faculty
Library at Oxford have been marvellous. Thanks to Vera, Tina,
and Helen especially. Meeting Iain McCalman has proved to be
as enjoyable as reading his work. Parts of Chapter 1 have
appeared in the *British Journal for Eighteenth-Century Studies*; I
am grateful to the editor, Brean Hammond, for permission to
reproduce them here. The later stages of preparation for this
book have been made much easier by the support and encouragement of Ian Higgins, Ben Penny, and Gillian Russell. It goes
without saying that none of the above are responsible for any
of the infelicities or inaccuracies to be found in the following
pages.

J.M.

Contents

List of Illustrations

(*between pp 112–113*)

Abbreviations

BIQ	*Blake: An Illustrated Quarterly.*
BR	G. E. Bentley, Jr., *Blake Records.*
BRS	—— *Blake Records Supplement.*
CWP	*The Complete Writings of Thomas Paine*, ed. P. S. Foner, 2 vols.
'EV'	'The Economy of Vegetation', Part I of Erasmus Darwin's *The Botanic Garden.*
Ossian	*The Poems of Ossian*, trans. James Macpherson, 2 vols.
'LP'	'The Loves of the Plants', Part II of *The Botanic Garden.*
Mathias	Thomas Mathias, *The Pursuits of Literature: A Satirical Poem in Dialogue.*
PL	*Paradise Lost* in *Milton: Poetical Works.*
PWS	*The Political Works of Thomas Spence*, ed. Dickinson.

For publication details, see the bibliography.

A Note on Texts

ALL Blake quotations are from *The Complete Poetry and Prose of William Blake* (New York, revised edition, 1982) edited by D. V. Erdman, henceforth abbreviated as E followed by page number. References within the poems are given in the form of the plate (Pl.) or page number (p.), whichever applies, followed by the lines quoted.

All quotations from Milton's poetry are taken from *Milton: Poetical Works*, ed. Douglas Bush. The quotations from Coleridge's 'Religious Musings' are from the version first published in *Poems on Various Subjects* (1796), while those from Erasmus Darwin, Thomas Gray, Thomas Mathias, and Macpherson's translations of Ossian are from *The Botanic Garden* (1791), *Gray and Collins: Poetical Works*, ed. Roger Lonsdale, *The Pursuits of Literature* (1797), and *The Poems of Ossian*, respectively (see the bibliography for details).

Introduction: Blake the Bricoleur

FOR some time now Blake's affiliations with the radicalism of the 1790s have been recognized. From its earliest beginnings Blake biography offered accounts of his ardent support for the French Revolution. Frederick Tatham, writing in the 1830s, described him proudly wearing the cap of liberty and mixing with the radicals who circulated around the publisher Joseph Johnson. Another persistent anecdote, retold by biographers of both Blake and Paine, has been the story that he was instrumental in Tom Paine's escape from prosecution for treason. The latter tale is of dubious authenticity, but no anecdotal evidence is needed to evince the radical tendencies of works like *The Marriage of Heaven and Hell* (1790–3), *The French Revolution* (1791), and *America* (1793). In this book I want to argue that the radicalism of Blake's rhetoric in the 1790s is much more fundamental than is often recognized. His work can be shown to be steeped in political significances and to gain an extra dimension in the context of the controversy over the French Revolution. All this is not just a matter of references to contemporary events. Radical discourse is often operative in what may seem the most unlikely places and informs Blake's language at almost every level.[1]

Any historical approach to Blake has to address the weighty presence of David Erdman's *Blake: Prophet Against Empire*, originally published in 1954. It was this work which offered the first thoroughgoing account of Blake's deep involvement with his own time. Subsequent historical scholarship has generally been involved in following up leads offered by Erdman. That is no less true of this book. Yet, while acknowledging this debt, I would like to begin my own account of Blake's political rhetoric with a discussion of what I take to be some of the limitations of Erdman's approach.

My primary criticism is that Erdman has a tendency to identify the political dimension of the poetry and designs with

---

[1] The anecdotes mentioned are to be found in *BR*, 40 and 530.

the representation of historical events. This tendency means that, at its very outset, historicist Blake criticism underestimated the radical significance of the formal dimension of the works. Blake's formal practices have as much political significance as his representation of historical revolutions in poems like *The French Revolution* and *America*. What is intended here is not just a restatement of the truism that everything admits of a political reading. My point is that Blake's rhetorical practices operate across a consistent political topology. They do not offer the route to some irreducible and invariable ideology, but they can be shown to be part of a complex political perspective which is directly involved with the discourse of radicalism in the 1790s. The point extends to generic issues too. When Blake explicitly presented *America* and *Europe* (1794) as prophecies, he was placing them in relation to a particular sort of prophetic politics which, as I shall show in my next chapter, played a vigorous part in the Revolution controversy.

The potential dangers of Erdman's approach are perhaps clearest in relation to a poem like *The Book of Urizen* (1794), which, unlike *America* and *Europe*, is devoid of any explicit historical or political references. Since Erdman tends to identify political poetry with the representation of historical events, this absence has to signify either a retreat from the political domain or some kind of shadowing of history by an allegorical mythopoesis. Unlike many critics, Erdman, committed to a political reading of Blake, prefers the latter. There is much to recommend his powerful readings of the poems and designs, but his approach ironically makes it easier for those critics who wish to evacuate politics from the texts. What is quite explicit about *The Book of Urizen* is its biblical quality. Many critics gleefully light on the poem's parodic reworking of Genesis as evidence of a retreat from politics, but this only holds if we limit political signification to the mimesis of historical events. The experience of reading the poem is rather different if we recognize the centrality of the Bible to the Revolution controversy. *The Book of Urizen* then seems to become crucially involved in the critique, widespread amongst radicals in the 1790s, of the role of the Bible and its conventional exegetes in the maintenance of the social order.

In some respects then my approach amounts to an archaeology of reading; it includes an effort to seek out the encoded politics of Blake's rhetoric. But it is important to emphasize that my attempt to relate Blake's rhetorical practices to the larger patterns of the Revolution controversy is not an attempt to explain anything away. The chapters below aspire to an historical approach which does not close down but opens up the texts it addresses. Central to this endeavour will be my use of the notion of 'bricolage'; a term which implies diversity in the object of study and looks beyond the attempt merely to fix and limit texts within already unified intellectual traditions. I have developed my understanding of 'bricolage' from Claude Lévi-Strauss's discussion of the distinction between modern and primitive modes of thought in *The Savage Mind*. Lévi-Strauss identified the magical perspective of the latter with the 'bricoleur': 'someone who works with his hands and uses devious means comparable to those of a craftsman'. The response of the bricoleur to a problem is conditioned by 'a heterogeneous repertoire which, even if extensive, is nevertheless limited'. Lévi-Strauss contrasted the bricoleur's use of whatever diverse materials lay at hand with the situation of the engineer, the term he uses to denote a modern, scientific perspective. The engineer seeks to forge new tools to fit each specific task and envisages a language 'wholly transparent with respect to reality'. Crucial to my understanding of 'bricolage' is the fact that, although 'pre-constrained' by 'a heterogeneous repertoire', each time the bricoleur resorts to that language it involves 'a complete reorganization of the structures' that have been inherited. Acknowledging Derrida's point that all textual constructions (including those of the engineer) are always already formed by received languages, I shall be using 'bricolage' to denote an approach which unapologetically recombines elements from across discourse boundaries such that the antecedent discourses are fundamentally altered in the resultant structures.[2]

---

[2] See Lévi-Strauss's *The Savage Mind* (2nd edn., London, 1972), 16–20. Derrida discusses Lévi-Strauss's distinctions in *Writing and Difference* (London, 1978), 279–95.

The historian Iain McCalman has already made an important application of the notion of 'bricolage' in the historical and political milieux with which I am concerned.[3] He has shown how ultra-radicals in the period 1795–1840 produced a variegated political discourse that was an eclectic combination of a variety of received repertoires. These radical bricoleurs produced texts which do not easily fit into any single intellectual tradition, indeed they frequently drew on resources which might seem to the modern scholar to be mutually exclusive. McCalman's paradigmatic example is Thomas Spence, who had a long career as a radical activist. Spence began in Newcastle upon Tyne, where he formulated a theory of land reform and promoted it through cheap tracts and his own debating society. He moved to London, probably in the late 1870s, and became an early member of the London Corresponding Society, producing his own pamphlets, prints, tokens, and the serial *Pig's Meat* (1793–5) to promote the case for revolution. The variety of vehicles that Spence was prepared to use is paralleled in the disparateness of his rhetorical resources. He combined, among other things, the millenarian tendencies of popular enthusiastic culture with the scepticism we associate with the rationalist Enlightenment. Of particular importance to Spence from the latter current was C. F. Volney's *The Ruins* (English translation, 1792). Spence's *A Letter from Ralph Hodge, to his Cousin Thomas Bull* (1795), for instance, contains a dialogue between those whose 'labours support and nourish society' and 'the civil, military, and religious agents of government' which is taken almost word for word from Volney's book. In contrast, *A Fragment of an Ancient Prophecy* (1796) rejoiced in the utopian expectations of the millenarian popular culture, happily quoting the Bible to support its vision of post-revolutionary bliss: 'Then

---

[3] His paper at the 1990 Historicizing Blake Conference was an intriguing placement of Blake's work in the milieu of his *Radical Underworld* (Cambridge, 1988). The work done by the notion of bricolage in the following chapters could perhaps have been sustained by the Bakhtinian notion of heteroglossia, which similarly gives weight to a discursive eclecticism across social and discourse boundaries, but since this term tends to be used mainly in relation to the novel and given the precedents of McCalman's and Ronald Paulson's (see below, p. 8) use of bricolage, I have decided to retain the latter term.

shall the whole earth, as Isaiah saith, be at rest and in quiet; and shall break forth into singing; and they shall say, Now we are free indeed!' We are familiar with similar biblical aspects of Blake's work, but perhaps less ready to admit that strains of Volney's scepticism are also evident.[4]

McCalman's recognition of both of these elements in Spence's work has led him to place Spence within 'a long history of convergence between millenarian religious ideas and popular forms of scepticism and materialism'. Whatever the prehistory of that convergence it surfaces repeatedly in the 1790s. It is a recurrent feature of Daniel Isaac Eaton's *Politics for the People* (1793–5) and can also be traced in Paine's *Rights of Man* (1791–2), where a submerged millenarianism, built up through biblical allusions, is coexistent with a sturdy rationalism. The latter point is exemplified in one of Paine's many direct appeals to the reader: 'Lay then the axe to the root, and teach governments humanity.' What might seem to be a direct appeal to natural rights theory, calling for the clearing away of the impediments that have grown up to obscure the original state of liberty, is, in fact, couched in the language of the Bible (Matthew 3: 10): 'The axe is laid unto the root of the trees therefore every tree which burgeons not forth good fruit, is hewen down, and cast into the fire.' The flexibility of Paine's political rhetoric is demonstrated by his preparedness to turn to the language of popular religion at a point where he sought to appeal directly to the disenfranchised reader.[5]

Part of the complexity of Blake's work from the 1790s onwards stems from the fact that he drew on disparate discourses to create a bricolage which has features in common with the work of Spence, Paine, and other radicals. Initially, at least, two separate aspects of Blake's eclecticism can be identified. The first, which most closely equates to the notion of bricolage invoked above, is a matter of seemingly disparate discourses operating in a single text. The subsequent chapters

---

[4] See Spence, *A Letter*, 8–12, and *A Fragment of an Ancient Prophecy*, in *PWS*, 46. McCalman, *Radical Underworld*, discusses Spence's debts to Volney, pp. 24 and 66, and his popular millenarianism, pp. 63–7.

[5] See McCalman, *Radical Underworld*, 65, and Paine, *CWP*, i. 266.

of this book are organized around what I take to be four of these discourses. The first and longest chapter will offer an account of the enthusiastic aspects of the work Blake produced in the 1790s. In particular it will trace the relationship of his writing to popular traditions of millenarianism and antinomianism and the part these played in the Revolution controversy. Later chapters will discuss his use of more respectable discourses; literary primitivism, mythography, and, finally, scriptural criticism. Similarities with writers, such as John Toland and Joseph Priestley (and indeed Paine), whose rationalism is often presented as making them irrelevant to Blake studies will also be explored in these later chapters. As with Spence, what seem contradictory currents of rationalism and enthusiasm are assimilated in Blake's works.[6]

From such interactions between discourses Blake constructed a rhetoric that was alive with political resonances. At the same time he was also responding to developments which, especially in the intensely ideological decade of the 1790s, were already emergent in the discourses themselves. Biblical criticism, for instance, which might seem the very stuff of dry scholarship, was taken to be intimately involved with the ideological struggles of the Revolution controversy. The Bishop of Lincoln at least was convinced that the defence of the constitution necessitated the protection of the integrity of the Bible.

The same captious and restless spirit which leads men to cavil at the articles of our religious faith, and to reject the mysteries of the Gospel, because they surpass their comprehension, causes them to be dissatisfied with our civil constitution, and to represent its essential parts as useless and dangerous, because they do not agree with their own imaginary ideas of unattainable perfection.

   [6] The four discursive fields which form the basis of this account are not being presented as an exhaustive catalogue of Blake's rhetorical resources. His involvement, for instance, in the attitudes and concerns of the civic humanist tradition of history painting, recently discussed in John Barrell's *The Political Theory of Painting from Reynolds to Hazlitt* (London, 1987), might have been included. The critical relationship with Milton's poetry and its historical interpretations, which I discuss at various points, could have been treated as a participation in another distinct discourse with important political aspects.

Such suspicions were not just held of the directly political attacks on the scriptures made by Paine and Volney but also of innovative biblical scholarship which threatened to subject the text to rational investigation.[7]

Particular aspects of Blake's rhetoric can be linked with specific discourses in clear-cut ways. The second aspect of Blakian bricolage to which I want to draw attention is the facility with which it produced forms, plots, and figures which stand at significant confluences between discourses. Sometimes these confluences preceded Blake's own formulations. The association of the Celtic bard with the Hebrew prophet, for instance, was a well-established product of syncretic tendencies in literary primitivism, biblical studies, and historiography. But even given these larger trends, Blake seems to have taken a particular interest in such confluences, extending those which were already established, and evolving others which seem uniquely Blakian. A typical example is the complex referentiality of Blake's Tree of Mystery, which makes its first appearance in *The Book of Ahania* (1795). By placing the Tree in a context which links druidism with Christian priestcraft this configuration suggests, like Paine's *The Age of Reason* (1794-5), that Christianity perpetuated barbaric pagan practices. Perhaps less obviously, the image also takes up one of the most emotive and contentious configurations of the Revolution controversy. Burke had presented the British state as the product of an organic and legitimate evolutionary process; in doing so he gave new life to the traditional symbol of the English oak. For radicals this image of natural maturation was a mystification of 'the tree of feudal tyranny' which Paine sought to cut down and replace with the Tree of Liberty. The secret noxious growth of Blake's Tree of Mystery reveals his sense of the corrupt reality hidden by Burke's rhetoric. The point is made even more explicitly in the later works where the image transmutes into

---

[7] G. Pretyman-Tomline, *A Charge delivered to the Clergy of the Diocese of Lincoln* (London, 1794), 15-16. For a fuller discussion of the issues raised in this paragraph, see Ch. 4 below.

feudal tyranny

Ch 2

'Tyburn's fatal tree', the gallows on which the power of Burke's established order was most nakedly displayed.[8]

The organization of an account of Blake's rhetoric around the notion of bricolage provides for a dialectical approach. Aspects traceable to the issues and language of one discourse can also be made sense of in other discursive contexts so that simplistic notions of sources and influence have to be abandoned. Devoting chapters to separate contexts allows for the treatment of particular features of Blake's work from different perspectives. It can accommodate the fact that Blake's anticlerical scepticism admits both of rationalist antecedents and analogues and parallel responses from the populist culture of religious enthusiasm. Yet the notion of bricolage can be pushed beyond an heuristic efficacy in relation to Blake. Many writers involved in the Revolution controversy seem to have shared Blake's rhetorical eclecticism. Ronald Paulson's work on the representation of the Revolution has suggested that the response was necessarily 'a kind of bricolage'. The various new styles of verbal and visual representation which emerged in conjunction with the Revolution were made up from adaptations of received modes in what Paulson sees as an attempt to come to terms with the unprecedented nature of events in France. While Paulson does offer a valid model for much of the discourse of the Revolution, bricolage seems to me to be especially typical of popular radicalism. My point is not that it is a rigidly class-determined strategy, but that those barred from orthodox channels of knowledge and its transmission were particularly disposed to such a procedure.[9]

Ever since E. P. Thompson's *The Making of the English Working Class*, the unprecedented contributions of the disenfranchised lower classes, especially artisans and the petite bourgeoisie, have been seen as one of the most distinctive features of the Revolution controversy. Although there was a

---

[8] For a fuller discussion of Blake's development of this image, see Ch. 2. The phrase 'the tree of feudal tyranny' is taken from J. Gerrald's *A Convention the Only Means of Saving us from Ruin* (London, 1793), 89.

[9] See R. Paulson, *Representations of Revolution* (1789–1820) (New Haven, Conn., and London, 1983), 18.

popular political culture before the 1790s, it is clear that the
London Corresponding Society had amongst its members many
who were freshly involved in the political process with no
tested tradition of political discourse standing behind them. The
memoirs of activists like John Binns and Francis Place offer
evidence of the intellectual awakening experienced by many of
these newly involved radicals. It is scarcely surprising that
autodidacts and those without formal education were often
eclectic in their use of language and prepared to use received
protocols in unusual ways. Blake can be numbered among these
artisan radicals, though like Thomas Spence he had produced
politically aware writings prior to 1789. Not having encountered ideas in the aspic of sanctioned tradition, there was little
reason for such figures to write in terms of any homogeneous
academic discourse.

   T. S. Eliot recognized something of the relevance of this for
Blake when he wrote: 'We have the same respect for Blake's
philosophy . . . that we have for an ingenious piece of home-
made furniture; we admire the man who has put it together out
of the odds and ends of the house.' For Eliot, in search of a
culturally ratified, unitary tradition of poetry, it was a source of
lament that Blake had no available 'framework of accepted and
traditional ideas' in which to work. But Blake and many other
lower-class radicals of the 1790s rejoiced in their freedom from
such a framework. They found in the dominant culture a
variety of rhetorical resources which they sought to refashion
and recombine in challenging frameworks of their own. Blake
was not Eliot's 'naked man'. Along with figures like Spence
and Eaton, Blake took full advantage of the potential the
complex nexus of languages he inherited opened up for subversion and parody. Many radicals in the 1790s took up the role of
the bricoleur; they relished breaking down those discourses
which had cultural authority and creating from them new
languages of liberation. Blake's attachment to this poetic of
transgression receives one of its clearest statements in Plate 14
of his *The Marriage of Heaven and Hell*. There he wrote of his
'printing in the infernal method, by corrosives, which in Hell
are salutary and medicinal, melting apparent surfaces away, and

displaying the infinite which was hid' (E 39; Pl. 14). So taken have many critics been with the figural allusion to the engraving process which produced the Plate that they have often failed to give due weight to the fundamentally subversive nature of the method declared here.[10]

Blake's poetic is deeply concerned with the disruption and transformation of hegemonic discourses. Examples are legion. *Europe*, for instance, invokes and works through Milton's 'Ode on the Morning of Christ's Nativity', revealing Milton's deferral of 'truth and justice' to be a compromise with the 'allegorical' rewards and punishments of the religious establishment. More broadly, there are Blake's transvaluations and disruptions of biblical paradigms. What I want to emphasize here is that while these processes might seem to be spectacular examples of Blake's peculiar 'Poetic Genius', they are also typical of the strategies and priorities of a range of radical texts in the 1790s.

So far I have argued that bricolage is a striking feature of the organization of Blake's poetry, a feature shared by many whose writing responded to and was shaped by the Revolution controversy. Another quality common to many of the radical texts produced in the controversy (which might even be seen as an aspect of bricolage) was a preparedness to reuse the same material in different contexts. Thomas Spence, for instance, would print songs and ballads both in his serial *Pig's Meat* and circulate them on separate broadsides. Similarly, he would reproduce designs on token coins and individual prints. Much the same is true of Blake. His designs often appear both within the illuminated books and as separate prints or paintings. He was also never afraid to rework plots and images in different texts (and even within a single text). Again this process is clearest in Blake's use of biblical material. A typical example is the reworking of the trope of the Deluge or Flood in *The Book of Urizen* (and indeed across a range of other texts). What is a single event in the Bible becomes a recurrent metaphor. To some extent this is an extension of the Bible's own rhetorical procedures. Robert Lowth's influential *Lectures on the Sacred*

---

[10] See T. S. Eliot, *The Sacred Wood*, 7th edn. (London, 1980), 156 and 158.

Poetry of the Hebrews (1787), for instance, had noted the Bible's frequent metaphorical reapplication of events that had a 'conspicuous place' in Hebrew history. But whereas the Bible clearly distinguished between its actual account of the Flood and subsequent uses of the Flood as a trope, Blake presents a series of deluges none of which is privileged as *the* Flood. I shall argue later in this chapter that Blake's conception of the Bible involved him in a struggle to liberate its poetic aspects from the legalistic Word. His development of the Bible's own procedures can be seen as part of this process, but Blake's use of the trope of the Flood has a radically different signification from that of the Bible. In conventional biblical exegesis the Flood was seen as a type of righteous punishment for the transgression of holy laws. Blake turns this on its head so that the introduction of such punishment becomes part of the primal catastrophe, an example of the 'unrelenting vindictiveness' Paine found in the Old Testament God.[11]

At the root of Blake's attitude to the Bible lies a hostility to the very notion of the pure text, the text which gains authority from its claim to be sacred, invariable, and original. In his annotations to Bishop Watson's *Apology for the Bible* (1798) Blake described 'the Bible or <Peculiar> Word of God' as an 'Abomination' (E 615). Perhaps the paradigmatic expression of Blake's attitude to the whole notion of the sacred text lies in Plate 11 of *The Marriage of Heaven and Hell*, which offers a telescoped account of the origins of 'forms of worship' in the corruptions of 'poetic tales':

The ancient Poets animated all sensible objects with Gods or Geniuses, calling them by the names and adorning them with the properties of woods, rivers, mountains, lakes, cities, nations, and whatever their enlarged & numerous senses could perceive.

And particularly they studied the genius of each city & country. placing it under its mental deity.

Till a system was formed, which some took advantage of & enslav'd the vulgar by attempting to realize or abstract the mental deities from their objects: thus begun Priesthood.

---

[11] See Lowth, *Lectures*, vol. i, Lecture 9, and Paine, *CWP*, ii. 474.

Choosing forms of worship from poetic tales.
And at length they pronounced that the Gods had orderd such
things.
Thus men forgot that All deities reside in the human breast. (E 38)

This Plate invokes in stark terms an opposition which functions
throughout Blake's work: the opposition between scripture,
represented as an oppressive mode of writing associated with
the law, and poetry, a mode of writing which is open, multi-
form, and seeks the imaginative participation of the reader. The
same opposition is personalized in the conflict between bard-
prophet and druid-priest in the figures of Los and Urizen.

The details and variations of these configurations will be
discussed below, particularly in Chapters 2, 3, and 4. What I
want to stress here is Blake's opposition to the notion of a text
which claims a transcendent authority. Throughout Blake's
work this sort of text is associated with the figure of Urizen.
The various 'books of metals formd' which Urizen is continually involved in engraving are parodic versions of the stone
tablets of the Mosaic dispensation and their continuation in
what Blake called the 'State Religion' (E 618) of his own time.
The blind copying from the tablets of the law with which
Urizen is shown busying himself on the frontispiece of The
Book of Urizen (see Pl. 1) is effectively an illustration of Plate 11
of The Marriage of Heaven and Hell. Urizen is characteristically
involved in the process whereby 'poetic tales' are reified into
'forms of worship'.

One distinct strand of Blake's opposition to 'books of metal
formd' is his hostility to allegory. The 'allegorical' is a negative
term in Blake's rhetoric, associated with delusion masquerading
as absolute truth. Enitharmon's 'heaven' in Europe, for instance,
is stigmatized as 'an allegorical abode' (E 62; Pl. 5, l. 7). Blake's
conception of allegory is made explicit in the notebook essay 'A
Vision of the Last Judgement' (1810), where he defines 'Fable
or Allegory' as 'a totally distinct & inferior kind of Poetry' (E
554). He specifies allegory as the poetry of moral virtues, that
is, the scripture of law and the commandments: 'Allegories are
things that Relate to Moral Virtues Moral Virtues do not Exist

they are Allegories & dissimulations' (E 563). The paradigm of
poetic tales being turned into forms of worship can be explained
in relation to this pervasive hostility to the notion of allegory.
Thomas Blackwell, the influential precursor of the eighteenth-
century primitivists discussed in Chapter 3, represented allegory
as a corruption of the metaphorical creations of the earliest
poets: 'Metaphor is the Language of Passion; as Simile is the
Effect of a warm Imagination, which when cooled and regulated
explains itself in diffuse Fable and elaborate Allegory.' Both
Blake and Blackwell presented this development as a conscious
manipulation fuelled by 'the Avarice of the Priests'. A similar
suspicion of allegory, more pointedly directed at the priestcraft
of Christianity than Blackwell's, is evident in many of the
radical texts of the late eighteenth century. Perhaps the most
daring exponent of this sort of criticism before the Revolution
controversy was Joseph Priestley, a close associate of Blake's
sometime employer Joseph Johnson, who in his *History of the
Corruptions of Christianity* (1782) attacked allegorical interpretations of the scriptures as a pagan influence on Christianity. This
same sort of observation was central to attacks made on the
Bible in the 1790s by radicals such as Volney and Paine.[12]

Blake's work seeks to reverse the process whereby priestly
authority usurped the poetic function and maintained the Bible
as a moral allegory. It was a politically sensitive tactic in the
1790s, when, as Robert Hole has recently shown, there was a
new emphasis on religion as the teaching of 'Moral Virtues'
which would function as the guarantors of political and social
stability. Although Blake's mythopoesis is often taken to
approximate to allegory, it is more accurate to say that this
similarity is an invocation of allegorical form which is sub-
verted or parodied as part of a process of contesting the
hegemony of Moral Virtues.[13] Whereas strict allegory depends

---

[12] See Thomas Blackwell, *Letters Concerning Mythology* (London, 1748), 71
and 275. Blackwell was a republican and, significantly for my discussion of
Macpherson in Ch. 2, James Macpherson's tutor at Aberdeen. See C. Robbins,
The Eighteenth-Century Commonwealthman (Cambridge, Mass., 1959), 211, and
F. Stafford, *The Sublime Savage* (Edinburgh, 1988), 28–37.

[13] W. J. T. Mitchell has written of the 'schematic, allegorical surface of

on a stable relationship between signifier and signified, each term consistently standing, say, for some moral principle, Blake's metaphorical procedures are more complex. His vocabulary is often reversible. Particular images have positive and negative variants. An example is Blake's use of the serpent as a signifier in *Europe*. The fiery serpent of the poem's title-page seems to be associated with the liberating energy of revolt. It is akin to the serpentine Orc of *America*. The 'temple serpent-form'd' described in the poem itself represents the petrifaction of that energy into the oppressive authority of State Religion. The latter, of course, is analogous to the rigidity of scripture; the former has the fluidity Blake associates with poetic tales.

Blake is constantly seeking to break down the notion of scripture as monolithic authority. It is generally true of radical writing in the 1790s that it similarly sought to contest the authority of hegemonic texts and their established readings. As with Blake, this contestation frequently centred around the Bible, the key text of the Christian state. Perhaps the prime example is Paine's *The Age of Reason*, the book which Blake set out to defend against Bishop Watson's *Apology for the Bible*. While Blake's annotations to his copy of the latter do not reveal him to have been a Painite in any straightforward sense, they do imply that he was much more sympathetic to Paine's attitude to the Bible than is often allowed. Some critics find it difficult to get beyond what they see as the irreconcilable facts of Paine's deism and Blake's explicit hostility to natural religion. This is much less of a problem when we bear in mind how far radical bricoleurs (and that might include Paine himself) were prepared to cross scholarly boundaries between irrationalism and rationalism, the vulgar and the polite. In Chapter 4 I shall deal in some detail with the similarities between Paine's comments on the Bible and Blake's. For the moment it is worth noting that, like Blake, Paine sought to stress the poetic nature of the

Blake's prophetic books', *Blake's Composite Art* (Princeton, NJ, 1978), 118. For Robert Hole's discussion, see *Pulpits, Politics, and Public Order in England 1760–1832* (Cambridge, 1989), 101–2.

valuable parts of the Bible: 'the Jewish poets deserve a better
fate than that of being bound up, as they are now with the trash
that accompanies them, under the abused name of the Word of
God'.[14]

Paine's hostility to notions of scriptural authority extended
beyond his views on the Bible. His entire political attitude was
based on a suspicion of received authority unverified by experience. His *Rights of Man*, among the most popular and influential
radical texts of the 1790s, defined its opposition to the eighteenth-century *ancien régime* as an aversion to scriptural authority:
'I am contending for the rights of the living against the
manuscript assumed authority of the dead.' It would not be a
distortion to adopt this statement as the slogan of Blake's poetic
enterprise, at least in the 1790s. Indeed so thoroughgoing is
Blake's suspicion of 'manuscript assumed authority' that he was
constantly taking measures to ensure that his own work was
not received as such.[15]

What Stephen Leo Carr has recently described as 'the radical
variabilty' of Blake's illuminated books prevents their assuming
the authority of scripture. The various 'copies' of the same text
have differences of detail and even in the ordering of their
plates, which means each varies substantively from the others.
Perhaps the most obvious example is *The Book of Urizen*, none
of the seven extant versions of which have the same format. In
each copy the plates are ordered differently, the position of the
full-page designs being particularly variable. Carr has suggested
that underlying such variations is a 'logic of difference' which
works against conventional notions of the authoritative text.
His point is made in the context of Walter Benjamin's discussion
of the 'aura' of the work of art. Carr's view is that Blake's
whole productive method militates against the authoritative and
original presence which constitutes Benjamin's idea of aura.
The aura of the work of art depends on the notion of the master
copy, the single or original from which all copies or reproduc-
tions are taken. No single version of *The Book of Urizen* can

[14] See Paine, *CWP*, ii. 477.
[15] Ibid. i. 252.

claim this status. None is the singular original which authorizes the others as copies.[16]

J. J. McGann has made similar claims about what he calls Blake's 'indeterminacy'. McGann finds indeterminacy to be operative in *The Book of Urizen* in two basic ways. The first is in the variations in ordering across the versions mentioned already above. The second is to be found in the internal variations within each version of the poem. There are episodes which are replayed in variant forms. The reader is offered, for example, more than one version of Urizen's genesis. This second aspect also extends across different poems. *The Book of Ahania* and *The Book of Los* (1795) both recount parts of the narrative of *The Book of Urizen* but either from a different perspective or with details which differ from the latter's account. It is exactly this aspect of Blake's rhetoric which leads Carr to conclude that 'there is no ur-myth in Blake's work only the repetition of variable performances either in terms of the repetitions of plots across poems or in the revision of a single work'.[17]

McGann historicizes Blake's indeterminacy by reading it as an attempt to challenge the authority of the received Bible in the context of eighteenth-century developments in scriptural criticism. What McGann omits to note is the importance of similar sorts of challenge to the Revolution controversy, an issue I have raised already in this chapter and shall return to in Chapter 4. McGann is also perhaps too reticent in his account of where indeterminacy operates in Blake's work. He does not take account of those illuminated books produced prior to *The*

---

[16] See Carr, 'Illuminated Printing: Toward a Logic of Difference', in *Unnam'd Forms: Blake and Textuality*, ed. N. Hilton and T. A. Vogler (Berkeley, Calif., 1986), 182, 177, and 182–3.

[17] See McGann's chapter 'The Idea of an Indeterminate Text: Blake's Bible of Hell and Dr. Alexander Geddes' in his *Social Values and Poetic Acts* (Cambridge, Mass. 1988), and Carr, 'Illuminated Printing', 180. For another discussion of Blake's reworking of passages in different contexts see W. Kumbier, 'Blake's Epic Meter', *Studies in Romanticism*, 17 (1978), 169–70. Kumbier notes that there is an indication that Blake wrote reminders to himself to do this sort of thing. On p. 55 of *The Four Zoas* manuscript, for instance, Blake wrote 'Bring in here the Globe of Blood as in the B. of Urizen.'

Book of Urizen. McGann does claim that the reworking of narrative sections across *The Book of Urizen*, *The Book of Ahania*, and *The Book of Los* can be assimilated to the principle of indeterminacy. None is allowed to stand as an authoritative version of a particular plot. But the same could be said, for example, of reworkings of plot in *America* and *Europe*. The account of the struggle between Orc and Urizen in the latter replays a section of the narrative of *America* with different details. *Europe*, like *The Book of Urizen*, is unstable both in its order and contents. Early versions lack the prefatory plate containing the mocking fairy song, while the two full-page designs occur in different positions in different copies of the poem. McGann's insights could also be extended to a consideration of the interaction between text and design in Blake's illuminated works. Heather Glen's conception of the 'ambiguous, sometimes ironic, and always dialectical difference between text and illustration' suggests that the relationship is very much an indeterminate one. Indeed it is misleading to refer to the designs as illustrations since this suggests that they are merely an annexe of the text. Some designs bear no obvious relation to the text with which they share a plate, while others apparently illustrate text which appears on another plate. Often the text and design are played off against each other. In Plate 7 of *America*, for instance, Albion's Angel's representation of Orcian revolution as a monstrous rebellion is contradicted by the tranquil pastoral scene shown in the design. Although the relationship between text and design often has specific implications for particular contexts, it can be generally asserted that it seeks to stimulate the imaginative energy of the reader, who is brought in to play as an active intelligence that must strive to make sense of the difference.[18]

The indeterminate relationship between text and design opens up the illuminated book to the reader. The same is true of other aspects of Blakian indeterminacy. For instance there is the doubling of plots within the prophecies *America* and *Europe*, where the narrative of the poem proper seems to offer the

[18] H. Glen, *Vision and Disenchantment* (Cambridge, 1983), 71.

prospect of a partial elucidation of the elliptical Preludium. The reader is called upon to make sense of the parallel but tangential relationship between the two dialogic narratives in the one text. This is not to suggest that there is a single meaning which the reader must discover. Blake would presumably have called a text which operated in such a way an allegory. Rather both prophecies strive to involve the reader in an hermeneutic process which Blake believed, in an almost Godwinian way, necessarily lead to a commitment to truth and justice. The text is not offered as a univocal and invariable authority. It is contingent and contradicts itself, other copies of itself, and elements similar to itself which appear in other poems. In total these features are part of Blake's attempt to achieve a style which 'rouzes the faculties to act' (E 702). They seek to promote the rights of the living reader against manuscript authority. The reader is enfranchised within the text, a development which could be compared to Daniel Eaton's decision to publish his readers' contributions in the pages of his *Politics for the People*. Indeed the reader might be seen as the keystone of the Blakian bricolage.

It is ironic then that Blake never achieved a significant readership while he lived. Central to the democratization of the text pursued by radicals in the 1790s was an attempt to reach an expanding popular audience with political ideas. Paine's populist style was part of a conscious effort to make the political sphere accessible to this audience. He succeeded to the extent that Blake considered the popularity of *Rights of Man* to be a 'miracle' (E 617). Blake, in contrast, failed to reach an audience of any kind. My Conclusion will discuss this failure in more detail. It is a matter which should not be shied away from as often as it is in Blake studies. But equally it should not be assumed that Blake sought the isolation that he found or that his visionary rhetoric is unconcerned with earthly matters. I believe, on the contrary, that the texts discussed in this book are profoundly involved with the ideas and images of the culture of the 1790s. If the modern reader finds little like Blake's illuminated books in the other literature of the time, it is because our knowledge is filtered through the canonical con-

struction of Romanticism. The subsequent chapters offer a
different kind of cultural history as a context for reading Blake,
a context which reveals the origins and animates the complexities of Blake's dangerous enthusiasm.

1

'Every Honest Man is a Prophet': Popular Enthusiasm and Radical Millenarianism

THIS chapter examines Blake's relationship to the popular culture of religious enthusiasm and the distinctive voice that culture had in the Revolution controversy. I shall argue that the prophetic rhetoric of Blake's poetry in the 1790s has more in common with an enthusiast like the visionary Richard Brothers than the perhaps better known millenarianism of Dissenters like Richard Price and Joseph Priestley. Whereas the latter pair sought to use the Bible to justify the French Revolution, Brothers and Blake went further and offered to supplement and even replace the received prophetic canon with their own visionary experience. For Blake and Brothers divine inspiration was an ongoing possibility, potentially available to anyone. Such enthusiasm was felt by many contemporaries to be a vulgar feature of the popular culture, whereas the millenarianism of Price and Priestley was couched in a much more respectable rationalist discourse. Yet, deeply implicated though Blake's writing is in the perspectives of the culture of enthusiasm, the differences should not be overlooked. His writing is characteristically less deferential to conventional religious notions than many enthusiastic texts and reveals the traces of other discourses besides the biblical basis of Blake's rhetoric. The final section of my discussion goes on to suggest some parallels between Blake's dangerous enthusiasm and radical attempts both to undermine the hegemonic moral vocabulary and to bring the vulgar language into the public domain.

I want to begin by specifying what is meant by describing Blake's rhetoric as prophetic. Blake is often described as a prophet, but the formal implications of the title are rarely examined. Only two of Blake's poems, *America* and *Europe*, explicitly lay claim to the status of prophecy in their subtitles,

but his other poetry shares with them features of form, style,
and allusion which indicate that he was self-consciously seeking
to write prophetically throughout the decade. The most
obvious of these features is the dependence on the language of
the Old Testament and the Book of Revelation. Blake presents
the revolutionary activity of the late eighteenth century as the
fulfilment of biblical prophecy. Typical is Plate 6 of *America*, an
anonymous speech introduced by an allusion to the voice from
the temple which proclaims the fall of Babylon in Revelation
16: 17:

> The Spectre glowd his horrid length staining the temple long
> With beams of blood; & thus a voice came forth, and shook the
>   temple.

(E 53; Pl. 5, ll. 6–7)

The speech itself goes on to represent the American rejection of
British authority as the beginning of the end of Babylonian
oppression:

> The morning comes, the night decays, the watchmen leave
>   their stations;
> The grave is burst, the spices shed, the linen wrapped up;
> The bones of death, the cov'ring clay, the sinews shrunk &
>   dry'd.
> Reviving shake, inspiring move, breathing! awakening!

(Pl. 6, ll. 1–4)

The whole Plate is a medley of allusions to the prophecies of
Ezekiel and Isaiah and their vision of the ultimate liberation of
the Hebrews. This vision reached a partial fulfilment in the life
of Christ for the orthodox Christian of Blake's time, who had
to await its completion in the Second Coming at the end of
time. An acceptance of this deferred liberation and the crucial
role of the reappearance of Christ himself was vigorously
promoted in conservative sermons and anti-Jacobin polemics in
the 1790s. W. B. Cadogan's *Liberty and Equality* (1792) is
representative: 'After all the noise that has been made in the
world about "liberty", no people are "free" but they who are
made so by Jesus Christ.' Blake's *America* implies, in contrast,

that the ultimate fulfilment of biblical prophecy is to be found
in the process of liberation which seemed to be renewing itself
in the American and French Revolutions. The Christ who
returns from the grave is Blake's Orc, the embodiment of the
revolutionary impulse.[1]

It is not only through its rendition of biblical eschatology that
Blake's writing participates in prophetic discourse. Many of the
distinctive formal features of his work are also to be found in
the Authorized Version and, especially, the books of the
prophets and Revelation. Indeed the basic notion of an illuminated book, which came to be Blake's preferred literary
medium in the 1790s, can be seen as a development of eighteenth-century conceptions of prophecy, the visual nature of
which was widely accepted. Revelation, in particular, was seen
as appealing predominantly to the visual sense. The pamphlet
Prophetic Conjectures on the French Revolution (1794), for instance,
approached Revelation as a series of 'emblematic representations'. Likewise James Bicheno's *Signs of the Times* (1793) saw
the biblical book as 'a number of scenic pictures'. Convention-
ally it was accepted that the words of St John were a direct
translation of his visions. Blake's illuminated books, of course,
eschew any such transparent relationship between the media.
They challenge the reader to an actively hermeneutic role and
seek to induce vision in the reader rather than merely presenting
it for consumption. This feature of the illuminated books may
have origins in the enthusiastic desire to free religious experience
from the mediation of commentaries, ceremonies, and even
texts themselves. I shall return to discuss this point later in the
chapter.[2]

[1] See Cadogan, *Liberty and Equality*, 1. Ezek. 37: 7–8 and Isa. 65: 25 are both
echoed in Plate 6 of *America*. The 'Let . . .' construction in the middle of the
Plate is common in Old Testament prophecy; e.g. Isa. 42: 11–12.

[2] See *Prophetic Conjectures*, 6; and Bicheno, *Signs of the Times*, 3. My point
about the perception of prophecy as a visual medium is made at more length
in J. A. Wittreich's 'Painted Prophecies: The Tradition of Blake's Illuminated
Books', in *Blake in his Time*, ed. Essick and Pearce, 101–15. A precursor of
Blake's illuminated books should be seen in William Lilly's *Monarchy or No
Monarchy* (1651). In this book Lilly was engaging in the Revolution controversy
of his own day, trying to refute Royalist uses of ancient prophecies by

If Blake's choice of media has prophetic significance so too do most aspects of his written style. Blake's versification, for instance, adapts the 'parallelism' which Robert Lowth had identified as the basis of biblical verse in the 1750s. Blake adopted a variety of metrical forms but what can be said in general about them is that they are not primarily based on the counting of syllables. Lowth had revealed that the basic versification of the Bible rested on 'a certain equality, resemblance, or parallelism between the numbers of each period'. Blake's poetry seems to be structured around such parallelism much of the time. The following passage from the Preludium to *Europe* exemplifies my point:

> Unwilling I look up to heaven! unwilling count the stars!
> Sitting in fathomless abyss of my immortal shrine.
> I sieze their burning power
> And bring forth howling terrors, all devouring fiery kings.
>
> Devouring & devoured roaming on dark and desolate mountains
>   In forests of eternal death, shrieking in hollow trees.
> Ah mother Enitharmon!
> Stamp not with solid form this vig'rous progeny of fires.
>
> I bring forth from my teeming bosom myriads of flames.
> And thou dost stamp them with a signet, then they roam
>   abroad
> And leave me void as death.

(E 61; Pl. 2, ll. 1–11)

The passage contains two of Lowth's varieties of parallelism. The repetition of syntactic structures, which he called 'Synthetic or Constructive Parallelism', is illustrated in the repeated adverbial use of the present participle in the first stanza. 'Synonymous Parallelism', the reiteration of a particular idea, underlies Blake's

---

presenting his own republican interpretations. Lilly concluded his book with nineteen pages of pictures in which he attempted to prophesy the history of England beyond his own time. Lilly's republican prophecies were known in the 1790s since they were reprinted by radical enthusiasts like Garnet Terry and George Riebau discussed below. *Monarchy or No Monarchy* itself is listed as lot 105 in *A Catalogue of an Extensive and Valuable Library of Books, sold by Phillips* (London, 1809).

different configurations of the painful birth of 'fiery kings'. Though line-length and rhythm vary in Blake's poetry, such parallelism remains a constant feature of his versification. I should add, as a coda, that I am not suggesting that the features discussed here and below were taken by Blake from Lowth. It is more likely that Blake had a familiarity with the language and cadences of the Bible from an early age which any sub-sequent contact with Lowth's theories served only to heighten.[3]

If Blake's versification betrays an intimate knowledge of biblical form, the sublime settings and imagery of Blake's prophetic narratives emulate what Lowth described as the 'parabolic style' of the Old Testament. Blake himself used the term 'Parabolic' of the Bible in his annotations to Watson (E 618). Lowth defined this style as 'a general mode of amplifying and elevating the subject, rarely and cautiously descending to circumstantial detail'. The 'parabolic' quality of Blake's style is evident in the vast amounts of space and time covered by the narratives of poems like *Europe* and *The Book of Urizen* and the violent, hyperbolic imagery which is a feature of all of Blake's poetry (except perhaps *Songs of Innocence*).[4] Key features of the parabolic style of biblical prophecy were 'bold ellipsis' and 'studied brevity' which elided history into a concentrated nar-rative as does, for instance, Blake's *The Song of Los*. The condensed history of religious mystification which forms the basis of the 'Africa' section of that poem is a particularly good instance of Blake's use of prophetic ellipsis. It is interesting that the historical perspective opened out in this section of the poem is not chronological. Blake's catalogue of the key moments in the development of religious systems puts its emphasis on identity rather than sequence. The opening lines of 'Africa' offer a mythic paradigm, focused on the unhistorical figure of

[3] See Lowth, *Lectures*, ii. 34, 49, and 35.

[4] Ibid. ii. 67–8 and 66. Another aspect of the prophetic style, according to Lowth, was the frequent reference to events that had a 'conspicuous place' in Hebrew history. These conspicuous events included the Chaos or Creation, the Flood, the destruction of Sodom, the Exodus, and the descent of Jehovah on to Sinai. I have already indicated the extensions Blake makes to this aspect of biblical style in my Introduction.

Urizen, of which all the historical epiphanies become incidents. Thomas Howes, in a development of Lowth's theories, had claimed that prophetic rhetoric typically discarded what he called 'chronological order' in favour of an 'oratorical' ordering which drew together disparate events in support of a particular argument. I shall return to the implications of the parabolic history offered by 'Africa' in a later chapter; what is important to note here is the essentially prophetic nature of Blake's narrative organization in the poem. Other of Blake's poems seem to contain similar sweeps of history, such as Enitharmon's dream in *Europe* and Los's prophetic struggles in *The Book of Los*, but the relationship of the narratives of these two poems to historical events is much more opaque. It is the prophetic basis of Blake's opacity to which I wish to turn now.[5]

The parabolic style and complex narrative organization of biblical prophecy contributed to its 'obscurity'; a term which Lowth used to define prophecy's most distinctive feature. Blake's poetry can be said to become increasingly 'obscure', in the technical sense offered by Lowth, as the 1790s went on. The narratives of Blake's illuminated books, for instance, become increasingly difficult to relate to historical events as they come to be more and more dominated by his personal pantheon of mythical figures and the disjunctive, complicated plots with which they are involved. Written at the beginning of the decade, *The French Revolution* is relatively free of this obscurity. Nevertheless it does still make use of a distinctively prophetic style which presents historical revolution in terms of cosmic upheaval in a way which Lowth had claimed was typical of biblical rhetoric:

> Gleams of fire streak the heavens, and of sulphur the earth,
>   from Fayette as he lifted his hand;
> But silent he stood, till all the officers rush round him like
>   waves
> Round the shore of France, in day of the British flag, when
>   heavy cannons

[5] See Lowth, *Lectures*, i. 98 and 102, and Thomas Howes, *Critical Observations on Books Antient and Modern*, 2 vols. (London, 1776–83), ii. 149 and 139.

Affright the coasts, and the peasant looks over the sea and
    wipes a tear;
Over his head the soul of Voltaire shone fiery, and over the
    army Rousseau his white cloud
Unfolded, on souls of war-living terrors silent list'ning toward
    Fayette.

(E 298; ll. 278–83)

Such distinctively prophetic features aside, *The French Revolution* is much more of 'a visualization of history' than most of
the narrative poetry Blake produced in the decade. *America*, for
instance, even though it is ostensibly involved in representing a
particular historical event, is much more complex and less
closely tied to historical detail than *The French Revolution*. The
historical basis of the plot is both framed and inhabited by
figures from Blake's own pantheon. *Europe* goes even further
in this direction. The exotic cast of names is expanded and there
are virtually no explicit references to contemporary history
(though the political concerns of the poem are signalled by a
conclusion 'in the vineyards of red France' (E 66; Pl. 15, l. 2)).
Evidence of Blake's determination to frustrate any attempt to
allegorize the poem against contemporary history can be
gleaned in alterations he made to the cancelled Plate b of *America*
when it was incorporated into Plate 9 of *Europe*. The latter
describes the collapse of a council house in the midst of the
struggle between Orc and Urizen. The cancelled Plate of
America makes it clear that this council house is the British
Parliament where 'George the third holds council. & his Lords
& Commons meet' (E 58; l. 9). The narrative Blake actually
published obscures any simple historical referent. This process
is taken even further in poems like *The Book of Urizen* and *The
Book of Los*, the narratives of which are difficult to reduce to
any kind of straightforward story, made up as they are of
disorientating disjunctions and confusing internal repetitions
and contradictions.[6]

    I believe Blake's obscurity is part of a specific rhetorical

---

[6] See Lowth, *Lectures*, i. 200, and Erdman, *Prophet Against Empire*, 3rd rev.
edn. (Princeton, NJ, 1977), 202.

strategy, modelled on biblical prophecy. Lowth held that the
'obscurity' of prophecy had a definite rhetorical function: 'It
whets the understanding, excites an appetite for knowledge,
keeps alive the attention, and exercises the genius by the labour
of the imagination.' Blake offered concrete evidence that his
own rhetorical procedures were part of a similar strategy when
he wrote that 'the wisest of the Ancients consider'd what is not
too explicit as the fittest for Instruction because it rouzes the
faculties to act' (E 702). If rousing the faculties to act is accepted
as the purpose of Blake's obscurity, then his poetic development
in the 1790s can be seen as an intensification of his desire to
stimulate the reader into a fuller hermeneutic engagement with
the text.[7]

Lowth's stress on the rhetorical function of prophecy is
important since it was central to his representation of the Old
Testament prophets as public figures involved in the transmission of 'history and politics, as well as the principles of
religion and morals'. This aspect of Lowth's account exemplifies
and indeed profoundly influenced the common eighteenth-
century notion of the public and even political nature of the
prophetic office. Thomas Howes went so far as to equate the
prophetic office with a radical political stance. For Howes the
prophets of the Old Testament were 'members of the opposition . . . who took very free, yet necessary liberties in criticising
and condemning the measures of their kings, nobles, priests,
and people'.[8] Both Howes and Lowth concentrated on the
hortatory, rather than the predictive, function of prophecy,
which was conceived of not as a vision of the future but as an
attempt to persuade the people to act in a particular way. The
same outlook seems to underlie Blake's most direct definition
of the prophetic role:

---

[7] Lowth, *Lectures*, ii. 168.

[8] See Lowth, *Lectures*, i. 87. Lowth was obviously influenced by contemporary theories of the bard which are also operative in Macpherson's Ossian
poems: see the next chapter for a fuller discussion of this issue. For Howes, see
his *Critical Observations*, i. 214–15. A general account of the trend towards
reading the Bible as a primitive historical poem, which includes a discussion of
Blake, can be found in Murray Roston's, *Poet and Prophet* (London, 1965).

Every honest man is a Prophet he utters his opinion both of private &
public matters I Thus I If you go on So I the result is So I He never
says such a thing shall happen let you do what you will. a Prophet is a
Seer not an Arbitrary Dictator.   (E 617)

It is a definition which shares Lowth's stress on the hortatory
aspects of prophecy. Prophetic discourse is a place to speak
from which can be taken up by any 'honest man'.

The prophetic platform, expressing social grievances and
utopian visions in terms of the biblical paradigms of Babylonian
oppression and millenarian expectation, was in fact one long
established in the rhetorical resources of the popular culture by
the time Blake wrote. Modern historians have perhaps paid
most attention to the role of prophetic writings in the politics
of the Civil War period. Keith Thomas, in his *Religion and the
Decline of Magic*, claimed that political prophecy waned after the
Restoration and linked the decline to a rising tide of rationalism
which undermined the belief in prophetic inspiration. E. P.
Thompson has suggested, however, that Thomas has overem-
phasized the decline of such beliefs. Thompson believes the
language of prophecy maintained a stronghold in the popular
culture. His research into anonymous protest letters in the
eighteenth century certainly reveals an enduring attachment to
the rhetoric of prophecy for the expression of social grievances.
Other historians have shown the discourse continued to flourish
in the popular culture. Clarke Garrett, for instance, claims that
by the 1790s millenarian visions had long been 'a staple of
popular literature'. What is certain is that the political upheavals
of the 1790s engendered an outburst of visionary activity
unequalled since the Interregnum and found 'a public eager to
read prophetic utterances of all kinds'.[9]

Perhaps the most famous exponent of the prophetic genre in

---

[9] See K. Thomas, *Religion and the Decline of Magic* (London, 1971), 144. E.
P. Thompson's 'The Crime of Anonymity', in *Albion's Fatal Tree*, ed. D. Hay
and others (London, 1975), reproduces a series of prophetic protest letters. He
takes issue with Thomas in his 'Anthropology and the Discipline of Historical
Context', *Midland History*, 1 (1972), 53–4. See also C. Garrett, *Respectable Folly*
(Baltimore and London, 1975), 169 and 169–70, and J. F. C. Harrison, *The
Second Coming* (London, 1979), 11–38.

the 1790s was Richard Brothers, who was notorious enough to provoke a public controversy around his writings. Brothers had been born in Newfoundland in 1757, the year of Blake's birth. He came to England as a boy and subsequently joined the navy at 14 as a midshipman. He was promoted to lieutenant at the end of the American War of Independence and discharged on half pay. The crucial turning-point in this hitherto unremarkable life came in 1789, when he refused on religious grounds to swear the oath of loyalty to the crown required for him to be able to draw his pay. His enthusiasm quickly lead to poverty and he was placed in a workhouse in 1791. When he left in the following year he began to write letters to the government warning them against joining the monarchical alliance against republican France. Apart from a brief stay in Newgate for non-payment of rent, little is known about Brothers's activities from 1792 to 1794, when he achieved national fame with the publication of his *A Revealed Knowledge of the Prophecies and Times*.

Brothers claimed that the two volumes of his book were written under direct inspiration from God. They comprise a mixture of his own visions with supporting reinterpretations of the Bible. The content is very much in line with Howes's definition of the prophet as a member of the political opposition: 'The English government, both what is called civil and ecclesiastical, in its present form, will, by the fierce anger and determined judgement of the Lord God, be removed, annihilated, utterly destroyed.' Some of Brothers's followers downplayed the political aspects of his prophecies. Many others saw it as essential to his mission and drew attention to the biblical precedent for visions of the destruction of 'NAMES, titles, ecclesiastical dignities, orders &c.' None were more explicit in their revolutionary ardour than the anonymous author of *The Age of Prophecy!* (1795), who eagerly awaited the time 'when that augean invention of Parliaments shall be dissolved, and a Convention substituted!' For this writer Brothers was 'surely a Democrat and a Prophet!' The radical tendency among Brothers's followers explains why Gillray's satirical cartoon of Brothers, *The Prophet of the Hebrews—The Prince of Peace conducting the Jews to the Promised Land* (1795), represented him as a sansculotte carrying the leaders of the British opposition with him (see jacket illustration).[10]

There are significant parallels between the enthusiasm of Brothers's *A Revealed Knowledge* and the millenarian temper and prophetic form of Blake's work in the 1790s. I began this chapter with a sketch of the prophetic aspects of Blake's style. Brothers similarly sought to authenticate his claim to divine inspiration by adopting the style of biblical prophecy. His writing, though different in many particulars from Blake's, is another example of prophetic 'obscurity'. To his supporters his occluded style was evidence of the truth of his claim to divine inspiration. Opponents read his 'exceedingly dark and mysterious' words as vulgar fanaticism: 'He introduces names unknown to the world, and runs on in such a bombastic style, that reason has evidently left her seat.' A poem like Blake's *Europe* might have elicited a similar response when it was first published in 1794.[11]

Apart from the general point that both Blake and Brothers adopt the parabolic and obscure language of prophecy in their publications, there are some interesting instances of specific similarities. Let me give an example of one of these. A recurrent motif in the Bible is the figure of Jerusalem as the bride of God. The other side of this coinage is the representation of the desolate Jerusalem as a grieving widow or lamenting woman. The Preludium to Blake's *Europe* makes use of this figure, drawing on the biblical books of Jeremiah and Lamentations, in its account of the 'nameless shadowy female' (E 60; Pl. 1, l. 1). Lamentations is delivered through the figure of 'a female, solitary, afflicted, in a state of widowhood, deserted by her friends, betrayed by her dearest connections, imploring relief and seeking consolation in vain'.[12] This description would fit Blake's 'nameless shadowy female', who is also betrayed by her

[10] See Brothers, *A Revealed Knowledge of the Prophecies and Times*, 2 parts (London, 1794), ii. 74, *Prophetic Conjectures*, 70; and the anonymous *The Age of Prophecy!* (London, 1795), 46.
[11] See [W. C. Oulton], *Sound Argument Dictated by Common Sense* 3rd edn. (Oxford, 1795), 48.
[12] The description of Lamentations is taken from Lowth, *Lectures*, ii. 138.

children and left imploring her mother, Enitharmon, for relief from their predations. Blake's account of these events even contains explicit verbal echoes of Lamentations. The daughter sees her children 'consumed and consuming' (l. 10) before being offered a vision of hope wrapped in 'swaddling bands' (E 61; Pl. 2, l. 14) at the close of the Preludium. Though Blake typically changes the significance of this vocabulary, it does seem to have its source in Lamentations 2: 22: 'Thou hast called as in a solemn day my terrors round about, so that in the day of the LORD's anger none escaped nor remained: those that I have swaddled and brought up hath mine enemy consumed.'

The grieving widow of Lamentations is a symbol of Jerusalem brought to ruin: 'The subject of the Lamentations is the destruction of the holy city and temple, the overthrow of the state, the extermination of the people.'[13] The Bible ascribes the blame for this situation to the failure of the people of Jerusalem, and especially their King, to listen to the warnings of the prophet Jeremiah. Indeed the rulers of the city actively seek to suppress the prophetic voice and stop Jeremiah preaching to the people at the city gate. Jeremiah's continual conflict with Zedekiah and the Hebrew religious establishment marks him as the epitome of Howes's prophet of opposition. The rulers of Jerusalem fail 'to proclaim liberty' to 'all the people' (Jeremiah 34: 8) and refuse to withdraw from monarchical war. The daughter in Blake's Preludium is also tormented by the tyrannies of 'all devouring fiery kings'. In 1794 when the poem was published, Britain was part of a monarchical alliance against republican France and attempting to suppress its own Jeremiahs from preaching to the people through the proclamation against 'divers seditious and wicked writings' of 1792 and the treason trials of 1794. Blake's obscure Preludium seems to invoke these events and place them in a biblical context which prophesies national ruin if such oppression persists.

Such a prophecy of national destruction was much more explicitly a feature of Brothers's radical millenarianism as we have seen, but what I want to emphasize here is the extent to

---

[13] Ibid. ii. 137.

which Blake and Brothers shared the same prophetic language. Brothers also made use of the figure of Jerusalem as the desolate widow, though his discussion of the trope focuses on a passage from Isaiah rather than Lamentations:

The married wife means Jerusalem at a former time, when rich and full of inhabitants; the desolate wife means Jerusalem at present: although she is a heap of rubbish and levelled with the ground, the Jews will return in such great multitudes, that when rebuilt, her extent and number of people will be far greater than at any former period.

Brothers explicitly identified the fallen Jerusalem with London and prophesied the latter's descent into destruction if the counter-revolutionary war prevailed:

While war continues in the World, Jerusalem the capital of the King of Peace is decreed to lie desolate: the restoration of the Jews will commence with the destruction of war, to favour their return, and build the city; when all Nations will rejoice with them, and once more receive from Jerusalem the commands of the living God.

The Preludium to *Europe* is much less explicit than Brothers's prophecies in its mapping of biblical eschatology on to British politics, but it is partially elucidated by the poem proper, which doubles the narrative of the Preludium. The torments suffered by the nameless, shadowy female in the Preludium are placed in the context of Enitharmon's rule in the main part of the poem. The latter details the growth of state religion and the parallel development of a code of war. Blake's annotations to Bishop Watson's *Apology for the Bible* make his view of the relationship between war and religion much more explicit: 'To what does the Bishop attribute the English Crusade against France. is it not to State Religion, blush for shame' (E 613). Erdman reads *Europe* as a specific allegory of late eighteenth-century history which culminates in 'red France'. While I would query the specificity of his reading, there is little doubt that the mythologized history of the growth of state religion is meant to carry critical implications for the Britain of Blake's time. The poem's closing reference to 'red France' is a partial elucidation of the vision of hope offered the shadowy female of the

Preludium, an elucidation that looks to the Revolution as the way out of the destructive cycle of 'fiery kings' in which she is trapped.[14]

The flurry of prophetic activity which manifested itself in response to Brothers in the 1790s indicates that millenarianism was a strong latent feature of popular culture. Among other things, the Brothers controversy stimulated a multitude of reprints from earlier prophetic texts, including those of seventeenth-century enthusiasts discussed below. These republications suggest that there existed in the popular culture a strong self-awareness of the prophetic heritage. Some publishers went so far as to set up short-lived prophetic serials filled both with old material and the more recent visions of contemporaries like Brothers. Examples include George Riebau's *God's Awful Warning* (1795) and Garnet Terry's *Prophetical Extracts* (1795). Riebau invited his readers to contribute accounts of their own visions, which implies that he thought such powers widely available. Entire pamphlets were also published which drew on their authors' own visions in support of the mission of Brothers. Sarah Green, for instance, claimed to have had inspired dreams which confirmed the authenticity of Brothers's prophecies. William Bryan felt himself empowered to prophesy the demise of 'all despotic kings and oppressive rulers'. Obviously prophetic inspiration was felt to be a continuing reality amongst such enthusiasts. Indeed many of the pamphlets are insistent on this point. The Advertisement to the fourth edition of *Wonderful Prophecies* (1795) claimed that there had been 'a general and

---

[14] Blake's uneven obscurity, the way he gives a vision in brief in his Preludium and then seems to expand upon it in the poem proper, can once again be related to the model of biblical prophecy. The biblical books of Ezekiel and Revelation both tend to work by giving a similarly brief initial statement with a subsequent elaboration in more detail. Lowth recognized that within the general pattern of prophetic obscurity some passages were more perspicuous and designed as a catalyst to rouse the reader to an interpretation of the rest. See *Lectures*, ii. 78–83. Brothers himself left some prophecies 'dark' to work on the minds of his readers. On Blake's conception of the French war as a crusade sponsored by state religion, compare Thomas Dutton's, *A Vindication of the Age of Reason* (London, 1795), 128: 'I am grieved to think that we are at the very moment that I write these pages fighting for religion in our crusade against the French.'

constant revelation of the divine will'. Others, such as William Bryan, were well aware of respectable hostility to such a belief: 'You think every man insane who dares profess to speak or write by inspiration of the divine Spirit.'[15]

Brothers's claim to be 'the Nephew of the Almighty' has been contrasted with Blake's more democratic conception of the prophetic role. Unfortunately the distinction fails to take account of the wealth of visionary material written and published by supporters of Brothers. These enthusiasts did not believe that Brothers had any monopoly on prophetic inspiration. Indeed many of their publications had a wider polemical concern with showing that prophecy had not stopped with the biblical period and that its practitioners were not 'confined either to the Jews or any other particular rank, age, sex, or condition of men'. Equally, Brothers and his publisher Riebau seem to have been happy to sponsor such pamphlets. Although Brothers did claim to have a special role, in practice he also recognized that visionary powers were generally available and did not 'assume the least pretence of monopolizing all knowledge of the Scripture and of the present times'. The real significance of Blake's claim that 'Every honest man is a Prophet' lies in its assertion of the continuing and general availability of prophetic inspiration. Brothers's publications and the response to them suggest that such a belief was still powerfully alive in the popular culture.[16]

[15] Only the first number of Riebau's *God's Awful Warning to a Giddy Careless Sinful World* seems to have been published. Riebau's request appears on the title-page. Riebau's relationship with Brothers is discussed in Garrett, *Respectable Folly*, 186–7, 199, 205, 215, and 219, McCalman, *Radical Underworld*, 62; and Harrison, *Second Coming*, 62, 223, and 265. Terry will be discussed in more detail below. As well as Terry's *Prophetical Extracts*, other collections of prophecies include *Prophetic Conjectures*, Riebau's *Prophetical Passages concerning the Present Times* (1795), and Ritchie's *Wonderful Prophecies* (1795). See p. 5 for the quotation. For Sarah Green, see her *A Letter to the Publishers of Brothers Prophesies* (1795), esp. 7–8. Bryan's remarks appear in his *A Testimony of the Spirit of Truth* (1795), 33 and 13.

[16] The distinction between Blake and Brothers was made in one of the first pieces to pay any detailed attention to the latter in the context of Blake studies, Morton D. Paley's, 'William Blake, the Prince of the Hebrews, and the Woman Clothed with the Sun', in *William Blake*, ed. Paley and M. Phillips (Oxford, 1973), 273. See *Wonderful Prophecies*, 5. Brothers made his claim

A general feature of the texts insisting on the continuing reality of prophetic inspiration which flooded out in the mid-1790s is their heterogeneity and lack of finish. Terry's *Prophetical Extracts*, for instance, throws together prophecies both ancient and modern of varying lengths, sometimes with editorial comments, in a rich millenarian stew. Of course this might be read as an unlearned editor's lack of organizational ability, but formal diversity and disjointed obscurity had a sanction within the culture of enthusiasm which suggests there is something more significant at issue. Those who sought to celebrate the operations of divine illumination were suspicious of received literary forms which smacked of a book-learning and legalism antithetical to inspiration. Terry, for instance, attacked 'framed studied speech, manufactured out of a scrap of scripture' as 'lecturing scientifically'. From his perspective a disrupted text looked like evidence of a genuine movement of the spirit and the obscurity proper to the true prophet. Congregations read the combustible language favoured by popular preachers as a sign of inspiration, just as the roughness of Brothers's own writing convinced some of his followers of the authenticity of his mission. Likewise, the collection *Wonderful Prophecies* defended 'a manner dubious and obscure' as typical of the true prophetic style. The same perspective informs one of Blake's Proverbs of Hell: 'Improvement makes strait roads, but the crooked roads without Improvement, are roads of Genius' (E 38; Pl. 10).[17]

The religious enthusiast's suspicion of received forms of written authority could even extend to the Bible. Terry warned his readers that not all of the Bible was inspired: 'That which the prophets and apostles spoke by dictation of the Holy Ghost, makes but a small part of the whole of the scriptures.' Brothers

---

about the general availability of prophetic inspiration after his imprisonment, see 'An Exposition of the Trinity' (1796) in *The Writings of Mr. Richard Brothers* 6 parts (London, 1798), 3. He went on to exclaim: 'I may be persecuted, but God will raise up fresh witnesses; I may be confined, but he will take care that his judgement shall not' (p. 33).

[17] See [Garnet Terry], *Letters on Godly and Religious Subjects*, 2 vols., 2nd edn. (London, 1808), i. 30; and *Wonderful Prophecies*, 9.

declared that he had been sent to correct mistakes in the biblical text. His prophecies obviously proclaim a freedom to supplement the canon and it was not unheard of for extreme enthusiasts to claim that what they received by vision had as much status as the biblical text, if not more. The disjointed collections of prophecies published by Terry, Riebau, and others can be seen as employing the friction between the *mélange* of extracts they reproduce to rouse the spiritual faculties of their readers. The editor of *Wonderful Prophecies* defended the prophetic obscurity of the collection as designed to 'exercise human sagacity'. Blake's own challenging use of text and design together with his other formal innovations may be an extension of a desire to break through the deadness of the letter to the life of the spirit typical of the culture of enthusiasm. His revisions and inversions of biblical paradigms go much further in their iconoclasm than most enthusiastic examples, but they may share origins in the same visionary self-confidence.[18]

There is another more strictly eschatological issue which I would like to mention before I move on. Recent scholarly discussions of millenarianism have been at pains to distinguish post-millennialism from pre-millennialism. The former, representing the Millennium as a progressive improvement, stresses the continuity between the world as it is and shall be. Rational Dissent is often associated with this sort of millenarianism. The confidence of someone like Joseph Priestley in the progress of a providential, general enlightenment was easily transmuted into an ostensibly de-Christianized belief in human perfectability by Godwin. Pre-millennialism, in contrast, involved a desire for a sudden and apocalyptic transformation of the temporal world by direct divine intervention.[19] To an extent, the distinction revolves around Christ's role. Those who foresaw a radical discontinuity believed Christ would precede the Millennium

[18] See [Terry], *Letters*, ii. 227, Brothers, *A Revealed Knowledge*, vol. ii, pp. iii–iv, and *Wonderful Prophecies*, 9. Brothers was also critical of the accuracy of the English translation of the Bible in his 'A Letter from Mr. Brothers to Miss Scott', *Writings*, 57–8.

[19] For a recent discussion of the distinction, see W. H. Oliver, *Prophets and Millenialists* (Oxford and Auckland, 1978), 20–3.

and act as the primary agent of transformation. For post-millennialists the Second Coming followed the Millennium; it marked the final dissolution of the human achievement rather than its commencement. Ultimately, however, these are scholarly distinctions and the enthusiast rarely committed him or herself to one or the other. Usually popular millenarianism was committed to the sudden apocalyptic perspective of pre-millennialism, but Brothers, for instance, maintained this emphasis while still representing the developments of the French Revolution as a human fulfilment of God's will. After he was imprisoned Brothers devoted himself to detailed plans concerned with the migration to and reconstruction of Jerusalem. It would not descend from the clouds but be built by human hands in the Palestine of his own time. Blake's *America* displays a similar duality in its millenarianism. The role of Orc is similar to that of the messianic Christ of pre-millennialism, but ultimately the success of the apocalyptic American Revolution devolves on to the citizens who reject British authority in Plate 14:

> Fury! rage! madness! in a wind swept through America
> And the red flames of Orc that folded roaring fierce around
> The angry shores, and the fierce rushing of th'inhabitants
> together:
> The citizens of New-York close their books & lock their chests;
> The mariners of Boston drop their anchors and unlade;
> The scribe of Pensylvania casts his pen upon the earth;
> The builder of Virginia throws his hammer down in fear.
>
> Then had American been lost, o'erwhelmed by the Atlantic,
> And Earth had lost another portion of the infinite,
> But all rush together in the night in wrath and raging fire
> The red fires rag'd! the plagues recoil'd! then rolld they back
> with fury.
>
> (E 56; Pl. 14, ll. 10–20)

Even in the poetry Blake published after *America*, where historical characters have no explicit part in the apocalyptic struggle, the onset of the Millennium is a complex struggle between Orc, Los, and Urizen (to name but three). The denouements of all

Blake's prophetic narratives present an apocalyptic process which opens out rather than marks an end of history. Perhaps his eschatology is best summarized in the terms Iain McCalman has used to describe the complexion of Thomas Spence's millenarianism. McCalman identifies in Spence's prophetic rhetoric both a kinship with 'scholarly post-millennialists who envisaged the millennium as arriving gradually through human action' and a populist tone which 'was that of the more apocalyptic pre-millennialists who believed that Christ's advent would precipitate an abrupt transformation'.[20]

Spence did not merely interpret biblical prophecy but claimed for himself the faculty of vision. If his pre-millennialism showed the impatience of a popular enthusiast, so too did this willingness to cast himself in the role of a contemporary prophet. It is a willingness he shared both with Brothers and Blake. So far this chapter has concentrated on the kind of prophetic radicalism manifested in these three visionaries, but it was not only enthusiasts of this sort who took a millenarian interest in the French Revolution. Much more rationalist and respectable Dissenters sympathetic to the Revolution interpreted it almost immediately as the prelude to the earthly Millennium. Typical of this perspective were Richard Price and Joseph Priestley. The latter, in his sermon published as *The Present State of Europe Compared with Antient Prophecies* (1794), claimed that the Revolution marked the onset of the dissolution of ecclesiastical and civil government that would precede the Millennium. Priestley, like Brothers, saw Revelation being fulfilled in contemporary events. His associate, the influential Cambridge Dissenter William Frend, even wished for the power of the prophetic voice so as to be able to denounce the counter-revolutionary war: 'Oh! that I had the warning voice of an antient prophet, that I might penetrate into the inmost recesses of palaces, and appall the haranguers of senates.' But Frend's phrasing here is instructive. He only wishes for prophetic power. He does not actually declare himself prophetically inspired. From the polite perspectives of Cambridge Dissent, the era of prophetic inspiration,

[20] McCalman, *Radical Underworld*, 65.

however much admired, was closed. Notwithstanding attempts by Burke to discredit figures like Priestley and Frend by comparing them to Oliver's preachers, it was Brothers who had more in common with the radical sectaries of the seventeenth century. Like many of the latter Brothers claimed to have experienced direct inspiration for himself; he shared with them an emphasis 'on the holy spirit within one, on one's own experienced truth as against traditional truth handed down by others'. Brothers drew on a culture which denied such illumination had ceased and claimed for himself the power of an Old Testament prophet. He issued his own prophecies. Frend and Priestley did not go this far. They never claimed to add to the settled and unrepeatable prestige of the Bible, even if they did challenge its established meaning. Their 'hope that a glorious period is at hand', in the words of the *Evangelical Magazine*, led to an often radical application of biblical prophecy to contemporary history, but Frend and Priestley were involved in a very different exercise from those, like Brothers, who, 'not content with so sober and commendable enquiry, have been bold enough to boast of a prophetic spirit'. Blake's proximity to the popular tradition manifested in Brothers can be gauged by the fact that, where Lowth described prophecy and Frend invoked it, he actively practised the prophetic role. It is in this context that the radical challenge of subtitling *America* and *Europe* 'A Prophecy' can be appreciated.[21]

Perhaps the point can be best illustrated by a more strictly poetic comparison between Blake's *Europe* and Coleridge's 'Religious Musings', two poems which are clearly the products of a millenarian interest in the French Revolution and which share a number of striking similarities. Despite the parallels, which I shall discuss below, I believe that Blake's prophecy has much more of popular enthusiasm about it than the poem Coleridge wrote while still under the influence of Joseph Priestley and Cambridge Dissenting circles. Both *Europe* and

---

[21] See W. Frend, *Peace and Union Recommended to the Associated Bodies of Republicans and Anti-Republicans* (St Ives, 1793), 48, C. Hill, *The World Turned Upside Down*, 2nd edn. (Harmondsworth, 1975), 368, and the *Evangelical Magazine*, 4 (1796), 303.

'Religious Musings' begin with a vision of the Incarnation
which foreshadows the Second Coming looked to at the end of
the two poems. *Europe*, however, is the more unconventional
in its treatment of these matters. Its version of the Nativity
leads to an account of the swamping of Christ's liberating
potential in the institutions erected in his name. More specifically, I shall suggest it parodies the pious hopes of Milton's 'On
the Morning of Christ's Nativity'. Coleridge's poem also
invokes Milton, and even seems to refer to the 'Nativity Ode',
but with more straightforward approbation than Blake's
enthusiastic critique.[22]

The central portion of Coleridge's poem is devoted to a litany
of the sufferings to be abolished at the return of Christ. It
implies that the French Revolution represents the opening of
the fifth of the seven seals (l. 324) and looks forward to the
ultimate descent of divine justice:

> And lo! the Throne of the redeeming God
> Forth flashing unimaginable day
> Wraps in one blaze earth, heaven, and deepest hell.

> (ll. 426–8)

Interestingly, Blake parodies exactly this conventional representation of the Judgement in the design on Plate 11 of *Europe* (see
Pl. 2). There Blake makes use of the iconography of popular
anti-Catholic prints to offer a vision of the enthroned deity as a
winged demon supported by the angelic hypocrisy of state
religion. David Erdman has noted the similarity between the
facial features of the central figure and caricature representations
of George III.[23] When *Europe* does finally offer an apocalyptic
denouement it is the product, not of divine Providence, but of
the energy of Blake's own invention, Orc, manifested in the
French Revolution:

[22] Details of Coleridge's relationship with radical Dissent in Cambridge are
to be found in Nicholas Roe's *Wordsworth and Coleridge: The Radical Years*
(Oxford, 1988). See esp. 84–117. I take Coleridge's mention of 'Milton's TRUMP'
(l. 387) to be a specific reference to the 'wakeful trump of doom' (l. 156) of the
'Nativity Ode' which is discussed in relation to *Europe* below.

[23] See Erdman's *Prophet Against Empire*, 213–14.

But terrible Orc, when he beheld the morning in the east,
Shot from the heights of Enitharmon;
And in the vineyards of red France appear'd the light of his fury.

(E 66; Pl. 14, ll. 37–9)

Coleridge, however, does not merely represent the apocalyptic promise of the French Revolution as the fulfilment of divine Providence. He lists an Elect who have brought closer the Millennium of enlightenment his poem seeks. This Elect includes Milton, Newton, Hartley, Franklin, and Priestley. Blake's poem explicitly mocks the notion that Newton has brought the Millennium closer. Newton blows the 'Trump of the last doom' in *Europe* (E 65; Pl. 13), but what he produces is a travesty of the conventional Judgement Day. Instead of the resurrection of the dead,

> . . . the myriads of Angelic hosts,
> Fell thro' the wintry skies seeking their graves,
> Rattling their hollow bones in howling and lamentation.

(ll. 6–8)

The suspicion of Newton expressed here and elsewhere in Blake's writing, where he is often linked with Locke, is typical of popular enthusiasm. Brothers, writing from the madhouse in 1801, claimed that the principles of Newtonian physics were established by habit not truth. John Wright, a follower of Brothers, believed Locke to be only 'a supposed famous writer' and that his work was 'exactly in opposition' to inspiration. These perspectives are borne out of a bitterness at being excluded from both the political and cultural means of representation, something Brothers made very clear; 'the vulgar are precluded from being judges of this or any other, because they are not learned—a very silly reason indeed'. It should come as no surprise that an autodidact like Blake, who was continually being denied the status of artist and poet (as well as sometimes lacking sufficient work to practise his trade as an engraver), should have shared an antagonism to those who valued 'Learning above Inspiration' (E 546).[24]

----

[24] See Brothers, *Description of Jerusalem* (London, 1801), 77–9, and J. Wright, *A Revealed Knowledge of some Things that will Speedily be Fulfilled* (London, 1794), 22.

Coleridge's background made it much easier for him to represent the Millennium as the culmination of a gradual enlightenment which comprised scientific and political changes within the public culture. Like most Rational Dissenters, Coleridge tended to post-millennialism, what Priestley called 'the general Enlargement of Liberty'. Vulgar enthusiasts, often suspicious of all institutionalized book-learning, tended to put their faith in sudden inspiration, though this could still accommodate a vision of the Millennium which foregrounded the role of human agency in its arrival.[25] Coleridge's poem is very careful to caution patience in its millenarianism. It is, of course, widely recognized that the commitment to the French Revolution shown by Rational Dissenters in the earliest years of the 1790s began to wane around 1795 in response to the excesses of the Jacobin Terror. It is equally the case that the relatively polite constituency of Rational Dissent had always been wary of popular enthusiasm and the notion of a genuinely mass participation in the Enlightenment. Priestley himself by 1794 had retreated from the unqualified radical commitment of the early 1790s. In his fast-day sermon of 1794 he stressed that the final destruction of Antichrist was 'reserved for the coming of Christ in person'. Priestley was criticized by more determinedly radical Dissenters for presenting this view of the Second Coming. J. L. Towers, for instance, claimed it was a contradiction of the views Priestley had expressed in his *Institutes of Natural and Revealed Religion* (1772–4), where he had allowed a metaphorical reading of the account of the Second Coming in the Bible: 'the utter destruction of Antichrist is often denominated in the scriptures by the coming of Christ . . . so that this coming also will not be a literal one, but figurative'.[26] Coleridge seems to have shared something of Priestley's later ambivalence about the imminence of the Millennium. He assures the 'Children of wretchedness' (l. 321) that 'Yet is the day of Retribution nigh' (l. 323), but he also takes

[25] See J. Priestley, *Letters to the Right Honourable Edmund Burke* (Birmingham, 1791), 141.

[26] See Priestley, *The Present State of Europe Compared with Antient Prophecies* (London, 1794), 26, and J. L. Towers, *Illustrations of Prophecy* 2 vols. (London, 1796), ii. 641.

care to counsel them that 'More groans must rise | More blood must stream, or ere your wrongs be full' (ll. 321–2). He twice cautions those impatient for apocalyptic change to 'Rest awhile' (ll. 320 and 327). Interestingly, the same cautious reflex is evident in Milton's 'Nativity Ode', a poem which Blake seems to invoke and challenge in *Europe*.

Several commentators have drawn attention to the verbal echoes of the opening of Milton's poem in the first lines of Blake's prophecy:

> The deep of winter came;
> What time the secret child,
> Descended thro' the orient gates of the eternal day:
> War ceas'd, & all the troops like shadows fled to their abodes.
>
> (E 61; Pl. 3, ll. 1–4)

The reflection on the Nativity in his ode leads Milton to look eagerly towards the triumph of 'Truth and Justice' (l. 141). Ultimately, however, the poem marginalizes this desire as impatience and presents the deferral of the Second Coming as a necessary part of God's providential plan:

> But wisest fate says no,
> This must not yet be so;
> The babe lies yet in smiling infancy,
> That on the bitter cross
> Must redeem our loss,
> So both himself and us to glorify;
> Yet first, to those ychained in sleep
> The wakeful trump of doom must thunder through the deep.
>
> (ll. 149–56)

Where Milton is content to celebrate the Incarnation as a step in the right providential direction, Blake's poem is less sanguine. The bard Los, perhaps playing out Milton's role, concentrates on 'the peaceful night' (E 61; Pl. 3, l. 7) of the Nativity and so fails to recognize or anticipate its usurpation by the children of Urizen who 'sieze all the spirits of life and bind | Their warbling joys' (E 62; Pl. 4, l. 3). This binding is continued in Plates 5 and 8, now by the children of Enitharmon. Blake implies that these are the representatives of the various dynasties and churches that have appropriated the Incarnation to their version of state religion: Palamabron is a 'horned priest' (E 62; Pl. 8, l. 3), Elynnitria 'a silver bowed queen' (l. 4), and Rintrah a 'furious king' (l. 12). The description of Enitharmon's children extends Blake's engagement with Milton by travestying stanzas xviii to xxvi of the 'Nativity Ode', which record the dispersal of the 'brutish gods' of various idolatrous heathen sects at the Incarnation. Both accounts take the form of a catalogue of strange and exotic personal names, but Blake inverts Milton's perspective by suggesting that Christian state religion has been a continuation of the brutish idolatry Christ was supposed to have destroyed. Paine made the same point more explicitly in *The Age of Reason*: 'The Christian theory is little else than the idolatry of the ancient Mythologies, accommodated to the purposes of power and revenue.' Blake's ironic revision of Milton's poem is resumed on Plate 13 of *Europe* with Enitharmon's complacent satisfaction at the sight of her subjects 'with bands of iron round their necks' (E 64; l. 29). Milton had accepted that 'those ychained in sleep' would not be released until the 'wakeful trump of doom' sounded at the end of time. *Europe* represents this acceptance as an acquiescence in the moral and political constraints of Enitharmon's dominion, politicizing Milton's metaphor by taking it literally. On Plate 12 the literalization is augmented by a translation into visual terms since the design shows a prisoner chained in a dungeon. It is an illustration of the consequences of Milton's compromise which might equally have been Blake's comment on Coleridge's 'Religious Musings'.[27]

---

[27] For a discussion of Blake's treatment of the 'Nativity Ode', see Michael Tolley's '*Europe*: "To those ychain'd in sleep"', in *Blake's Visionary Forms Dramatic*, ed. D. V. Erdman and J. E. Grant (Princeton, NJ, 1970). Paine's description of Christian's continuation of pagan practices is taken from *The Age of Reason*, *CWP*, ii. 467. The same perspective was also retained by more enthusiastic opponents of established religion: 'The sciences falsely so called, like the professors of them, motley tribe, decked with all the trumpery of Rome, are danced on the wires of human invention, to the great admiration of the present refined age, and the no small profit of Diana's priestly craftsmen. An attempt to draw the veil of ignorance, from the minds of the multitude, has ever been considered as high treason against these rulers, principalities, and powers of darkness.' See the editor's preface to Garnet Terry's reprint of Samuel How's

   The difference between the enthusiasm of Blake's *Europe* and
the more restrained Dissenting perspectives of Coleridge's 'Religious Musings' is evident in the forms of the two poems. The
subtitle of *Europe* indicates its prophetic status. Its formal aspirations are very much those of biblical prophecy. I have already
drawn attention to the parallelism which seems to operate at the
basis of Blake's versification in *Europe*. Its parabolic language,
the enigmatic pantheon of figures, and the complexities of its
narrative all conform to a model of prophetic obscurity. Coleridge's poem does not present itself as prophetic in this way. It
does tend towards the parabolic language suitable to its sublime
subject and is unsurprisingly full of biblical allusions, but its
most immediate model is Miltonic rather than biblical as evi-
denced by the extended similes and blank verse. Towards the
close of the poem Coleridge makes it clear that he is not himself
laying claim to visionary powers. He writes that his 'Fancy Falls'
(l. 409) at the prospect of describing the events of the Last Days.
The poem concludes with the acceptance that divine inspiration
is not enjoyed by mere mortals:

> I haply journeying my immortal course
> Shall sometime join your mystic choir! Till then
> I discipline my young noviciate thought
> In ministries of heart-stirring song.

> (ll. 436–9)

Coleridge's acceptance of the discipline of song in part explains
the generally favourable reviews his poem received at a time
when all the reviewers were wary of visionary enthusiasm.
Indeed one reviewer was quite explicit in confirming that, while
the poem sailed close to the dangerous wind of prophecy, it
succeeded in navigating a poetic course:

Often obscure, uncouth, and verging to extravagance, but generally
striking and impressive to a supreme degree, it exhibits that ungov-
erned career of fancy and of feeling which equally belongs to the poet

---

The Sufficiency of the Spirit's Teaching, 8th edn. (London, 1792), which is
discussed in more detail below.

and enthusiast. The Book of Revelations maybe a dangerous fount of prophecy, but it is no mean Helicon of poetic inspiration.

The millenarianism of Coleridge's poem stayed on the safe side of the divide between poetry and prophecy. Blake's more fully enthusiastic style, together with the explicit claim in the subtitles of *America* and *Europe* to be writing prophecy, may explain his lack of commercial success in the 1790s. His work smacked too much of 'the dangerous fount of prophecy' which even the relatively liberal *Monthly Review* feared.[28]

In making this distinction between vulgar enthusiasm and Rational Dissent I do not want to underplay the radicalism of the positions taken up by Priestley and Coleridge in the 1790s. Both were committed to a millenarianism which sharply contrasted with the conservative view of the Judgement as the ultimate tribunal at which transgression of the laws of state religion could be punished. Most loyalist writers in the 1790s chose to present this day as deferred to a very distant future, though a few did offer millenarian accounts of the French Revolution which portrayed the Republic in the role of the Beast of the last days. Garrett has shown, for instance, that the Pitt government sponsored millenarian texts which sought to counter the varieties of radical millenarianism and to prepare the people for patriotic war against France. An example is *A Prophecy of the French Revolution and the Downfall of Antichrist* (1793), which encouraged gratitude in the reader for the 'inestimable Blessings' provided by Church and King. Yet the identification of the French Republic with the Beast involved a difficult contortion of Protestant millenarian tradition since the Catholic monarchy of France, along with Rome, had historically long been cast in that role. Brothers and

---

[28] See *Monthly Review*, 2nd ser., 20 (1796), 197–8. A brief overview of the initial response to Coleridge's poem can be found in D. Roper's *Reviewing Before the 'Edinburgh', 1788–1802* (London, 1978), 85–90. The necessity of a distinction between poetry and prophecy was also emphasized by the *Analytical Review*, which noted that 'Prophecy and poetry are so nearly allied, that in most nations they have been more or less confounded' in a discussion of the dangers of Brothers's enthusiasm. Interestingly, the review notes one difference as being that poetry is less obscure than prophecy. See *Analytical Review*, 21 (1795), 213.

his supporters were able to draw on this tradition in their republications of old prophecies.[29]

Significantly, the authors and publishers of loyalist millenarian tracts seldom laid claim to prophetic inspiration themselves. I would argue that the actual practice of prophecy was read as intrinsically threatening by the status quo. There is a distinct uneasiness, for instance, in the begrudging coverage given by respectable journals to the prophetic literature which poured out in 1795. Even where a prophetic intervention was made against Brothers, as in Eliza Williams's *The Prophecies of Brothers Confuted from Divine Authority* (1795), the *Critical Review* could give her pamphlet's loyalist sentiments only muted assent because 'though we may give an account of, we never take on us to review prophets or prophetesses'. The cautious nature of this response reflects a nervous antipathy to the prophetic genre. The *Critical Review* feared that 'in no instance has the public credulity been more grossly played with . . . than in the discovery of pretended prophecies as relating to the French Revolution'. Writing on the popular interest in Brothers, the *British Critic* commented 'if such enthusiasts were in all times to be found, wicked men were never wanting to make them, if possible, the instruments of mischief'. Behind the latter statement lay a recognition of the historical relationship between prophetic activity and political discontent. Given this recognition, it is no surprise to find that there was a statute in force throughout the eighteenth century against seditious prophecy. All in all, the ruling classes saw too much of what the *Critical Review* called 'the dangerous nature of enthusiasm' in the very idea of the practice of prophecy to rest easy whatever the particular prophecy's ideological message.[30]

The fear aroused by what the *Gentleman's Magazine* described as 'visionary impertinence' had its origins in the perceived threat

---

[29] See Garrett, *Respectable Folly*, 167, and the 'Publisher's Preface' to *A Prophecy of the French Revolution and the Downfall of Antichrist* (1793).

[30] See *Critical Review*, 15 (Oct. 1795), 218, 8 (Aug. 1793), 405, 15 (Sept. 1795), 18, and *British Critic*, 5 (1795), 437. Paley's 'William Blake, the Prince of the Hebrews, and the Woman Clothed with the Sun', 261–2, has an account of the statute against seditious prophecy.

to the received authority of the Bible. To most Anglicans at least
the Bible was a closed text; the era of genuine prophecy which it
described was now emphatically over. As the author of *Sound
Argument Dictated by Common Sense* (1795) put it: 'God hath
already revealed his will; and it is impious to suppose that, after
his Son, he would send such an humble prophet as Brothers.' To
attempt to add to the received canon of God's word was to
suggest that the era of divine inspiration was not closed. More
pointedly it implied that areas of knowledge and power existed
outside of those officially sanctioned. Blake himself implied
much the same thing when he wrote 'the Beauty of the Bible is
that the Most Ignorant & Simple Minds Understand it Best' (E
667).[31] Such a perspective was obviously particularly suspect in
the context of the French Revolution and amid demands by
British radicals that the unlearned should be enfranchised. A
belief in the continuing possibility of the practice of prophecy
complemented the Painite commitment to 'the rights of the
living' over 'manuscript assumed authority' by implying that the
conventional sources of authority and knowledge could be
superseded. In fact there were definite links between popular
radicalism and millenarian culture in the 1790s. Blake's friend
William Sharp, for instance, was both a member of the Society
for Constitutional Information and a follower of Brothers. The
publishers of radical tracts often performed the same service for
millenarians. George Riebau, one of Brothers's most loyal followers, was also a member of the London Corresponding Society. Connections such as these have led Harrison to conclude
that 'political radicalism and religious millenarianism were not
alternatives so much as different aspects of the same phenomenon'. The *British Critic* had no doubt about the political affiliations of the followers of Brothers:

The truth is, that in almost every instance, we see democracy and the
real or pretended belief in this creature united. The shops that sell the
pamphlets of Eaton, deal also in the prophecies of Brothers. In many
cases it appears that the contagion of insanity has actually caught the

---

[31] See the *Gentleman's Magazine*, 65 (1795), 223, and [W. C. Oulton], *Sound
Argument Dictated by Common Sense*, 52.

friends of anarchy: how else has it happened, that a very eminent engraver, whose political opinions are but too notorious, has executed a fine print of Brothers?

The engraver referred to is Sharp, and while the *British Critic* had a political investment in presenting reformist principles in general as a species of fanaticism, the evidence does suggest that in the artisan culture at least there were very strong links between enthusiasm and radicalism.[32]

The fear of popular prophecy was heightened by contemporary theories of the psychopathology of enthusiasm. From Locke onwards enthusiasm had been presented as a contagious disease capable of rapidly infecting the lower orders. To many the Methodist revival seemed to be corroborating evidence of this weakness in the popular mind. Brothers's prophecies looked like a virus of radicalism suited to exploit such vulgar susceptibilities. Hence the anonymous author of *A Word of Admonition to the Right Hon. William Pitt* (1795), typically using a metaphor of infection, urged the government to take action against 'the poisonous prophetic that is infused and making rapid progress through the great body of society'. He was convinced that Brothers's prophecies were more likely to overturn the state than any other variety of radicalism. The *Gentleman's Magazine* echoed this point of view when it argued that the enthusiasm of Brothers's books together with their cheapness made them particularly attractive to 'the bulk of the people, whose minds in these days do not need disquiet'.[33]

The most definite biographical evidence of Blake's acquaintance with the religious enthusiasm which the *Gentleman's Magazine* feared so much is his association with Swedenborgianism. It is important to emphasize that there is no clear proof that Blake was ever a member of the Swedenborgian Church of the New

---

[32] See Harrison, *Second Coming*, 223 and 79. The comments of the *British Critic* are taken from its review of *The Age of Prophecy!* in 5 (1795), 555.

[33] See *A Word of Admonition to the Right Hon. William Pitt* (London, 1795), 14, and the *Gentleman's Magazine*, 65 (1795), 208. Southey, looking back on the phenomenon of Brothers's popularity, wrote: 'When a madman calls himself inspired from that moment the disorder becomes infectious' (*Letters from England by don Manuel Alvarez Esprella*, 3 vols. (London, 1807), ii. 256).

Jerusalem, though he did move in Swedenborgian circles before the Church was set up and attended a conference at which he signed his name to a manifesto of principles. By the time Blake was writing *The Marriage of Heaven and Hell* he had clearly lost most of his earlier sympathy for the Swedish prophet: 'Swedenborg boasts that what he writes is new; tho' it is only the Contents or Index of already publish'd books' (E 42). Perhaps the most coherent account of Blake's anti-Swedenborgianism has been put forward by John Howard. Howard claimed that *The Marriage of Heaven and Hell* was Blake's response to the growing conservatism of the Swedenborgian movement in the late eighteenth century, a conservatism most obviously manifested in the creation of the institution of the Church of the New Jerusalem. What had been a movement with a broad appeal, attracting interest amongst the populations of manufacturing towns such as London, Manchester, and Birmingham, was developing into 'a small and prosperous denomination'. So intent was this denomination on respectability that in 1792 it publicly declared its loyalty to the government to clear itself from the radical associations of religious nonconformity.[34]

What was really original about Howard's thesis was the link it made between Blake's antagonism to Swedenborg in *The Marriage* and the circle of writers which surrounded the publisher Joseph Johnson in the 1790s. Joseph Priestley, for instance, became involved in a public controversy with Robert Hindmarsh, self-styled printer to the Prince of Wales and an important conservative influence in the New Church. At the same time the *Analytical Review*, published by Johnson, never lost an opportunity to ridicule the Swedenborgians and the visionary pretensions of their prophet. Howard claimed that *The Marriage of Heaven and Hell* was specifically written to participate in this

---

[34] See Garrett, *Respectable Folly*, 152. On the increasing conservatism of the Church of the New Jerusalem, see M. Butler, *Romantics, Rebels and Reactionaries* (Oxford, 1981), 46–7, R. Hindmarsh, *The Rise and Progress of the New Jerusalem Church*, ed. E. Madeley (London, 1861), 54 and 70–1, and J. Howard, 'An Audience for *The Marriage of Heaven and Hell*', *Blake Studies*, 3 (1970), 24–6. Much of the discussion in the next few pages is taken from my article 'The Radical Enthusiasm of Blake's *The Marriage of Heaven and Hell*', *British Journal for Eighteenth-Century Studies*, 14 (1991), 51–60.

anti-Swedenborgian polemic with the Johnson circle in mind as its audience.[35]

That Blake had contact with the Johnson circle is undeniable. In his trade as an engraver Blake did more work for Johnson than any other publisher.[36] Subsequent chapters of this book will suggest many instances in which Blake's rhetoric seems to be implicated in the language and concerns of Johnson's associates, but it is necessary to be aware that the enthusiasm of *The Marriage of Heaven and Hell* would probably have alienated the intellectuals of the Johnson circle as much as similar features of Swedenborg's writings. That is not necessarily to say that enthusiastic features of Blake's rhetoric are to be regarded as Swedenborgian. There is a tendency within Blake criticism to limit the enthusiastic dimensions of Blake's texts to Swedenborgian sources. This tendency began as early as Frederick Tatham's manuscript biography, which was eager to distinguish Blake and Swedenborg from Brothers in order to distance the first two from the last's unrespectability: 'Brothers is only classed with Swedenborg in order to ridicule Swedenborg & bring him into Contempt. Blake and Brothers must not be classed together.' My approach, on the contrary, has shown that Blake's prophetic radicalism has features in common with a whole range of texts produced from the broader culture of enthusiasm.[37]

Some of the features of Blake's rhetoric often linked to a

---

[35] See Priestley's *Letters to Members of the New Jerusalem Church* (London, 1791); and Hindmarsh's *Letters to Dr. Priestley* (London, 1792). Accounts of this dispute can be found in Howard, 'Audience', 30–2, and Heather Glen's *Vision and Disenchantment*, 58–60. Howard gives the following references to attacks on Swedenborg in Johnson's journal: *Analytical Review*, 5 (1789), 61–4; 6 (1790), 80 and 332–3; 10 (1791), 546; 11 (1791), 517–20; 14 (1792), 190–3. In addition there are reviews and comments on Swedenborgian material in vols. 2 (1788), 97–8; 3 (1789), 459; 5 (1789), 352; 6 (1790), 453; 8 (1790), 332–3; 9 (1791), 546; 14 (1792), 190–3.

[36] Johnson was easily Blake's most consistent employer, especially in the 1790s. He published engravings by Blake from 1780 right up to his death in 1804. During this period Blake engraved 96 plates for Johnson. The most he executed for anyone else was 48 for Longman from 1805 to 1819. See *BR*, 620.

[37] For Tatham's comments, see *BR*, 520.

Swedenborgian influence could just as easily be traced to this broader culture. Let me give a simple example. Central to Blake's *The Marriage* is a series of 'Memorable Fancies' in which the author experiences visions, is transported across the spiritual universe, and has dinner with the prophets Ezekiel and Isaiah. These 'Memorable Fancies' are usually related to Swedenborg's 'Memorable Relations'. That they are to some extent a parody of Swedenborg is very probable, but this ready source should not obscure the fact that such visionary adventures were commonplace in the literature of enthusiasm. Blake's 'Memorable Fancies' take up the use of visions and prodigies that was a staple of popular culture. During the Brothers controversy there was a particularly spectacular crop of such material.[38]

One such pamphlet is *God's Awful Warning to a Giddy Careless Sinful World* (1795), which contains at least one vision which is worth considering in relation to Blake's *The Marriage of Heaven and Hell*. Plates 17–20 of the latter are taken up with a 'Memorable Fancy' in which an Angel shows Blake the dreadful fate that awaits him if he continues in his sinful ways. The Angel reveals a vision of hell centred on a monstrous Leviathan:

His forehead was divided into streaks of green & purple like those on a tygers forehead: soon we saw his mouth & red gills hang just above the raging foam tinging the black deep with beams of blood, advancing toward us with all the fury of a spiritual existence.

(E 41; Pl. 18–19)

But once the narrator is left alone, this terrible vision is transmuted into a pastoral idyll. The implication is that hell is a fable invented by established religion to secure obedience, a charge made more explicitly against the Angel on Plate 19: 'All that we saw was owing to your metaphysics; for when you ran away, I found myself on a bank by moonlight hearing a harper' (E 42). Thomas Webster's vision in *God's Awful Warning*

[38] Both Howard, 'Audience', 46–7, and Scrivener, 'A Swedenborgian Visionary and *The Marriage of Heaven and Hell*', *BIQ* 21 (1987–8), 103, follow the critical consensus of reading the Memorable Fancies as Swedenborgian in origin.

similarly begins with the appearance of a nightmarish 'ill-form'd beast'. Webster's beast, like Blake's Leviathan, undergoes a benign transformation. It becomes a docile leopard which in turn conjures 'fertile land' out of a 'barren heath'. Beneath the account of Webster's vision is an interpretation, allegedly by Brothers, which reads the beast as the army of the French Republic about to bring 'the restoration of peace to the people' and the downfall of received authority in England and Spain. In loyalist propaganda, the French Revolution was often presented as a return to bestial savagery. Brothers's commentary on Webster's vision subverts this conservative convention by representing what loyalists saw as monstrous as the prelude to universal peace. The transformation is similar to that at the centre of Blake's 'Memorable Fancy', which implies that the fruits of disobedience or rebellion are not necessarily eternal damnation. A more politically developed version of this insight appears in 'A Song of Liberty' at the close of *The Marriage of Heaven and Hell*. There the upheavals of the French Revolution are ironically treated both as a Fall from Heaven and the descent of the New Jerusalem. Political disobedience, a fall into sin from the establishment perspective, opens up the potential of a liberating Millennium: 'Empire is no more! and now the lion & wolf shall cease' (E 45; Pl. 25).[39]

Blake's *The Marriage of Heaven and Hell* seems to record a disillusionment with Swedenborg and a move to the sort of radical enthusiasm which came to the fore in the Brothers controversy. Blake was not the only figure in the 1790s who made such a move. Indeed such mobility was typical of the whole culture of enthusiasm, in which seekers often moved from group to group looking for a community within which

---

[39] See *God's Awful Warning*, 2–4, for Webster's vision and Brothers's commentary. Webster's vision was reprinted separately by Riebau with a crude engraving, 'an exact representation', of the vision: see *A Description of a Remarkable Vision seen by Thomas Webster* (London, 1798); the engraving is dated 1794. Webster's vision was evidently popular since one of Joanna Southcott's letters discusses it and disputes some aspects of Brothers's interpretation: *Letters &c to the rev. Stanhope Bruce* (London, 1801), p. A2. Other of the letters in this volume are addressed to Blake's friend William Sharp.

they could feel free from received error. John Wright and William Bryan were two such artisan enthusiasts whose careers provide ready comparisons with Blake's since they also moved from Swedenborgianism in the late 1780s to a commitment to a radical millenarianism in the mid-1790s.[40]

John Wright gave an account of his movements within the culture of enthusiasm in *A Revealed Knowledge of some Things that will Speedily be Fulfilled in the World* (1794), a tract which offers some revealing parallels with Blake's *The Marriage of Heaven and Hell*. Both texts share the sort of heterogeneous and unfinished structure which I have claimed typifies the rhetoric of enthusiasm. Blake's text is the more diverse; making use of poetry, prose, and design as well as taking up the genres of vision, prophecy, and proverb collection. Wright's pamphlet is consecutively divided into spiritual autobiography, a section of obscure millenarian prophecies, and a collection of aphoristic spiritual maxims. The diverse nature of both texts reflects the suspicion of standardized forms within the culture of enthusiasm, a suspicion which sought to avoid what William Bryan called 'the accumulation of error' in 'the multitude of books . . . already in this world'.[41]

The first section of Wright's pamphlet takes on a form which was very common in popular literature—the spiritual autobiography, full of the visionary inspiration sought by the enthusiast.[42] Indeed Wright's immediate interaction with the spiritual world is strikingly demonstrated in the very first sentence: 'In the month of April, so called, 1788, at which time I lived in Leeds, Yorkshire, the Holy Spirit told me, I must go to London, without mentioning the reason, or saying anything more to me.' Later in this section of the pamphlet it becomes clear that Wright was directed to the Swedenborgians in London by their northern missionaries Salmon and Mather.

[40] For contemporary accounts of Wright and Bryan, see Hindmarsh, *Rise and Progress*, 47, and Southey's *Letters from England*, iii. 237–52.

[41] See Bryan, *Testimony*, 1 and 11.

[42] *The Marriage of Heaven and Hell*, of course, contains quasi-autobiographical elements in what Scrivener calls 'bold assertions of visionary experience': 'Swedenborgian Visionary', 103.

Once in London, however, Wright responded to the New Jerusalem Church in much the same way as Blake. Wright declared he saw there 'nothing but old forms of worship established by man's will'. Blake likewise claimed that Swedenborg had written 'all the old falshoods' (E 43; Pl. 21) and accused him of being the source of 'Lies and Priestcraft' (E 609). Both Wright and Blake seem to have been disappointed by the reification of Swedenborg's ideas into scripture and to have shared the enthusiast's typical impatience with laws and ceremonies which attempted to mediate between the human and divine.[43]

Wright's disgust with the New Jerusalem Church led him, again at the prompting of the Holy Spirit, to undertake a journey, in the company of William Bryan, to France in search of a more suitable spiritual community. Their goal was the Avignon Society, a group of aristocratic mystics that the two English artisans had probably come into contact with through their Swedenborgian associations.[44] By 1791 Wright and Bryan had returned to England and were soon to become followers of Brothers. In the second section of his pamphlet Wright drew on his experiences at Avignon to offer a validation of Brothers's mission. He printed a series of 'Remarkable prophecies' revealed to the Society which represent the political upheavals of the 1790s as the onset of the biblical Apocalypse and, though less emphatically than Brothers's prophecies, suggest that the French Revolution was the beginning of the fulfilment of God's Providence:

The sun, the moon, and the stars will fill the earth with troubles. The end of this age will be a long series of calamities which will extend to all the nations in every place. The face of Religion will be changed,

[43] See Wright, *A Revealed Knowledge*, 4.
[44] See Garrett, *Respectable Folly*, 117, for details of the Avignon Society's response to the French Revolution. Robert Southey certainly read the Avignon Society as a radical political organization which helped to 'raise the storm' of the French Revolution. He described the group as 'a society of political Jesuits' seeking 'some imaginary amelioration', *Letters from England*, iii. 251-2. For evidence of contacts between the London Swedenborgians and the Avignon Society, see Hindmarsh, *Rise and Progress*, 41-7, and Garrett, 109.

ostentation will be suppressed, and temporal authority will pass over into other hands.[45]

This prophetic section of Wright's pamphlet is involved in the same radical millenarian discourse as Blake's 'A Song of Liberty', which proclaims that the Apocalypse will see the demise of state religion: 'Let the Priests of the Raven of dawn, no longer in deadly black, with hoarse note curse the sons of joy. Nor his accepted brethren, whom, tyrant, he calls free: lay the bound or build the roof. Nor pale religious letchery call that virginity that wishes but acts not!' (E 45; Pl. 25.) The Millennium described in Revelation, preceded by the calamities described by Blake and Wright, is presented by both as an earthly revolution.[46]

Wright's pamphlet continually returns to the notion that this revolution would involve the transgression and destruction of human laws: 'Here is the time in which God will break the laws made by the children of the earth. Here is the time wherein he will reprove the science of men, and here is the time of his Justice which is that of his prodigies.'[47] A similar emphasis on liberating transgression has long been recognized as operative in *The Marriage of Heaven and Hell*: 'No virtue can exist without breaking these ten commandments: Jesus was all virtue, and acted from impulse: not from rules' (E 43; Pl. 23–4). It is a tendency which is perhaps most in evidence in Blake's 'Proverbs of Hell', the section of *The Marriage of Heaven and Hell* which provides the most obvious parallels with Wright's *Revealed Knowledge*. One section of Wright's pamphlet was devoted to a collection of 'Sentence's. Moral Maxims. and Spiritual Instructions'. Blake's 'Proverbs' have much more in common with Wright's maxims than with Lavater's aphorisms to which they

[45] Wright, *A Revealed Knowledge*, 29. William Bryan tends to be more politically outspoken than Wright. The following passage is typical of Bryan's pamphlet: 'They are the Antichrist, the man of sin, which is to be revealed in this latter day, (that is) all the craft and serpentine subtilty with which they contrive to get to themselves all rule and authority, both civil and ecclesiastical, to enrich themselves by oppressing others, shall be discovered and abolished' *Testimony*, (38).
[46] Wright, *A Revealed Knowledge*, 29.
[47] Ibid. 30.

are often linked. Where Lavater's aphorisms are elegant and balanced, seeking on the whole to recommend the prudence and restraint of their form, both Wright and Blake's collections display the hyperbole and energy associated with enthusiasm and explicitly promote impulse against prudence.[48]

Typical of Blake's 'Proverbs' is the claim 'Exuberance is Beauty' (E 38; Pl. 10). Several of Wright's maxims demonstrate a comparable emphasis on the breaking of bounds. Wright calls on the reader to 'tread under thy feet the prudence of men' and at more length exhorts: 'Follow the bent, follow the desires to be the child of promise, and leave corruption to run in the sepulchre of the old man.'[49] The implications of the latter are much the same as Blake's famous 'He who desires but acts not, breeds pestilence' (E 35; Pl. 7). The hostility to legalism common to both Blake and Wright, and especially the hostility to the ten commandments evident in *The Marriage*, can legitimately be described as antinomian. So far I have concentrated on the role of millenarianism in the Revolution controversy of the 1790s, but, if a longer perspective is taken on the eighteenth century, antinomianism comes to seem the more significant feature of popular enthusiasm. Indeed the words 'enthusiast' and 'antinomian' often come close to being used as synonyms by those alarmed at the progress of popular heresy in the period. Before going on to discuss the place of antinomianism in the 1790s, let me attempt to define the term and its provenance in the late eighteenth century more carefully.

Literally the word antinomian means 'against the law' and describes a heretical hostility to the authority of the moral law which plagued the Christian Church more or less from its inception; but perhaps the best way to begin is by offering a definition from a work contemporary with Blake. John Evans, in his *A Sketch of the Denominations of the Christian World*, described antinomianism as 'the doctrine of imputed righteousness' taken to lengths which could destroy 'the very obligation to moral obedience'. The heresy described by Evans has its

---

[48] Ibid. 30.
[49] Ibid. 54 and 52.

biblical origins in passages such as 1 John 3: 9: 'Whosoever is born of God doth not commit sin; for his seed remaineth in him: and he cannot sin because he is born of God.' Antinomian responses to such passages had a range of manifestations. The claim that the ten commandments were not binding upon Christians who had found salvation could be merely theoretical, maintaining an actual obedience to the law. Practical antinomianism, on the other hand, involved a conviction of a finished state of salvation in the here and now which led to an active rejection of the authority of the law, sometimes to the point of rejoicing in sinfulness as an occasion for the outpouring of God's grace. The examples from *The Marriage of Heaven and Hell* quoted above would seem to be manifestations of this extreme variety of antinomianism. Many of the 'Proverbs of Hell' effectively represent grace as the reward of transgression. Not all antinomianism so militantly promoted transgression. A more passive variety, often equally alarming to the established Church, promised unconditional forgiveness for what it still recognized as sin. The stress on forgiveness in Blake's prophetic writing after 1800 might be regarded as antinomian in this sense.[50]

Central to the antinomian emphasis on the quickening of the spirit over the letter of the law was the downgrading of the ceremonial aspects of religion. The antinomian tended to favour those biblical texts where Christ announced the end of the Mosaic dispensation and its attendant ceremonies. Throughout his writing Blake maintained an antinomian hostility to religious ceremonies. His annotations to Swedenborg's *Divine Love and Divine Wisdom*, probably written in 1789, assert that 'The Whole of the New Church is in the Active Life & not in Ceremonies at all' (E 605). The antinomian basis of this attitude is perhaps clearest in the annotations to Watson's *Apology for the Bible* where, writing in the late 1790s, Blake argued that 'The laws of the Jews were (both ceremonial & real) the basest & most oppressive of human codes. & being like all other codes

---

[50] See J. Evans, *A Sketch of the Denominations of the Christian World*, 8th edn. (London, 1803), 80–1.

given under pretence of divine command were what Christ pronounced them The Abomination that maketh desolate i.e. State Religion which is the Source of all Cruelty' (E 618). As late as around 1820 Blake seems to have maintained similar attitudes. He inscribed his engraving of the Laocoön with the antinomian maxim: 'The outward ceremony is Antichrist' (E 274).

A natural corollary of this distaste for the moral law and religious ceremony was anticlericalism, the mediating presence of the Church being unnecessary for those freed from the curse of the law. A more radical antinomianism often went further and sought to represent the established Church as the scion of Antichrist and an evil distortion of Christ's liberating message. Something of this point of view emerges in Blake's 'The Little Vagabond', a poem which implies that the Church had been actively involved in blocking the believer's experience of salvation:

> Dear Mother, dear Mother, the Church is cold,
> But the Ale-House is healthy & pleasant & warm;
> Besides I can tell where I am use'd well,
> Such usage in heaven will never do well.

> (E 26; ll. 1–4)

At its most radical the antinomian heresy could run over into complete rejection of civil and religious authority. It is this dimension that has attracted the attention of Marxist historians of the seventeenth century like Christopher Hill and A. L. Morton, but I shall argue below that a politically radical antinomianism can be traced in the London of the 1790s. Blake's antinomianism, of course, retains a firmly political perspective in its conviction, as the Chimney Sweeper of Songs of Experience puts it, that 'God & his Priest & King' make up 'a heaven of our misery' (E 23; l. 11).

The sketch of antinomianism provided above should make it clear that I do not consider antinomianism to be so much a specific heresy as a tendency. It seems to me a mistake to over-specify a particular antinomian tradition since the heresy often took on different sectarian guises mixed with other currents such as millenarianism. James Relly, for instance, is a prime example of an eighteenth-century enthusiast who moved beyond Methodism into antinomianism. Originally apprenticed to a cow-farrier, he was converted by Whitefield, and worked with the Methodist leader until a breach followed and Relly set up as a preacher in London. During his mission in London he was frequently attacked as an antinomian and accused of sexual misconduct (as were many enthusiasts). Among his detractors was Maria de Fleury, who argued in her *Antinomianism Unmasked* (1791) that the heresy was dangerously 'gaining ground'. She characterized Relly and his followers as believing 'sin is for ever pardoned and done away with'. Relly's later theology does seem to justify her accusation. He attacked the ceremonial law and the Decalogue as 'that yoke which galled the neck of the nations and made them sigh for deliverance'. Prepared to apply this antagonism practically, he told his followers that the Christian was absolved from the need to observe the sabbath and abstain from popular pastimes and sports. Walter Wilson agreed with de Fleury that Relly had been an antinomian who preached a 'finished salvation'. Wilson also thought Relly a dangerous universalist in that he believed ultimately 'all shall be restored to holiness and happiness'. It was a belief which could veer in directions reminiscent both of seventeenth-century radicals like Gerrard Winstanley and later enthusiasts like Blake: 'Christ is considered as compounded of the people, as the one body is of its various parts and members.' The *Analytical Review* claimed such universalism was still being promoted among the populace in the 1790s by the 'publication of pretended visions'.[51]

Relly is an example of the type of mechanic preacher that so

---

[51] See M. De Fleury, *Antinomianism Unmasked* (London, 1791), 2 and 37, and J. Relly, *Christian Liberty* (London, 1775), 6–7 and 38. Michael Ferber has stressed similarities between Blake and Gerrard Winstanley in their presentation of Christ as an aggregated humanity: see *The Social Vision of William Blake* (Princeton, NJ, 1985), 31–3 and 90–1. On antinomian universalism, see W. Wilson, *The History and Antiquities of Dissenting Churches*, 4 vols. (London, 1808–14), i. 358–60. For the *Analytical Review*, see 20 (1794), 39–41. Ferber discusses the popularity of Winchester's preaching, p. 190. See also Garrett, *Respectable Folly*, 137–8.

alarmed polite opinion throughout the eighteenth century. It was always assumed that such preachers had an investment in calumniating the established clergy and some commentators feared that they promoted tenets subversive of both civil and religious authority. This fear became much more pronounced in the 1790s, when popular preachers were suspected of being in league with Painite reformers and revolutionaries. W. H. Reid's *Rise and Dissolution of the Infidel Societies in this Metropolis* (1800) offered an extreme variant of this trend when he claimed that enthusiasm and Jacobinism were pretty much the same thing, a charge, as we have seen, frequently made during the Brothers controversy of the mid-1790s. Brothers's notoriety was perhaps matched by that of William Huntington, who was consistently accused of a subversive antinomianism from the 1780s to his death in 1813. These accusations were justified to the extent that there were clear antinomian tendencies in the sermons and tracts put out by Huntington. He was even conscious of his seventeenth-century forebears and provided a preface for the 1792 edition of John Saltmarsh's *Free Grace*, originally published in 1645, a text which is blatantly antinomian:

The Spirit of Christ sets a believer as free from hell, the law, and bondage, here on earth, as if he were in heaven; nor wants he anything to make him happy in enjoyment of it, but a revelation of it to him.

Ironically enough Michael Ferber has actually quoted this passage as evidence of a similarity between Blake's view of sin and the antinomianism of seventeenth-century radicals without noticing that the text of *Free Grace* would have been available to Blake in a new edition in the 1790s.[52]

Events in the congregation of William Huntington's Providence Chapel lend support to Reid's case about the allegiances between religious enthusiasm and political radicalism. Hunting-

[52] See J. Saltmarsh, *Free Grace*, 11th edn. (London 1792), 154, and Ferber *Social Vision*, 124. The recommendation by Huntington and Terry's advertisement show an explicit knowledge of Saltmarsh's antinomian reputation. *Free Grace* was also republished in 1700 and 1814. For other of Saltmarsh's works published in Blake's lifetime see the bibliography.

ton himself was a fierce loyalist, but he had considerable difficulties in controlling his own flock's political applications of his theology. Some members of Providence Chapel seem to have been unhappy that he did not follow his populist condemnations of monopolists and the clergy through into a radical politics. In *The Utility of the Books* Huntington had responded to social unrest over war and famine with a sermon that described the first task of Christ at the Second Coming as avenging 'the poor and needy, by an entire destruction of this engine of the devil called OPPRESSION', but he also went on to condemn those who 'let fly the anguish of their souls in open rebellion against the higher powers'. These sentiments were hissed by one section of his audience: 'a knot of young wise men among us, who were great readers and admirers of Tom [Paine]'. Clearly Huntington's deferral of social justice to the last days was too orthodox for those members of his congregation attracted by Brothers's more imminent apocalyptic vision and the political radicalism of Paine, both of whom Huntington warned his followers against.[53]

The disaffected in Providence Chapel did not only include the 'knot of young wise men'; Huntington spoke of others 'who lay near to my heart' being turned against him. One prime candidate for inclusion in this group is the engraver Garnet Terry, evidently one of many in that trade with radical opinions in the 1790s. Others include Blake, Thomas Bewick, and William Sharp. It appears Terry was rescued by Huntington from the unsuccessful practice of his trade some time in the 1780s and set up as a bookseller. His name can be found on the title-page of most of Huntington's publications from the late 1780s till 1795. After 1795 Terry is no longer listed among

[53] See W. Huntington's *The Utility of the Books*, 2nd edn. (London, 1796), 33–4, and *A Watchword and Warning from the Walls of Zion* (London, 1798), 82. See also the attacks on Paine and Brothers in *Discoveries and Cautions from the Streets of Zion*, 2nd edn. (London, 1802), 10–15, and *The Lying Prophet Examined*, 2nd edn. (London, 1813). For further details of problems Huntington experienced in controlling the politics of his flock, see T. Wright, *The Life of William Huntington, S. S.* (London, 1909), 105–7, and Huntington, *God the Guardian of the Poor*, 10th edn. (London, 1813), Part II, 43 and 45, and *A Watchword and Warning*, 56.

Huntington's booksellers, a break which gives support to the idea that there was a political and religious rift between the two men at about that time.[54]

I have already mentioned Terry in the context of the flood of millenarian publications produced in the mid-1790s. His involvement in such projects is likely to have caused problems for him with Huntington since the latter was vehemently opposed to the prophetic aspirations of Brothers and warned his congregation away from similar interests. Writing in 1806 about the 1790s Huntington claimed that Terry had always seemed disaffected with the religious and political establishment: 'When I have been enforcing obedience to rulers, he has afterwards exclaimed against me before a Mr. Wildish. He laboured hard also with Mr. Stephen Mesnard, of Shed Thames, in recommending Tom Paine's *Rights of Man.*' Elsewhere Huntington described Terry as 'the same in religion as he is in politics—a leveller and for all things common'. Nor was Huntington alone in making such charges against Terry. The Calvinist minister Vigors M'Culla claimed that Terry was preaching 'avowed rebellion against Christ, Church, King, and State' in order to 'level all posts and offices'.[55]

Corroboration for these charges can be found in the other millenarian publications Terry put out in the 1790s. The earliest of these, *A Description accompanying an Hieroglyphical Print of Daniel's Great Image* (1793) already records a move towards the radicalism of Brothers. Terry's commentary on his engraving treats Daniel's prophecies as a promise of the ultimate destruction of civil authority, an interpretation Huntington denounced when attacking Brothers two years later. *Prophetical Extracts,*

---

[54] Ibid. 83. Huntington gives an account of Terry's career in *Onesimus in the Balance and Obedience to the Civil Powers Proved* (London, 1806), 5–13. E. P. Thompson has written of 'the line of radical engravers that runs from Blake and Bewick through to Walter Crane': see his 'History from Below', *TLS* (1966), 279.

[55] See Huntington, *Obedience to the Civil Powers Proved*, 13, and *The Eternity of Hope*, 59. For M'Culla's attacks, see his *The Bank Note: or. Engraver Carved* (London, 1806), 44 and 49. There are accounts of the dispute between Terry and Huntington in E. Hooper's *Facts, Letters, and Documents* (London, 1872), 41–2, and Wright's *Life of Huntington*, 142–3.

the serial Terry briefly published in 1795, approximates even more closely to the republican millenarianism of Brothers. Numbers four and five of Terry's serial are explicitly devoted to prophecies 'Relative to the Revolution in France, and the Decline of the Papal Power'. Among the texts, some of which were also reprinted by Riebau, are prophecies which identify the French monarchy with the Beast of Revelation. All this lends a ring of truth to Huntington's retrospective claim that Terry had been spreading radical millenarianism in Providence Chapel in the 1790s.[56]

David Bindman has suggested that Terry's engraving of Daniel's dream-image (see Pl. 3) participates in the same tradition of popular, religious hieroglyphics as many of Blake's designs and specifically his Laocoön engraving. There are more general comparisons to be made between Terry's millenarian publications and the illuminated books Blake was producing at roughly the same time. Both engravers combined interpretations of prophecy with their own designs to suggest the imminence of a political apocalypse.[57] One specific point of comparison bears investigation in more detail. Terry's Babylon is specified as a great centre of trade where morality has become a matter of commerce, 'to make merchandize of men, and to sell them by kingdoms, bishopricks, parishes, or parcels'. Brothers had also based his identification of London with Babylon on the fact that both were great trading powers which dealt in human slavery. A similar complex of ideas and images recurs in Blake's prophecies. In *America* it is typified by the claim 'pity is become a trade' (E 55; Pl. 11, l. 10). Both Blake and Terry seem to object to the ascendancy of the market over the moral economy, a shared perspective that can be related to

[56] See *Prophetical Extracts*, 1 (1795), 31.

[57] See Bindman, 'William Blake and Popular Religious Imagery', *Burlington Magazine*, 128 (Oct. 1986), 717. Quite apart from the fact that both were professional copy-engravers and likely to know each other through business, Bindman has pointed out that Blake may have known Terry in the 1790s through Alexander Tilloch, whose submission of a new banknote press was supported in a petition by Blake. Bindman fails to note that Terry and Blake were on opposite sides in this incident, however. It was Terry, as engraver to the Bank of England, who rejected the new press.

their socio-economic experience as reproductive engravers.
Both found difficulty commanding the rewards they felt their
skills deserved. Terry's description of the belly and thighs of
Daniel's image as 'the merchandize, arts, crafts' of Babylon
which the powerful 'often affect to despise . . . but not with-
standing, they cannot do without their ARTS and CRAFTS' perhaps
reflects the bitterness of the unsuccessful engraver of the 1780s.
Blake's own chequered career as an engraver and his inability to
establish himself as a writer-painter may equally lie behind the
demand;

> . . . who commanded this? what God? what angel!
> To keep the gen'rous from experience till the ungenerous
> Are unrestraind performers of the energies of nature.
>
> (E 55; Pl. 11, ll. 7–9)

Both men wanted to be something more than copy-engravers;
frustration in these aspirations probably inflamed their radical
political sentiments.[58]

William Huntington believed that Terry had been led to
radicalism by one influence in particular:

Nor should we have been favoured with these discoveries, cautions,
and warnings, if the book of an old ranter, long extant, had not fallen
into his hands. His whole mystical fabric is I have no doubt built upon
that man's wild rant, which pulls everything, but builds up nothing.

There are two possible candidates for the text referred to by
Huntington. One is the edition of Saltmarsh's *Free Grace* on
which Terry worked with Huntington. The other is an edition
of Samuel (Cobbler) How's sermon *The Sufficiency of the Spirit's
Teaching*, which Terry brought out in 1792. Significantly,
Terry's collaborator on this book was not Huntington, but J. S.
Jordan, an early member of the London Corresponding Society
and the first publisher of Paine's *Rights of Man*. The collaboration between Terry and Jordan is further confirmation of Reid's

---

[58] See Terry, *A Description . . . Daniel's Great Image* (London, 1793), 10 and
12. Terry evidently had also harboured ambitions to be a painter in the 1780s:
see the dismissive reference in Dodd's 'Memorials of Engravers', British
Museum, Add. MSS e. 33406, fo. 140.

claims about the political affiliations of religious enthusiasm. It also lends support to a separate point made by Reid, that there were parallels and continuities between the unrespectable radicals of the 1790s and the regicides and ranters of the Interregnum. Terry's editions of Saltmarsh and How were far from being the only texts from the earlier period to be reprinted in the 1790s. Brothers and Riebau used millenarian material from the earlier period, while Eaton republished tracts like John Cooke's *Monarchy no Creature of God's Making*. An article in Eaton's *Politics for the People*, 'The Reflexions of a True Briton', explicitly discussed a common link between the two periods:

In revolutions . . . Enthusiasts are necessary, who in transgressing all bounds, may enable the wise and temperate to attain their ends. Had it not been for the Puritans, whose aim was equally to destroy both Episcopacy and Royalty, the English would never have attained that portion of civil and religious liberty which they enjoy.

Eaton was very much conscious of the potential of radical enthusiasm as an auxiliary force to the infidel radicalism he espoused. What the partnership of Terry and Paine's publisher, Jordan, nicely illustrates is that enthusiasm and scepticism were far from being mutually exclusive in the popular radicalism of the period. The point is reinforced if we take into account W. H. Reid's claim that Paine's rationalist conviction that every man's mind was its own church had its origins in the beliefs of the sectaries of the seventeenth century. Indeed Reid specifically mentioned How's tract as the source of Paine's idea.[59]

Central to the lasting popularity of How's sermon was its claim that spiritual inspiration was more important than schol-

---

[59] See Huntington, *Obedience to the Civil Powers Proved*, 24; and *Politics for the People*, 2 vols. (London, 1793–5), vol. i, Part 1, 158. For Reid on the similarities between the radical enthusiasts of the 1790s and those of the 1640s and 1650s, see *The Rise and Dissolution of the Infidel Societies in this Metropolis* (London, 1800), 41, 53, and 83–4. He refers to How's tract, p. 69. Joseph Moser compared the millenarianism stirred up by Brothers to the period after the execution of Charles I when 'the reign of fanaticism commenced' and 'every week produced a new religion, every day a new prophet'. Saltmarsh is amongst the enthusiasts he mentions. See his *Anecdotes of Richard Brothers* (London, 1795), 8–9.

arship to preaching, a principle which was reiterated in the tracts put out by Brothers and Riebau in the 1790s. The latter's *An Impartial Account of the Prophets*, for instance, claimed that the Bible could only be understood 'by those that are spiritually learned, and informed thereof by inward revelation'. Terry's edition of How makes the more extreme claim that the poor and unlearned were more likely to be open to such illumination than the powerful and educated. How charged the learned with importing heathen corruptions into the original simplicity of the Christian faith. His populist antagonism to 'Plato and Aristotle, and a multitude more of heathen philosophers' is still operative in Blake's anti-classicism. In fact much of the structure of feeling of How's pamphlet is recurrent in the writing of both Blake and Terry. How's belief that the mysteries of the scriptures were open to 'mean and simple things as we are' reappears in their belief, which I shall return to below, that the poor understood the Bible best. How also believed that the Bible sanctioned any loose gathering of Christians as a church blessed with Christ's presence. The idea that a building of lime and brick was the temple of Christ or even that the performance of prayers was necessary was another priestly corruption. Blake seems to have shared these prejudices. There is no evidence that he ever attended church and he seems to have ceased his involvement with the Swedenborgians soon after their decision to constitute themselves as the Church of the New Jerusalem. Blake's attitude was that 'every man may converse with God & be a King & Priest in his own house' (E 615).[60]

The attraction of How's claim that the unlearned were better

---

[60] See the Preface of *An Impartial Account* (London 1795); the pamphlet was put out by Riebau with John Wright, and Samuel How, *The Sufficiency of the Spirit's Teaching without Human Learning*, 8th edn. (London, 1792), 47 and 54. Note that Terry's 'Advertisement' to his edition of How claimed; 'I have carefully revised and corrected it; studying, cautiously, to preserve the Divine, wherever I have taken the least liberty with the Cobler.' His confidence in having the 'liberty' to identify the 'Divine' in How could be seen as the equivalent of Brothers's confidence in his own prophetic power to supplement and correct the Bible. Terry is accused of having 'mangl'd Cobler How' in The Prodigal, *Huntington Unmasked and the Doors of his Face opened* (London, n.d. [1802?]), 97.

able to understand and preach the gospel than the 'wise, rich, noble, and learned' for those, like Blake and Terry, without formal education or access to the universities is fairly obvious. Such a claim offered a sense of autonomy and self-esteem to people normally cast in roles of economic and cultural dependency; 'to see with his own eyes, knowing that the just is to live by his faith'. The introduction to Terry's edition is militant in its antagonism to received cultural authority. It promotes How's sermon as 'an attempt to draw the veil of ignorance, from the minds of the deluded multitude, . . . high treason against the rulers, principalities, and powers of darkness'. The celebration of high treason in 1792, the year of the proclamation against seditious writings, suggests how religious enthusiasm could lend itself to radical politics. It was a vision of the world which often already suspected the powers that be of anti-Christian allegiances.[61]

Despite the similarities between Blake's antinomian and millenarian tendencies and the enthusiasm of figures like Garnet Terry and John Wright, it is necessary to acknowledge that there are also important differences. To clarify what seem to me to be the significant aspects of these differences, I shall return to the ostensible parallels between Wright's maxims and Blake's 'Proverbs of Hell'. Though many of Wright's maxims do undoubtedly come close to an antinomian justification of desire, there is another tendency which marks a deep ambivalence. Typical of this other tendency is the maxim 'Too much confidence blinds us, and pride leads astray, and precipitates into the abyss, because then truth flies from us.'[62] This sentiment is indicative of a pious strain in Wright's pamphlet, a strain which suggests a concern that the anticlericalism of enthusiasm should not run over into blasphemy. It is a concern which seems entirely absent from, say, Blake's *The Marriage of Heaven and Hell*. Wright's distrust of religious institutions and 'old forms of worship' does not lead him as far as Blake. Wright does recognize that 'the devil and his agents also make use of

[61] See How, *Sufficiency*, 43, 52, and A2.
[62] Wright, *A Revealed Knowledge*, 48.

the sayings of the Man of GOD', but he does not go so far as to challenge established conceptions of the Divinity. God remains in place as the transcendent authority and his will is to be obeyed: 'Happy he who knows his nothingness, for GOD smiles at the humility of his heart.'[63] Blake's radical enthusiasm is much more thoroughgoing in its rejection of received religious values, a fact made clear in two statements in particular: 'All deities reside in the human breast' (E 38; Pl. 11) and 'God only Acts & Is, in existing beings or Men' (E 40; Pl. 16).

Blake's work tends to show a much less respectful attitude to the Bible than the bulk of the literature produced in the Brothers controversy. Admittedly, extreme enthusiasts sometimes did claim that where scripture differed from their inspired belief it could be amended or even dismissed as pernicious. Brothers asserted that textual errors in the Bible had been revealed to him, but on the whole he treated the scriptures with reverence. He sought to revalue the orthodox signification of biblical prophecy by placing the revolutionary energy of the American and French Revolutions in the role of the Providence fulfilled at the Second Coming. Unlike more polite radical millenarians, such as Richard Price and Joseph Priestley, he also asserted the continuing possibility that the biblical canon was not closed but open to visionary supplementation. Yet if Brothers went beyond Rational Dissenters in claiming to possess prophetic powers himself, he did not go as far as Blake, who sought in his work of the early 1790s to actively disrupt and not merely reinterpret and supplement scriptural authority. The paradigms of the Bible are subjected to a radical rearrangement in Blake's *The Marriage of Heaven and Hell*. An obvious example is the way the Devils become a positive force in contrast to the repressive Angels, who are the continual butt of Blake's sarcasm: 'I have always found that Angels have the vanity to speak of themselves as the only wise; this they do with a confident insolence sprouting from systematic reasoning' (E 42; Pl. 21). Blake's irreverent use of Christian signifiers is demonstrated extensively in the mythic narratives of the prophecies *America*

[63] Ibid. 45–51.

and *Europe*. In those poems the Saviour who returns at the Apocalypse is transformed into Orc, a figure associated both with Christ and Satan. Orc is both the tempter, 'wreathed round the accurs'd tree', and a type of Christ who stamps to dust the stony law of the Decalogue. Thus Blake's Saviour disrupts one of the most basic of biblical paradigms: the opposition between Christ's inspiration and Satan's energy.

Blake's disruption of such received categories can be related to the broader desire among radicals in the 1790s to undermine and reinterpret hegemonic moral, religious, and political vocabularies. Paine's *Rights of Man* drew attention to the way language was used to mystify and control, frequently and ironically inverting the conventional meaning of words for polemical purposes. He pointed out, for instance, that it was 'a perversion of terms to say that a charter gives rights. It operates by a contrary effect, that of taking rights away.' Paine's book inspired a stream of publications which similarly sought to contest the official language. These sometimes took the form of dictionaries such as Pigott's *A Political Dictionary* (1795), which glossed 'Church', for instance, as 'a patent for hypocrisy; the refuge of sloth, ignorance and superstition, the corner-stone of tyranny'. A similar challenge to the moral vocabulary of the cultural hegemony is evident throughout Blake's work. Heather Glen, for instance, has given a detailed account of Blake's ironic use of terms such as 'pity' in *Songs of Innocence and of Experience*. His prophetic narratives continued this critique, transforming the received language of biblical prophecy into a novel rhetoric which seeks to legitimize revolutionary aspirations and demystify established authority.[64]

The pressure Blake places on the language of the Bible goes further than the examples of popular enthusiasm examined in this chapter, but it should be emphasized that the sort of

[64] See Paine, *CWP*, i. 415 and 319 and C. Pigott, *A Political Dictionary, explaining the True Meaning of Words* (London, 1795), 9. Some of the issues raised in this paragraph are discussed in Glen, *Vision and Disenchantment*, 88–92. Several popular radical texts had an approach to specifically biblical material which offers interesting parallels with the work Blake produced from 1790 to 1795. I shall return to this issue in my penultimate chapter.

scepticism evident in Blake's writing could have its origins in the perspectives of enthusiasm. Indeed it was a central tenet of Reid's reading of the subversive nature of popular religious heresy that it was an auxiliary to infidelity because it undermined the traditional deference given to hegemonic structures of religious and political authority. At the basis of much enthusiastic literature lay the conviction that 'the letter killeth but the spirit giveth life' (2 Corinthians 3: 6). It was an attitude which often placed the visionary illumination of the culturally and politically disenfranchised individual or community of believers above the authority of the scholar and priest. In the midst of the popular millenarian outburst of 1793–5 the perspective manifested itself in the stress on the continuing possibility of prophetic practice. Such an emphasis threatened to undermine the authority of the Bible as the revealed world of God in favour of a notion of ongoing revelation in the present. To question the cultural hegemony in this way could prove a small step towards, though still a long way from, Paine's deliberately iconoclastic claim that 'the Jewish poets deserve a better fate than that of being bound up, as they are now with the trash that accompanies them, under the abused name of the Word of God'. Some enthusiasts carried on along this path in the 1790s towards the convergence of visionary enthusiasm and scepticism that Iain McCalman has so ably described. It is a convergence hinted at in the collaboration of Terry and J. S. Jordan described above.[65]

Blake often emulates the sceptical iconoclasm of Paine. The most pungent example being this couplet on the Bible from the notebooks *circa* 1793:

> The Hebrew Nation did not write it
> Avarice & Chastity did shite it.   (E 516)

Sentiments such as these represent an extension of enthusiasm beyond that of Brothers, Terry, and Wright to a point where its

---

[65] See Paine, *CWP*, ii. 477. For an example of a shift from what seems like fairly straightforward religious enthusiasm to a more complex combination of visionary rhetoric with scepticism, see McCalman's account of Robert Wedderburn, *Radical Underworld*, 50–72.

disruption of received Christian discourse bears a paradoxical similarity to rationalist critiques of the Bible. Subsequent chapters will offer more detail on other sources of this disruption. Suffice it to say at this point that, despite their stress on the immanence of the divine, Brothers *et al.* still look to a transcendent source. Blake's notion of the divine is much more radically decentred. *The Marriage of Heaven and Hell* proclaims 'God only Acts & Is, in existing beings or Men'. Even *Jerusalem*, the last of Blake's illuminated books, still maintains a similar attitude:

> . . . Why stand we here trembling around
> Calling on God for help; and not ourselves in whom God
>   dwells
> Stretching a hand to save the Falling Man.

(E 184; Pl. 38, ll. 13–15)

If Blake went further beyond the parameters of conventional Christianity than contemporaries like Brothers and Terry, the fact that the basis of his rhetoric still lies in the culture of vulgar enthusiasm should not be obscured. His 'visionary impertinence' needs to be considered in the context of an important aspect of radicalism in the 1790s: its attempts to legitimize popular language and forms in the public space. The key text in this impetus is usually taken to be Paine's *Rights of Man*, which marks an attempt to achieve a style which confounded hegemonic distinctions between the polite and vulgar languages. Paine strove to write in a political language accessible to the disenfranchised: 'a style of thinking and expression different to what had been customary in England'. The implication was that the vulgar language and its speakers could participate in the public and political life of the country. Blake's prophetic rhetoric has similar implications since it proclaims the right of the discourse of popular enthusiasm to a public voice.[66]

That Blake believed the parabolic style of the Bible was integral to the rhetorical resources of the vulgar language is made abundantly clear in his angry annotations, made in 1827,

---

[66] Paine, *CWP*, i. 348. Olivia Smith's *The Politics of Language 1791–1819* (Oxford, 1984) offers a detailed consideration of the linguistic dimensions of the Revolution controversy.

the year of his death, to Thornton's new translation of the Lord's Prayer. Thornton's translation was part of a movement to replace the uncouth language of the Authorized Version with a more polished style. The hostility apparent in Blake's marginalia to the 'Classical Learned' (E 667) mode of Thornton reflects both the populist antagonism to book-learning evident in Terry's edition of Cobbler How and a conviction that the Authorized Version had become part of the common language. Where Samuel Johnson (quoted by Blake in his annotations) claimed that the Bible could not 'be understood at all by the unlearned', Blake argued that 'Ignorant & Simple Minds Understand it Best' (E 667). Terry seems to have shared Blake's beliefs:

> The scriptures are plain and easy—as is Christ's example clear and obvious to view: he is no hard master, nor are the scriptures a sealed book to you, but a plain clear guide, and easy to be understood, written to suit the meanest capacities, independent of the glosses of mercenaries who would make us believe to the contrary.

The comments of Blake and Terry alert us to a popular feeling that the Bible, and particularly the Authorized Version, belonged to the people. It had been appropriated to become an active part of the popular culture. Brothers's writings, for instance, were attacked because their practice of the parabolic style of the Bible was felt to be especially appealing to vulgar tastes. The *Gentleman's Magazine* felt that there would have been nothing to fear if Brothers had written in a more respectable manner, but warned 'it should seem they are calculated to worse ends, and written for the understanding, and adapted to the purchase of the lower class'. Terry believed what Lowth called prophetic obscurity to be 'plain and easy', revealing the enthusiast's conviction that what the learned found difficult could be directly illuminated by spiritual inspiration. Blake's poetic adaptation of prophecy represents in part an attempt to bring a vulgar language into the public domain, although the means of production he adopted precluded any of his work reaching a popular audience in the 1790s.[67]

[67] An account of 18th-century attempts to reform biblical style can be found

Utopian writing 'Spensonia'

Despite that caveat, Blake's prophetic rhetoric bears comparison with other artisan radicals of that decade. Thomas Spence, for instance, also resorted to the language of biblical prophecy to represent revolutionary change. Neither Blake nor Spence drew solely on the Bible for their political rhetoric. Spence and his followers are McCalman's prime example of the convergence of sceptical and enthusiastic traditions in artisanal radicalism. The subsequent chapters of this book should demonstrate something of the breadth of Blake's rhetorical resources. Both Blake and Spence were bricoleurs who sought to forge new systems of representation out of a variety of received protocols. Yet both incorporated popular millenarianism into their radical texts in a way that implies the right of this language and its vulgar practitioners to the public space.

---

in Tucker's 'Biblical Translation in the Eighteenth Century', *Essays and Studies* (1972), 106–20. See also *Gentleman's Magazine*, 65 (1795), 208, and [Terry], *Letters*, vol. i, p. iii.

2

'Northern Antiquities': Bards, Druids, and Ancient Liberties

MANY of the prophetic features of Blake's writing and designs discussed in the previous chapter have a double signification of origins which makes it difficult to ascribe them to a biblical model with complete certainty. The parabolic style of Blake's illuminated books draws not only on the Bible but also conforms in various ways to more general eighteenth-century conceptions of what primitive literature was supposed to be like. A further complication arises from the fact that the Bible was taken to be the supreme example of such literature, especially once Robert Lowth's theories became well known. Lowth had presented the Bible in the context of theories of the nature of ancient poetry established by scholars such as Thomas Blackwell. In this chapter I shall discuss the place of such antiquarian theories in the cultural politics of the 1790s and their part in Blake's development of his own brand of radical primitivism.

Blake's primitivism was part of a desire, widespread among radicals in the 1790s, to bring previously excluded currents into the public domain. The broader tendency represents the intensification into an explicitly political enterprise of the interest in the antique, exotic, and vulgar which typifies the cultural production of the second half of the eighteenth century. Joseph Ritson and Edward Williams (Iolo Morganwg), both discussed towards the end of this chapter, offer cases analogous to Blake's of a committed republican antiquarianism. At the same time primitivism feeds more directly into the Revolution controversy, which often restaged literary and philosophical arguments from preceding decades about ancient liberty and modern corruption with a new urgency. Burke represented the French Revolution as a regression orchestrated by primitivist intellectuals; a return to 'naked shivering nature' in which 'all the decent drapery of life is to be rudely torn off'. Radical intellectuals in Britain, such as Mary Wollstonecraft, presented their reformist beliefs as a paradoxical return to 'the real dignity of man'. Blake's writing and designs pick up and develop the notion of an original liberty, much of it staged around an antagonism between the inspired bard and repressive druid of northern antiquity which maps on to a parallel biblical opposition between prophet and priest.[1]

I want to begin, however, by looking at the relationship between Blake's verse and James Macpherson's alleged translations into English of the poetry of the ancient Celtic bard, Ossian. Macpherson's translations were the focus of one of the great literary controversies of the eighteenth century. His publication of fragments and later complete epics from the writings of the ancient Caledonians was greeted with relish by a Britain, and indeed Europe, fascinated by the cultural identities of the distant past, but there were also doubts voiced about the authenticity of Macpherson's originals. Modern discussions of Macpherson's publications have tended to be blighted by the latter issue. More importantly, in terms of cultural history, Macpherson's publications answered to a widespread conception of the nature of ancient poetry and conformed to a growing interest in northern antiquities. It is their contribution to and development of these conceptions and interests that will be the focus of my discussion in this chapter.[2]

Modern critics frequently comment on similarities between Blake's work and Macpherson's alleged translations.[3] Above

---

[1] See Burke, *Works*, 7 vols. (London, 1803), v. 151, and M. Wollstonecraft, *A Vindication of the Rights of Woman*, ed. M. Kramnick (Harmondsworth, 1975), 103. See also the many references to this debate in W. Stafford's, *Socialism, Radicalism, and Nostalgia* (Cambridge, 1987).

[2] For a good, general account of the evolution of Macpherson's translations, their content and influence, and the ensuing controversy surrounding their authenticity, see F. Stafford, *The Sublime Savage*. A shorter discussion of the contemporary importance and subsequent neglect of the Ossian poems is to be found in H. Gaskill's article '"Ossian" Macpherson', *Comparative Criticism*, 8 (1986), 113–46.

[3] One of the best recent extended discussions is David Punter's in 'Blake: Social Relations of Poetic Form', *Literature and History*, 8 (1982), 191–201. See

all, the rhythmic prose of Macpherson's English rendering of
his Celtic originals is cited as an important influence on the
evolution of Blake's versification away from the regularity of
conventional forms of poetic metre. Eighteenth-century theorists of primitive literature, like Hugh Blair, believed Macpherson's style epitomized the 'wild, harsh, and irregular' nature of
ancient poetry: 'freer from constraint in the choice and arrangement of words, it allows the spirit of the original to be exploited
with more justness, force, and, simplicity'.[4] Blake's poetry and
Macpherson's prose translations share many of the indices of
primitive style recognized by eighteenth-century theorists. Blair
believed, for instance, that the poetry of antiquity was typified
by 'a style always rapid and vehement; in narration concise,
even to abruptness and leaving several circumstances to be
supplied by the reader's imagination'. It was a style 'crowded
with imagery' to the point where, in Ossian's case, objections
could be made to the 'uniformity and too frequent repetitions
of the same comparisons'. There is something of this in the way
Blake's narratives often develop by piling up simple phrases to
create the air of millenarian expectancy discussed in the previous
chapter. Plate 13 of *America* exemplifies my point:

> . . . the flames coverd the land, they rouze they cry
> Shaking their mental chains they rush in fury to the sea
> To quench their anguish; at the feet of Washington down fall'n
> They grovel on the sand and writhing lie.
>
> (E 56; Pl. 13, ll. 2–5)

Macpherson's rhythmic prose likewise builds an atmosphere of
what was felt to be primitive intensity out of patterns of simple
phrases:

Chief mixed his strokes with chief, and man with man; steel, clanging,
sounded on steel. Helmets are cleft on high. Blood bursts and smokes
around. Strings murmur on the polished yews. Darts rush along the

---

also Erdman, *Prophet*, 33, 233–7, 253, 262, and S. F. Damon, *A Blake
Dictionary: The Ideas and Symbols of William Blake* (Boston, 1965), 312–13.
    [4] See H. Blair, *A Critical Dissertation on the Poems of Ossian* (London, 1763),
11 and 75.

sky. Spears fall like the circles of light that gild the stormy face of night.　(*Fingal*; *Ossian*, i. 233)

Both of these passages also display the 'exaggeration and hyperbole' that Blair claimed typified the verse of primitive societies.[5]

Any attempt to characterize these similarities directly in terms of influence faces the problem that many of the features common to Blake and Macpherson are also typical of the parabolic style Lowth found in the Bible. Earlier, for instance, I suggested that Blake's use of the trope of cosmic upheaval could be read as one of Lowth's categories of Hebrew metaphor. Yet the trope is equally a facet of Macpherson's prose: 'The winds come down on the woods. The torrents rush from the rocks. Rain gathers round the head of Cromla. The red stars tremble between flying clouds' (*Fingal*; *Ossian*, i. 255). Nor can the ascription of an influence on Blake's versification to Macpherson's rhythmic prose be acknowledged without noting that both seem to have a basis in the parallelism Lowth found in the Bible. If Macpherson's rhythmic prose is set out line by line, its dependence on parallelism becomes much more apparent. The opening lines of the epic *Fingal* will serve to illustrate the point:

> Cuthullin sat by Tura's wall:
> by the tree of the rustling sound.
> His spear leaned against a rock.
> His shield lay on a grass, by his side.
>
> (*Ossian*, i. 219–20)

It is likely that Macpherson had been influenced directly by Lowth's theories since they were well known in literary circles from the 1750s. This influence may have been intensified by Hugh Blair, who promoted Lowth's ideas in his lectures in Edinburgh which were eventually published as *Lectures on Rhetoric and Belles Lettres* (1783). Blair was also instrumental in encouraging Macpherson to collect the antiquities of the High-

---

[5] Ibid. 18 and 54. For a fuller discussion of theories of the constituents of primitive style see Smith, *The Politics of Language*, 26–8.

lands and take the further step of translating them into an epic poem.[6]

The authenticity of Macpherson's translations was judged against the style of the Old Testament, which was taken by many critics to be the archetypal primitive text. Blair himself mounted a defence of Macpherson against charges of forgery by pointing out the 'remarkable resemblance' between the Ossianic epics and the Bible. The similarities between the 'parabolic style' as described by Lowth and the rhythmic prose adopted by Macpherson have their origins in assumptions held by both men about the sort of verse produced by primitive cultures. What was original and exciting about Lowth's work was that he was perhaps the first scholar in Britain to historicize the Bible as literature in this way. He claimed that the poetry of the Bible seemed strange to the modern reader because it was produced by a culture 'farthest removed from our customs and manners' in 'the infancy of societies and nations'. Blair similarly wrote of the difficulties faced by the refined reader in appreciating the literary products of 'uncultivated ages'. Neither the parabolic style of the Bible nor Macpherson's translations conformed to the 'regular correct expression' Blair sought in 'Modern Poetry'.[7] Critics like Lowth and Blair valued the Authorized Version because its use of a relatively primitive English captured the parabolic style of the Hebrew. Lowth believed that the Authorized Version excellently captured the primitive style of the Hebrew original because 'it was made at a very early stage in our literature, and when the language was by no means formed: in such a state of the language the figurative diction of the Hebrews might be literally rendered without violence to the national taste'. Less historically minded critics found the English Bible 'uncouth, obsolete, and vulgar'. Even Lowth's appreciation of the parabolic style was dependent on its being confined to a primitive discourse in the past. Lowth

---

[6] For a discussion of the influence of Lowth on both Blair and Macpherson, see Stafford, *Sublime Savage*, 86–91.

[7] See Blair, *A Critical Dissertation*, 18–19, and *Lectures on Rhetoric and Belles Lettres*, 2 vols. (London, 1783), ii. 399. For Lowth, *Lectures on the Sacred Poetry*, i. 112 and ii. 163.

admitted that by modern standards the prophetic style of the
Bible appeared 'frequently harsh and unusual, I had almost said
unnatural and barbarous'.[8]

Blake's writing in the 1790s rejects such 'regular correct
expression' in order to achieve a primitive language for contemporary practice. To promote the uncultivated and incorrect was
a much more politically fraught business in the 1790s than when
Lowth and Blair wrote. A series of satirical poems, including
William Gifford's *Baviad* (1791), Thomas Mathias's *Pursuits of
Literature* (1794–7), and the efforts of Canning and his colleagues
in the *Anti-Jacobin*, sought to reinforce the hegemony of 'regular
correct expression' against the taste for the passionate simplicity
of the past. Written in refined couplets themselves, these satires
presented any deviation from the polished style as an index of
subversion and immorality:

> From laws of metre free (which idly serve
> To curb strong genius and its swelling nerve);
> In verse half veil'd raise titillating lust,
> Like girls that deck with flow'rs Priapus's bust.
>
> *(Pursuits, i; ll. 31–4)*

Burke's *Reflections* presented the French Revolution as the
ultimate, threatening manifestation of the primitive sublime in
history. From the conservative perspective the cultural and
literary trends of preceding decades, of which a major component was the primitivism of Rousseau, had culminated in the
Revolution. Burke and the satirists who followed his lead were
eager to point out the dangers of the same process being fulfilled
in Britain. Against this counter-revolutionary aesthetic, Blake
and a number of other writers were involved in an effort to
push the taste for the antique to radical conclusions.[9]

Blake's primitivism is all the more subversive because of the
way it dilutes the status of the Bible as the pre-eminent ancient
text. I have already mentioned the difficulties of determining
whether Blake's versification is biblical or Ossianic. His para-

---

[8] See Lowth, *Lectures*, i. 183 n. and 321, and *Critical Review*, 69 (1790), 172.
[9] See Ronald Paulson on Burke and the sublime in relation to the French
Revolution in his *Representations of Revolution*, 57–87.

doxically original primitive style invokes the parallelism both
of the Bible and the Ossian poems. Other aspects are suspended
equally ambiguously between biblical and Celtic precedents.
Take, for instance, Blake's use of the figure of the lamenting,
solitary female which, in the previous chapter, I traced to a
configuration of Jerusalem in the Bible. This trope is centrally
important to the lament of the eponymous heroine in *The Book
of Ahania*. Erdman has suggested that the name Ahania has an
Ossianic ring to it and gives a speculative etymology which
traces its origins to a compound of the name of one of
Macpherson's heroines, Annia, with Aha! If the name does
carry such an allusion, it is reinforced by other features of the
lament. The world depicted by Macpherson in his translations
was very much one on the verge of destruction. The dominant
tone is elegiac as Ossian himself looks back to a Golden Age
which is fast disappearing: 'Let the tomb open to Ossian, for
his strength has failed. The sons of song are gone to rest' ('The
Song of Selma', *Ossian*, i. 216). Furthermore, within the
narratives themselves the lament recurs as a formal device,
usually delivered by shadowy female figures mourning the loss
of their lovers. Hugh Blair noted that 'with apostrophes, or
addresses to persons absent or dead, which have been in all ages
the language of passion, our poet abounds'. The structure of
The Book of Ahania as a whole might be seen as typical of the
Ossian poems in this respect. The first part of the poem is
dominated by the struggle between the tyrant Urizen and the
rebel Fuzon. Ahania's lament is a coda to this struggle which
replicates the pattern of battle followed by grieving widow that
gives a basic structure to the Ossian poems.[10]

Some of the laments in Macpherson's translations have more
specific points of contact with Blake's use of the form. Ahania,
for instance, remembers her former anticipation of Urizen's
return from the hunt:

> I cannot touch his hand:
> Nor weep on his knees, nor hear
> His voice & bow, nor see his eyes

[10] See Erdman, *Prophet*, 253, and Blair, *A Critical Dissertation*, 65.

And joy, nor hear his footsteps, and
My heart leap at the lovely sound!

(E 88; Pl. 4, ll. 65–9)

Her memories are very similar to those Macpherson's Lorma has of her lover: 'When shall I behold his dogs returning from the chace? When shall I hear his voice, loud and distant on the wind?' ('The Battle of Lora'; *Ossian*, i. 403.) The parallels between Lorma's lament and the Preludium to Blake's *Europe* are even closer. The Preludium ends with 'the shadowy female' wondering about the fate of her offspring before she fades from view:

And who shall bind the infinite with an eternal band?
To compass it with swaddling bands? and who shall cherish it
With milk and honey?
I see it smile & I roll inward & my voice is past.

She ceast & rolld her shady clouds
Into the secret place.

(E61; Pl. 2, ll. 13–18)

Lorma's situation is different, she laments a lover killed in battle, though the shadowy female's children are also 'fiery kings' who live and die by violence, but Macpherson's description does contain the details of paleness and voicelessness as well as the parallelism of Blake's lines: 'She came. She found her hero! Her voice was heard no more. Silent she rolled her eyes. She was pale and wildly sad' (*Ossian*, i. 403). Blake's figuration of the daughter as 'rolld inward' may even have taken its cue from the rolling eyes of Lorma. Ultimately, however, I do not want to trace Blake's lines to a particular source in the Ossian poems. There are several other passages which share the same vocabulary of voiceless grief and rolling eyes. What I do want to stress is that the Ossianic context is clearly invoked in the laments in both *Europe* and *The Book of Ahania* and indeed in the numerous lamenting females who people the later prophecies.

Blake's adaptation of the lament in his poetry is a bricolage with biblical and Ossianic antecedents. The latter have some specific implications that I shall go on to discuss below. What is of more general importance to my argument is a recognition that Blake's parabolic style is not simply biblical. Its model is a generalized notion of primitive literature not confined to the hegemonic Christian tradition. One implication is that the Bible is but one among many examples of ancient inspiration which Blake believed made up 'the Word of God Universal'. Included in this transnational canon of primitive literature were 'the Songs of Fingal', together with others like 'the Edda of Iceland', 'the accounts of North American Savages (as they are calld)', and 'Homers Iliad' (E 615). The Bible, in the 1790s at least, was not the only divinely inspired text for Blake.

Clarke Garrett has suggested that the millenarian enthusiasm of the 1790s should be read as an indication of the need to fit what was new and unprecedented, that is the experience of the French Revolution, into familiar categories. This formulation overlooks the pressure put on the received language of the Bible by radical bricoleurs such as Blake. I have suggested that Blake's figuration of Orc in terms of both Christ and Satan undermines fundamental biblical categories. But Blake does more than this. He does not merely invert or conflate biblical paradigms. Orc is also presented as a version of the primitive hero of the Ossian poems.[11] Let me give a specific illustration from the 'Asia' section of *The Song of Los*, where Orc is described as 'a pillar of fire' (E 69; Pl. 7, l. 27) in the process of burning away the oppression of the Urizenic regime. This same phrase is frequently used to describe the eponymous hero in Macpherson's *Fingal*. Indeed, so frequently does it (or close variations) occur that it comes near to being the standard formula for describing Fingal.[12] In the world of the Ossian poems, Fingal represents all that is good. Not only is he brave and strong, but he is committed to the defence of the oppressed: 'My arm was the support of the injured; the weak rested behind the lightning of my steel' (*Ossian*, i. 275). He relieves his Irish cousins from the encroachments of the Norsemen and also defends the Celtic world from the Roman Empire. Where Fingal struggles against

---

[11] Garrett, *Respectable Folly*, 225.
[12] See *Ossian*, i. 255, 293, 301, and 319.

imperial ambitions, Orc struggles against Urizen's system. He promises to bring a liberation which is not simply figured as the Christian Millennium but is also represented in terms of a return to the primitive virtue of, in this case, Caledonian antiquity.

If the figure of Orc seems to operate through both Christian and Ossianic paradigms, the synchronism is even more pronounced in the evolution of Los, who comes to take the central role in Blake's prophetic narratives. Los is described almost interchangeably in terms of both bard and prophet, which parallels the way Blake's poetry is at one and the same time both bardic and prophetic. At the beginning of *The Song of Los*, for instance, he is placed in the role of the bard of northern antiquity, singing 'to four harps at the tables of Eternity' (E 67; Pl. 3, l. 2). In the same passage he is identified as 'the Eternal Prophet' (l. 1). Los is usually explicitly given the latter title while often being figured in a bardic context. Typically the role of Los in Blake's plots is as a residual link with primitive liberty in a world of Urizenic oppression. He first appears in this role in *The Book of Urizen*, where it is Los that the Eternals choose as their representative to watch over the fallen creation of Urizen:

> And Los round the dark globe of Urizen,
> Kept watch for Eternals to confine,
> The obscure separation alone.
>
> (E 73; Pl. 5, ll. 38–40)

It is a role Los maintains in the prophecies Blake produced after 1800. At the fulfilment of Blake's eschatology in *Jerusalem* he is remembered for having kept 'the Divine Vision in time of trouble' (E 193; Pl. 44, l. 15), a position which has led many commentators to identify Los with Blake as the bard-prophet struggling for inspiration and liberty in an indifferent world. What is equally clear, however, is that Los's position as the guardian of a threatened tradition is typical of the conception of the bardic role in the eighteenth century. Macpherson described Ossian as the last representative of a passing heroic age. Similarly, Thomas Gray's poem 'The Bard', which Blake illustrated several times in his career, was based on the tradition that Edward I had ordered the execution of all the Welsh bards. The poem describes the last of their number cursing Edward's descendants before leaping to his death from a cliff-top.[13]

The conception of the bard shared by Macpherson and Gray drew on the belief that the ancient poets had been intimately involved in the public affairs of their societies. Gray's bard is at the centre of a struggle for national independence. Ossian, the narrator, if not the hero of Macpherson's translations, is a warrior bard. It is this role to which Los seems to accede at the end of Blake's *Europe*. He first appears in a much more acquiescent role when, at the beginning of the poem, he celebrates the birth of 'the secret child' without anticipating or striving against the imposition of the oppressive systems of Enitharmon and Urizen. Perhaps his position is meant to be that of Milton, who fails in his bardic office by accepting the deferral of 'Truth and Justice' in his 'Nativity Ode'. By the close of Blake's poem, however, Los is an activist in the struggle against Enitharmon:

> Then Los arose his head he reard in snaky thunders clad:
> And with a cry that shook all nature to the utmost pole,
> Call'd all his sons to the strife of blood.

> (E 66; Pl. 15, ll. 9–11)

Los seems to be transformed into the radical prophet envisaged by Howes, but his transformation is also a function of his conception in terms of an ancient bard.

Macpherson's Ossian is an active, public figure, typical of the representation of the bard in eighteenth-century accounts of northern antiquity. Macpherson and Blair both drew attention to the public nature of the bardic office. Blair described the bards as 'highly respected in the state, and supported by a publick establishment'. The antiquarian conception of the Welsh bardic tradition offered much the same perspective. Blake's lost painting *The Ancient Britons* was set in the Welsh

---

[13] See I. Tayler, *Blake's Illustrations to the Poems of Gray* (Princeton, NJ, 1971), 14, 83–107, and 158.

context by his *Descriptive Catalogue* (1809). Apparently the painting showed the bard in a typically active role; 'The dead and the dying, Britons naked, mingled with armed Romans, strew the field beneath. Among these, the last of the Bards who were capable of attending warlike deeds, is seen falling, outstretched among the dead and dying; singing to his harp in the pains of death' (E 545).[14] Blake's painting showed the bard involved in a war of self-defence against Roman imperial ambitions. Antiquarian and literary accounts of the ancient poets tended to stress their role as defenders of liberty. Macpherson's Ossian was represented in the conventional way. Ossian supports Fingal's struggle against the imperial ambitions of the Romans, as does the bard in Blake's painting, and against the incursions of the bloodthirsty Norsemen. The civilization with which Ossian is associated was represented as freer and more tolerant than the powers which threatened it by both Macpherson and Blair. Similarly, Gibbon's *Decline and Fall of the Roman Empire*, drawing it seems on Macpherson's translations, had contrasted 'the untutored Caledonians, glowing with the warm virtues of nature' with 'the degenerate Romans, polluted with the mean vices of wealth and slavery'.[15]

Macpherson described Fingal's people as 'much less barbarous' than their Scandinavian counterparts. Such a distinction is typical of the goal of establishing a typology of primitive cultures pursued by eighteenth-century historiographers. M. M. Rubel has characterized the typology as revolving around the difference between 'savage' and 'barbarian' societies, though it should be stressed that eighteenth-century historiographers themselves did not always stick to these terms. One axis around which distinctions between primitive cultures were drawn was their attitude to war. Whereas the barbarian was believed to fight in order to conquer, the wars conducted by the savage were thought to have more gallant motives. Another aspect of this savage–barbarian distinction was that the former was often

[14] See Blair, *A Critical Dissertation*, 13.
[15] See Gibbon, *The History of the Decline and Fall of the Roman Empire*, 6 vols. (London, 1776–88), i. 132. On Gibbon's debts to Macpherson's historiography, see Stafford, *Sublime Savage*, 161 n.

associated with an egalitarian society and the latter with the birth of social hierarchy. The egalitarianism of savages was traced to their lack of private property, whereas the anarchy of barbarism was seen as a direct effect of the introduction of private property. When the Ossian poems were published they were seized upon as evidence of the egalitarian nature of the savage state. Blair and Macpherson drew attention to the fact that Ossian's society existed prior to the development of property and commerce. Macpherson claimed that it was 'free from the toil and business which engross the attention of a commercial people'. Blair believed such a society lacked the hypocrisy and deceptions of a more developed culture. It represented 'the most artless ages . . . before those refinements of society had taken place, which enlarge indeed, and diversify the transactions, but disguise the manners of mankind'. Ahania's lament, discussed above, makes use of the notion of a lost time of liberty and prosperity figured in terms of the primitive societies both of the Ossian poems and the Bible. The primitivism of Blake's style in general represents the endorsement of a form of society lacking the domination and exploitation which radicals were attacking in the 1790s. The same point could be made even if we insist that Blake's rhetoric is primarily biblical since Lowth represented Hebrew society as having a noble simplicity and primitive equality.[16]

The notion of an original, egalitarian state was central to Paine's *Rights of Man* and became a staple of radical propaganda. One recurrent example is the use made of the theory of the Norman Yoke which represented Anglo-Saxon England as a

[16] Macpherson gives his description of the Scandinavians in 'Cath-Loda'; *Ossian*, i. 11 n. See also Macpherson's 'A Dissertation Concerning the Poems of Ossian', *Ossian*, ii. 238, and Blair, *A Critical Dissertation*, 1. M. M. Rubel's discussion of the use of the Ossian poems in historiographical debates can be found on pp. 41–9 of her *Savage and Barbarian* (Amsterdam, New York, Oxford, 1978). Although her discussion of the distinction drawn between the 'savage' and 'barbarian' stages of pre-civilization in 18th-cent. historiography is extremely valuable, her model has to be handled with care since the two terms tend not to be used systematically by writers of the period. David Punter has also suggested that Blake identified with the egalitarian liberty of Ossian's society in his 'Social Relations of Poetic Form', 191–200. Lowth discusses the primitive egalitarianism of Hebrew society in his *Lectures*, i. 145–6.

quasi-democracy which had been destroyed by the feudalism imposed by the aristocratic Normans. E. P. Thompson has suggested that this theory reflected a mode of thought bound to the idea of an authentically English constitutional liberty which had to be regained. The further back this state of liberty was placed in history, the more radical the claims of the writer in question tended to be. Moderate Whiggish opinion usually identified it with the Bill of Rights of 1688. Paine's *Rights of Man* is commonly identified with a newer vein of thought which denied the need to appeal to such precedents and based its arguments for change on universal and inalienable rights. Yet Paine's rhetoric still had at its centre a desire to contend for history which drew on the notion of a primitive state of liberty and equality:

> Every history of Creation, and every traditionary account whether from the lettered or unlettered world, however they may vary in their opinion or belief of certain particulars, all agree in establishing one point, the unity of man, by which I mean, that all men are born of one degree and consequently that all men are born equal and with equal natural right.

Paine went back beyond any particular constitution or historical institution to suggest that freedom and equality were inscribed in the nature of things.[17]

Rousseau, of course, provided a similar perspective in his *A Discourse upon the Origin and Foundation of the Inequality of Mankind* (English translation, 1761). David Erdman has stressed the debts in Blake's radical primitivism to Rousseau's historiography. There is also no doubt that loyalists like Burke tried to present the appeal to an original state of freedom as a French and especially Rousseauist notion. What I have attempted to outline above is an indigenous discourse which made available very similar perspectives. Blake's writing and designs make use of both sources to the same end: a critique of contemporary society in the light of primitive liberty. Nor is it only in these two sources that such a critique is to be found. The notion of a

---

[17] See E. P. Thompson, *The Making of the English Working Class* 2nd edn. (Harmondsworth, 1968), 85–110, and Paine, *CWP*, i. 274.

return to a state of original liberty was alive in sections of the Revolution controversy which seem a long way from the discourse of the Enlightenment. Radical millenarians often figured the Second Coming as the rebirth of an Edenic state of nature. John Wright, for instance, claimed that 'the world will become again what it was in the beginning'. Richard Brothers's 'Notes on the Etymology of a Few Antique Words' (1796) searched for the true meaning of the word Albion and found it in the Welsh language obliterated by successive waves of tyrannical invaders:

Had not the Roman legions, the Saxon allies, the Danish robbers, and the Norman conquerors, furiously over-run England, each in their turn obliterating from the towns, villages, and rivers, their ancient Alliban distinctions we should have had at this day Can's, Car's and Aber's as common as they are still in Wales.

It seems that Blake's bricolage of Hebrew and Celtic antiquities was part, in a less developed form, of Brothers's writing too.[18]

The Ossianic elements in Blake's rhetoric deserve to be regarded as radical not only because they invoke the notion of primitive liberty but also because they undermine the received authority of biblical discourse. This point can be made more sharply if we recognize that Blake's use of Celtic antiquity marks a particularly profane admixture. Both Macpherson and Blair drew attention to the 'total absence of religious ideas' in the Ossian poems.[19] Macpherson claimed that the early Caledonians had had an organized religion administered by the druids, but that these were 'cunning and ambitious priests' who were disliked by Fingal and Ossian. This dislike was traced to the involvement of the druids in a civil war against Fingal's ancestors. The antagonism felt by Ossian towards religious institutions was not limited to the druids. Macpherson also

[18] For Erdman's discussions of Blake and Rousseau, see *Prophet*, 139, 143, 252, 260, and 290–2. See also Wright, *A Revealed Knowledge*, 27. Brothers's 'Notes' were originally published in the *Morning Chronicle*; I quote from the version published in *The Writings of Mr. Richard Brothers* (1798), 6. See also Harrison, *The Second Coming*, 80–3.
[19] See Blair, *A Critical Dissertation*, 20, and also Macpherson, 'Aera of Ossian', *Ossian*, ii. 219–20.

claimed that Ossian disputed with early Christian monks or culdees and Blair drew attention to a fragment which showed that Ossian resisted monkish attempts to transcribe his work. Obviously the religious attitudes of the Caledonian culture presented by Macpherson would have been attractive to Blake, who, as I showed in the previous chapter, shared the anticlericalism typical of radical opinion in the 1790s. Furthermore, Blake takes up and develops something of the rivalry between the bard Ossian and the druidic priests.[20]

Before embarking on a discussion of the place of this opposition in Blake's rhetoric I should emphasize that he did not make explicit use of the terms 'bard' and 'druid' as part of a rigid binary opposition. My concern is rather to suggest ways in which antiquarian accounts of bards and druids inform the struggle between the liberating agency of Los and the repressive system of Urizen. The word druid or its derivations did not appear in Blake's writing till *The Four Zoas*, begun as *Vala* around 1796, although I shall suggest below that he consistently represented Urizen in druidic terms earlier in the 1790s. Explicit mentions of druidism in Blake's writing are ambivalent. The *Descriptive Catalogue* identifies the druids with the resistance of the bards to Roman imperialism. Bards and druids also appear to be identical in Plate 9 of *Milton*:

And all Eden descended into Palamabrons tent
Among Albions Druids & Bards, in the caves beneath Albions
Death Couch, in the caverns of death, in the corner of the Atlantic.

(E 102; Pl. 9, ll. 1–3)

This identification of the druid and the bard seems to owe more to the Welsh tradition, promoted (and to an extent invented) by Edward Williams and William Owen Pughe in the 1790s and after, than Macpherson's account of an opposition between the

[20] For Ossian and the druids, see Macpherson, 'A Dissertation Concerning the Aera of Ossian', *Ossian*, ii. 217–20; and also Blair, *A Critical Dissertation*, 20, who claims that Ossian found the druids 'odious'. The mentions of Ossian's antagonism to the culdees come in 'Aera of Ossian', ii. 217–20, and Blair's 'Preface' to Ossian, *Fragments of Ancient Popular Poetry*, trans. J. Macpherson (Edinburgh, 1760), pp. iv–v.

bard and druid. Macpherson's negative perception of druidism is, however, more typical of Blake's treatment of druidism. The 'Druid Temples', which mark the first mention of the word in *The Four Zoas*, are associated with Oxford as a centre of the mystificatory scholarship of state religion. The druidic involvement in the fall from Rubel's 'savage' simplicity into 'barbarian' oppression is suggested in the *Descriptive Catalogue*:

Adam was a Druid, and Noah; also Abraham was called to succeed to the Druidical age, which began to call allegoric and mental signification into corporeal command, whereby human sacrifice would have depopulated the earth.   (E 542–3)

Here Blake suggests that the primitive religion of druidism had two forms; an original prophetic inspiration which degenerated into a corrupt cult. *Milton* and *Jerusalem* tend to use the term almost exclusively to apply to the latter; 'the whole Druid Law' (E 223; Pl 69, l. 39) which is destroyed by Christ. A simple chronological account of druidism which charts an increasingly negative attitude on Blake's part is not satisfactory, however, since the druidic representation of Urizen in the 1790s draws on the association of druidism with the fall from primitive liberty and the practice of human sacrifice. The ambivalences of Blake's presentation of druidism are also present in his use of the figure of the bard. As with Los in *Europe* the bard can be a poet of liberty and inspiration or an agent of the fall into the Urizenic system which is identified with druidism in *Milton* and *Jerusalem*. There is, none the less, the strong implication that the proper (original and redeemed) role of the bard is the former.[21]

The process Blake presented in the *Descriptive Catalogue* whereby 'allegoric and mental significances' were reified into 'corporeal commands' is first sketched in the description of the degeneration of 'poetic tales' into 'forms of worship' at the hands of a manipulative 'Priesthood' in *The Marriage of Heaven and Hell*. The same opposition between inspired bard and deluding priest is implied in *Europe*. Blake takes on the role of

---

[21] For further general discussions of Blake's attitude to the druids, see P. F. Fisher, 'Blake and the Druids', *Journal of English and German Philology*, 58 (1959), 589–612; and A. L. Owen, *The Famous Druids* (Oxford, 1962), 224–36.

the bard-prophet who seeks to reawaken humanity to a desire for the liberty and equality that he associates with primitive culture. Within the poem Los eventually awakens to his bardic role when, like the ancient bards resisting the Romans in *The Ancient Britons*, he calls his sons to the strife of blood. Los and his sons struggle against the system set up in the central portion of the poem by Enitharmon. Prior to this, on Plate 9, the poem takes up the narrative of *America* and its configuration of the struggle in terms of a contest between Orc and Urizen. The centre of the oppressive system of Urizen and Enitharmon is located in an ancient temple:

> In thoughts perturb'd they rose from the bright ruins silent
>   following
> The fiery King, who sought his ancient temple serpent-form'd
> That stretches out its shady length along the Island white.
> Round him roll'd his clouds of war; silent the Angel went,
> Along the infinite shores of Thames to golden Verulam.
> There stand the venerable porches, that high-towering rear
> Their oak-surrounded pillars, form'd of massy stones, uncut
> With tool; stones precious; such eternal in the heavens,
> Of colours twelve, few known on earth, give light in the
>   opake,
> Plac'd in the order of the stars, when the five senses whelm'd
> In deluge o'er the earth-born man; then turn'd the fluxile eyes
> Into two stationary orbs, concentrating all things.
>
>   (E 63; Pl. 10, ll. 1–12)

The druidic connotations of the 'ancient temple serpent-form'd' are quite specific and can be traced to the theories of the antiquarian William Stukeley. In his *Stonehenge* (1740) and *Abury* (1743) Stukeley had put forward the influential idea that the various stone circles around Britain had their origins in the hieroglyphic language of the druids. Stonehenge was the main metropolitan temple of the druids and so was built in a circle, taken by Stukeley to signify the omnipotence of the godhead. He claimed that Abury's serpent shape was a hieroglyphic of Christ. Stukeley obviously credited the druids with the bases of a Christian theology. Indeed this belief was at the centre of his entire thesis since he was trying to prove that the druids had received the religion of Abraham from philosophic priests who had arrived as part of a Phoenician colony during the patriarch's lifetime. The religion of Abraham was believed by Stukeley to be 'Patriarchal Christianity'. Blake's 'ancient temple serpent-form'd' appears to be a fusion of Stukeley's two temples, a combination of the hieroglyphic design of Abury with the role of Stonehenge as the main seat of religious authority. By placing the origin of his temple in the 'deluge' (l. 11), Blake also retained the Old Testament associations Stukeley claimed for Abury and Stonehenge.[22]

Stukeley's antiquarianism was essentially patriotic, an attempt to find biblical origins for the earliest British religion. Blake turns this theory on its head to suggest that pagan mystification continued in the Christianity of his day. The Old Testament origins of Blake's temple are established through his allusion to the Flood, but this invocation of biblical history carries a negative signification where Stukeley's was positive. Blake's deluge is of the five senses, representing a closing off of sensual enjoyment similar to that ordained by Enitharmon on Plate 5 of *Europe*. By restaging the biblical deluge as a founding moment in the history of institutionalized repression, Blake passes a negative comment on the covenant established between God and Noah after the Flood. Since Blake's version of the covenant witnesses the foundation of Urizen's temple, the God of the Bible becomes involved in the foundation of a druidic state religion. Plate 11 of the poem (see Pl. 2), showing Albion's Angel rising on 'the Stone of Night' (l. 1), is a more direct repudiation of Stukeley's patriotism. The design caricatures George III, the head of the Church of England, representing him as the patriarch of Urizen's system of druidic repression.[23]

On Plate 12 of *Europe* the 'vast rock' (E 64; l. 8), the altar of the druid temple, becomes the pulpit from which 'aged ignor-

---

[22] Both Stevenson (ed.), *Blake: The Complete Poems* (London, 1971), 232–3, and Owen, *The Famous Druids*, 231, with several other critics, trace Blake's druid temples to Stukeley. See Stukeley's *Abury* (London, 1743), 8–9 and 54, on the hieroglyphic significances of the shapes of the temples. For a detailed discussion of Stukeley's ideas see Owen, 117–30.

[23] See above, p. 40, on the design as caricature.

ance' preaches 'canting' (l. 7). 'Aged ignorance' is Blake's parodic version of Stukeley's 'Patriarchal Christianity'. In fact Blake's negative representation of druidic lore is similar to the very account of the druids Stukeley had set out to refute. Stukeley's two books on the druids were actually conceived as a reply to the deist controversialist John Toland's *A Critical History of the Druids* (1723). Toland had presented the druids as the epitome of manipulative priestcraft: 'no heathen priesthood ever came up to the perfection of the Druidical . . . as having been much better calculated to beget ignorance, and an implicit disposition in the people, no less than to procure power and profit to the priests'. The attack on druidism by Toland was a covert attack on the Church of England, which played on parallels between druidism and institutionalized Christianity. Stukeley's riposte took on board these parallels, but attempted to use them to prove that the druids had inherited their religion from the Old Testament patriarchs and that this had been passed directly on to the Anglican Church. From Stukeley's perspective the Church of England had become the custodian of the pure patriarchal religion untainted by the corruption of Rome.[24]

Although this sort of antiquarian historiography might seem a long way from the Revolution controversy, the debate between Burke and Paine on the origins of Britain's institutions gave such matters a renewed political charge. Paine's *Rights of Man* drew on the deist tradition of Toland to mount an attack on 'the superstitions which priestcraft united with statecraft had interwoven with governments'. This aspect of *Rights of Man* was developed into the extended critique of established religions in *The Age of Reason*, which echoed Toland's claim that the Anglican Church had retained heathen deceptions. A loyalist development of Stukeley's position can perhaps be identified in an anonymous poem of 1792 entitled *Stone Henge*. The poem is a vision of an ancient druid ceremony which covertly legitim-

---

[24] See J. Toland, *History of the Druids*, ed. R. Huddleston (Montrose, 1814), 56. For an account of the debate between Toland and Stukeley, see Owen, *The Famous Druids*, 112–130.

ates the English establishment by suggesting that the British state had developed consistently from the most ancient times. The ceremony presents the druids as the lawgivers of a united British nation whose authority is based on the principle of obedience:

> Obedience is the basis of our state
> Those who depart from that incur our hate.

Furthermore, the British are exhorted to maintain their unity in the face of foreign interlopers in a couplet that seems to participate in the anti-Gallicanism of loyalist propaganda in the 1790s:

> Watch well our state, nor let the stranger's art
> Bewray your thoughts, nor steal upon the heart.

The druids reinforce their authority by reference to the promise of future rewards and punishments in an afterlife:

> And after death their spirits restless roam
> In birds, or beasts of prey, that know no home,
> While future ease awaits the obedient mind,
> In herds, or flocks, they sanctuary find.[25]

The doctrine of future rewards and punishments was among the chief targets of deist attacks on the Christian establishment at the beginning of the eighteenth century. John Toland represented the doctrine as one among many importations from pagan theology which had corrupted primitive Christianity. During the Revolution controversy it again became an important point of attack for radicals like Eaton and Paine who eagerly drew attention to the doctrine's role in the coercive rhetoric of the state. Volney's *Ruins* concurred with Toland in tracing the origins of the doctrine to Egyptian 'kings and priests' who 'saw in it a new source of power, as they received to themselves the privilege of warding the favours or the censure of the great judge of all'.[26]

[25] These lines, together with those quoted above, are found in *Stone Henge: A Poem* (London, 1792) 13.

[26] See Paine, *CWP*, i. 299, and C. F. Volney, *The Ruins: or, A Survey of the Revolutions of Empire*, English trans. (London, 1792), 264–5.

Burke had claimed that this sort of scepticism would remove moral constraints and produce anarchy. From around 1793 pulpits began to respond to his warnings by placing a renewed stress on the Christian duty of obedience backed up by the prospect of eternal damnation for the disobedient. Publications such as the series of Cheap Repository Tracts reinforced this trend. These developments must have intensified the repugnance which many radicals felt for such doctrines. Blake's response was to place the theology of future rewards and punishments at the very heart of the druidical establishment of Enitharmon:

> Go! tell the human race that Womans love is Sin!
> That an Eternal life awaits the worms of sixty winters
> In an allegorical abode where existence hath never come.

(E 62; Pl. 5, ll. 5–7)

His representation of conventional promises of an afterlife as a deception marks one of those key points where Blake's rhetoric goes beyond enthusiasm and moves towards the patterns of a radical scepticism which we normally associate with figures like Paine, Volney, and Eaton. Blake is also echoing the deist tradition which informed the publications of Paine and Eaton when he subverts the notion that the druids were the venerable founders of the British state put forward by Stukeley and recycled by the author of *Stone Henge*. For Blake what was the venerable authority of the druid in Stukeley's theory becomes 'aged ignorance', the ideology of obedience 'canting'. Other radicals in the 1790s mediated their opposition to priestcraft through a negative account of the druids. 'Old Hubert' in the first part of his 'History of England', published in Eaton's *Politics for the People*, offered the following account of their practices: 'The Druids, by the severity of their manners, and by the mysteriousness of their religious rites, had obtained so complete an ascendancy over [the ancient Britons], as to be permitted . . . to make very numerous sacrifices of their miserable devotees.' Old Hubert is playing on the notion, much as Blake does in *Europe*, that the druids were the ancient founders of the British state. The implication was that the state was blighted at its inception by a system of priestcraft which still prevailed as he wrote, an obvious counter to Burke's notion that the British state had grown through a healthy and organic evolutionary process.[27]

Something of Old Hubert's identification of the druids with the practice of human sacrifice is present in Blake's *The Book of Ahania* (1795). Blake once again broadens the perspective by fusing his druidic references with a Christian context, this time the doctrine of Atonement. In Chapter 4 I shall chart the similarities between Blake's position and the distaste felt amongst Rational Dissenters like Priestley for the notion that the Crucifixion was a sacrifice to propitiate a vengeful God. The implication of Blake's druidic Crucifixion in *The Book of Ahania* is that the Atonement is another example of Christian theology 'sprung out of the tail of heathen mythology'.[28]

The theme of human sacrifice emerges in Chapter III of *The Book of Ahania*, where Urizen finally defeats the rebellious energies of Fuzon. Having killed his enemy, Urizen takes Fuzon's body and nails it to the 'accursed Tree of MYSTERY' (E 87; Pl. 4, l. 6). There follows a digression of origins which again invokes a druidic context for Urizen. Blake's account of the origins of the Tree of Mystery draws on Mallet's *Northern Antiquities* (English translation 1770), which contains an account of 'a great ash-tree' believed to be sacred to the religion of Odin. Like Blake's Tree of Mystery which 'grows over the Void', Odin's sacred tree entwines itself all around the universe; 'its branches cover the surface of the earth, its top reaches to the highest heaven, it is supported by three vast roots, one of which extends to the ninth world, or hell'. Blake places the origin of

---

[27] See 'History of England' in *Politics for the People*, vol. i, Part 1, p. 10. A comparable invocation of antiquity in a political context is Wordsworth's use of Stonehenge and human sacrifice in the unpublished 'Salisbury Plain'. It is interesting that Wordsworth should have used the same complex of ideas and images at the same time as Blake and Old Hubert. The poem was originally written in 1793–4, when Wordsworth was beginning to get closely involved with the circle around Joseph Johnson. For a discussion of Wordsworth's treatment of druidism in the poem, see A. Liu, *Wordsworth: The Sense of History* (Stanford, Calif., 1989), 192–7.

[28] See p. 200 below and Paine, *CWP*, ii. 467.

his tree in a cataclysmic rupture when 'Urizen shrunk away |
From Eternals'. Mallet's account of Odin's religion similarly
invoked a prior, more harmonious religious system which had
worshipped the deity as 'the active principle' and enshrined as
its only law 'to do no wrong to others, and to be brave and
intrepid in themselves'. This culture sounds very much like the
world of Macpherson's Ossian. Both, of course, are varieties of
a positive or 'savage' ancient culture. Mallet's book, however,
dwelt mainly on the 'barbarian' culture which followed it and
the religion of Odin, which he presented as bloody and
oppressive.[29]

   Mallet presented the religion of Odin as bloodthirsty not only
in its pursuit of war, but also in its practice of human sacrifice.
He described in detail the ceremonies dedicated to Odin which
culminated with the corpses of the victims being 'suspended in
a sacred grove'. Fuzon's 'dead corse' is similarly suspended by
Urizen on the Tree of Mystery in *The Book of Ahania* (E 86; Pl.
3, l. 52). On the basis of the importance of human sacrifice to
the worship of Odin, Mallet claimed that the religion was in
fact a species of druidism. Therefore those details of *The Book
of Ahania* taken from Mallet mark a continuation of Blake's
druidic conception of Urizen. Not that the belief that the druids
practised human sacrifice was exclusive to Mallet. The druids
had long been identified with human sacrifice in classical texts
and this tradition was deeply rooted in ideas about their religion.
James Foot's *Penseroso* (1771), for instance, described 'their
groves | The bloody shambles of misguided zeal, | And the vile

---

[29] P. H. Mallet, *Northern Antiquities*, 2 vols. (London, 1770), i. 102 and
77–81. In *The Song of Los* Blake followed Mallet in explicitly identifying Odin
with a 'code of war'. Blake presented Odin's religion as one who sought to
repress desire and 'catch the joys of Eternity' in 'nets & gins & traps', but he
suggests that such joys could not be erased only channelled into the degraded
forms of 'War & Lust'. The conception of the religion of Odin offered briefly
in *The Song of Los* reappears in the illustrations to the poems of Thomas Gray
which Blake worked on later in the 1790s. Blake's designs for 'The Descent of
Odin' present the god as a gloomy warrior, encased in armour so tightly that
it seems to be a second skin. The implication is that his energies have been
completely sublimated into the code of war he founds in *The Song of Los*. For
a fuller discussion of this illustration, see Tayler, *Blake's Illustrations to the Poems
of Gray*, 116 ff.

priests the butch'ring tools of Heav'n'. Deeply rooted though this tradition was, responses to it were complex. The apologists for the druid, of whom Stukeley is the most obvious example, were apt either to overlook the practice of human sacrifice or even to attempt tortuous justifications of it as evidence of a developed, if misguided, religiosity. The patriotic William Mason took the course of claiming that it was the druids of Gaul who had transmitted this barbarity to their British counterparts.[30]

The reluctance to criticize the druids did not only have its basis in the patriotic desire to present a virtuous version of Britain's earliest civilization. Stukeley's idea that the druids had learnt their religious practices from Hebrew patriarchs was widely accepted. Others, like William Cook in his *An Enquiry into the Patriarchal and Druidical Religion* (1754), promoted the same theory. The traditional identification of the druids with human sacrifice was difficult for the Christian to square with the notion that these ancient priests had received their religion directly from the Hebrews. What was difficult to explain away for Christian apologists was the very attraction for Blake of the tradition of representing the druids as primitive Christians since it enabled him to stress the continuing barbarity of state religion. *Politics for the People* made the same point when it compared what Blake called the 'English Crusade against France' to the worship of the 'ferocious Odin . . . the active roaring deity; the father of slaughter; the God that carrieth desolation and fire'.[31]

Blake's presentation of Urizen in *Europe* and *The Book of Ahania* fixes him as both a druidic and biblical figure. He is the

[30] See Mallet, *Northern Antiquities*, i. 136. The similarities between the religion of Odin and druidism are discussed by Mallet in several places, see i. 140, and vol. ii, pp. xv and xvi. For a discussion of the association of druids with human sacrifice, see Owen, *The Famous Druids*, 155–68. He quotes the lines from Foot, p. 160. See also, W. Mason, *Works*, 4 vols. (London, 1811), ii. 160.

[31] See *Politics for the People*, vol. i, Part 2, no. 2, p. 12. Writing of the fast days held in support of war, the same piece noted the clergy behaved 'as if he [God] had been more merciless and blood-thirsty than any divinity that ever disgraced Paganism'.

patriarchal druid of Stukeley's theory, but he is also the pagan sponsor of human sacrifice. Blake, like John Toland before him, made use of potential parallels between druid and Christian priestcraft to undermine the contemporary authority of the latter. He does this in *The Book of Ahania* by invoking the relationship between God and Christ in his configuration of Urizen and Fuzon. Urizen is described in the opening section of the poem as a 'cloudy God seated on waters' (E 84, Pl. 2, l. 12), which invokes both the God who 'moved upon the face of the waters' in Genesis 1: 2 and the 'cloudy God' who appears surrounded by smoke on Sinai. Fuzon is consistently placed in a Mosaic role in the plots of both *The Book of Urizen* and *The Book of Ahania*, but he is also figured in terms of Christ. The description of Fuzon as the 'Son of Urizen's silent burnings' (E 84; Pl. 2, l. 9), for instance, alludes to Christ putting on his father's wrath in *Paradise Lost* (VI. 734–6). Similarly, his 'chariot iron-wing'd' (l. 1) invokes the 'Chariot of Paternal Deity | Flashing thick flames' on which Christ subdues Satan's armies (*PL* V. 750–5). These references culminate in Fuzon's crucifixion at the hands of his paternal deity Urizen. The Crucifixion is revised as the sacrifice of the Son to the authority of the Father, exactly the reading of the Atonement which Priestley and others criticized as a heathen distortion of primitive Christianity. Blake makes the same point by identifying druidic practices of human sacrifice with the God of orthodox Christianity in the figure of Urizen. In doing so he points to continuities between pagan religion and Christianity which radicals like Paine and Eaton were also stressing in the 1790s.[32]

The Tree of Mystery, where Urizen sacrifices Fuzon, gains further resonance in the context of the Revolution controversy since the tree as a symbol of the state became an important and contested image in the 1790s. The oak, of course, had long been a symbol of England, but the identification received a new impetus in the 1790s from Burke's description of the organic

[32] The same subversive connection probably lies behind the version of the druids presented in Old Hubert's 'History of England' discussed above. For Priestley and Paine on the Atonement, see below, p. 200.

development of its institutions in his *Reflections*. Burke presented what he believed to be the unique liberties of the English
constitution as the fruit of a great tree which had been following
a course of steady and natural growth: 'Upon that body and
stock of inheritance we have taken care not to inoculate any
scion alien to the nature of the original plant.' This emotive
image of national development passed into a prominent position
in the political rhetoric of the next few decades. Coleridge in
his *Lay Sermons* (1816–17) took up Burke's theme reverentially,
for instance, when he represented the constitution as a mighty
tree which had to be ensured stable conditions if it were to
survive. The image was particularly popular in loyalist cartoons
in the years immediately following the publication of Burke's
polemic. A typical example is Gillray's *Le Coup de Maitre*
(1797), in which Charles James Fox, the leader of the Whig
opposition, is represented as a Jacobin taking pot-shots at the
liberty of England hung about the ancient tree of state. Another
dimension of the trope was the presentation of reformist
principles, identified with the Tree of Liberty, as Burke's alien
scion. Take this example from the anonymous anti-Jacobin
poem *Topsy-Turvey*:

> To propagate RAPINE AND SLAUGHTER,
> BLEST SCYONS OF LIBERTY'S TREE,
> WHICH WE PLANT, AND THE DEVIL WILL WATER.

Gillray's *Tree of Liberty—with, the Devil Tempting John Bull*
(1798) could serve as a graphic commentary on these lines (see
Pl. 4). Fox appears again, this time as the serpent wrapped
around the tree of good and evil attempting to seduce the
British people with his politics.[33]

It was not only Burke's allies who made political use of the
arboreal metaphor. Blake's Tree of Mystery has something in
common with radical responses to Burke's manipulation of the

[33] See Burke, *Reflections on the Revolution in France*, in *Works*, v. 75;
Coleridge, *Collected Works*, ed. K. Coburn (London, 1971–), vi. 21–3; and [R.
Huddesford], *Topsy-Turvy* (1793), 32. For a discussion of the caricatures, see
H. M. Atherton, 'The British Defend their Constitution in Political Cartoons
and Literature', *Studies in Eighteenth-Century Culture*, 11 (1982), 12–17.

symbol of the English oak. Writers making use of the Norman
Yoke theory presented the constitution Burke defended as an
alien tree in the Anglo-Saxon forest: 'The Norman conquest
planted by force that law of robbers, the tree of feudal tyranny.'
Paine represented the destruction of this tyranny in terms of an
improving farmer removing a troublesome tree from his fields
when he called on his readers to put 'the axe to the root'.
Perhaps developing Paine's rhetoric, other radicals replaced
Burke's figure of majestic organic growth with the idea that the
established order was 'a noxious weed in the sweet gardens of
liberty'. Such writers offered the Tree of Liberty as a positive
alternative to the blighted oak of old England. Eaton's *Politics
for the People* published a pseudo-botanical account of the Tree
of Liberty which contrasted its benign effects with the 'Upas,
or Poison Tree' of the monarchical order. The Upas has been
named by several critics as a source for Blake's 'A Poison Tree'
and 'The Human Abstract' in *Songs of Innocence and of Experience*
as well as the Tree of Mystery in *The Book of Ahania*. What has
not been noticed is that the tree, made famous by Erasmus
Darwin's *The Botanic Garden*, was given a political signification
by Eaton which has much in common with Blake's identification of his Tree of Mystery with Urizenic state religion. The
image is another example of how an apparently apolitical term
in his vocabulary is actually implicated in the language of the
Revolution controversy.[34]

The trope of the noxious growth of tyrannical government
was one of which Thomas Spence was particularly fond:

But take away those tall, those overbearing aristocratic trees, and then
the lowly plants of the soil will have air, will thrive and grow robust.
Nevertheless, take care, you leave not any roots of those lordly plants
in the earth, for though cut down to the stump like Nebuchadnezzar
yet if any vestige of the system remain, any fibre of the accursed roots,
though ever so small lie concealed in the soil, they would sprout again
and soon recover their pristine vigour, to the overshadowing and
destruction of all the undergrowth.

[34] See Gerrald, *A Convention,* 89; Paine, *CWP*, i. 266; and *King, or no King*
(London, 1791), 38. For the account of the Upas Tree in Eaton's journal, see
'The Tree of Liberty' in *Politics for the People*, vol. i. Part 1, pp. 7–10.

Spence's rhetoric here demonstrates his willingness to make use of the language of Christian eschatology to envision the downfall of the established order in a way which calls to mind Blake's millenarian rhetoric. Blake's description of the secret growth of the Tree of Mystery in *The Book of Ahania* also shares something of Spence's sense of the tenacious and threatening nature of the dominant forces in his society. The basis of Urizen's authority in the Tree of Mystery is figured in such a way as to suggest the continuation of patriarchal and druidic barbarity in the Christian establishment of Blake's day. Blake's development of this allusive web in his writing after the 1790s makes the political point if anything more clearly. The Tree of Mystery becomes 'Tyburn's fatal Tree'. Urizen's authority is now centred on the gallows of Tyburn, where the full force of the regime defended by Burke was brought to bear on transgressors. It also retains its associations with the Crucifixion when it is placed in the same landscape as Golgotha in *Jerusalem*. In *The Four Zoas* the druidic aspects of the image are given prominence. There Blake places the crucified Albion 'among the Druid Temples' which are beside 'Tyburn's brook' (E 314; p. 25, l. 7).[35]

The various druid temples which recur in different guises in Blake's mythical landscapes are an important part of his development of the opposition between druid priest and bard-prophet. Of similar importance is the use he makes of an antithesis between written and oral forms. Urizen is a figure associated with the process of transcription and the written law, most obviously on the title-page of *The Book of Urizen*, where he is shown as a blind scribe copying from one book to another without seeing what he writes (see Pl. 1). Urizen is typically described either transcribing or carrying a book of laws made from iron or brass. One obvious implication of these metal books is the inflexibility of the political and psychological order Urizen sponsors. A more specific background to the image may

---

[35] Spence, *A Fragment of an Ancient Prophecy* in *PWS*, 47. For other examples of Spence's use of the same image, see *The Restorer of Society* in *PWS*, 77 and 88–9.

be Rousseau's theory that the fall from savage freedom into barbarianism had centred around the discovery of iron. The struggle against the iron authority of Urizen's written laws is often figured in terms of orality. When Orc finds his voice in *The Book of Urizen*, for instance, it signals the beginning of a minor but positive movement in the poem sometimes overlooked by critics:

> The dead heard the voice of the child
> And began to awake from sleep
> All things. heard the voice of the child
> And began to awake to life.

(E 80; Pl. 20, ll. 26-9)

Similarly, the daughter of Urthona in the Preludium to *America* remains voiceless till liberated by Orc: 'dumb till that dread day when Orc assay'd his fierce embrace' (E 51; Pl. 1, l. 10), though the voice given by Orc in this instance only communicates 'rending pains', reflecting the unsatisfactory nature of Orc's male and still patriarchal revolt in relation to the daughter.[36]

Above all it is the bard-prophet who is typically figured as involved in oral production. At the opening of *The Song of Los*, for instance, he sings at the tables of eternity. When he succumbs to the enveloping power of Urizen's system in *The Book of Urizen*, Los loses his power to speak:

> A nerveless silence, his prophetic voice
> Siez'd; a cold solitude & dark void
> The Eternal Prophet & Urizen clos'd.

(E 77; Pl. 13, ll. 38-40)

The opposition Blake develops between repressive writing and liberated speech again fits in with Macpherson's account of the ancient Caledonian culture. Ossian was the representative of a strictly oral culture which 'did not think it lawful to record these poems in writing, but handed them down by tradition'. I

---

[36] Rousseau claimed that iron had 'civilized men' and 'ruined mankind'. See, *A Discourse on the Origin and Foundation of the Inequality of Mankind*, English trans. (London, 1761), 119-22.

have already mentioned Macpherson's account of Ossian resisting the attempts of early Christians to transcribe his work. Urizen's association with the written law is part of his complex association with the priestly function. Secret writings, designed to keep the truths of religion from the people, were linked with Egyptian priestcraft and the druids in eighteenth-century historiography.[37]

The question of Blake's configuration of the oral and the written in his work leads on to an issue I touched on in my Introduction; the status of his own writing. His use of the written book as a signifier of repression and mystery might seem paradoxical given his own commitment to the written form. What must be borne in mind, however, is that the structure of his illuminated books operates against logocentricity. One index of this fact is the number of full-page designs which are independent of the text. In copies A and B of *The Book of Urizen*, for instance, there are ten full-page designs out of twenty-eight plates in total. There are also many plates, where the design dominates the text, on which the visual component overshadows the written. The significant visual element clashes with the rigid division of the poem into biblical chapter and verse. When I come to discuss *The Book of Urizen* in more detail in Chapter 4 I shall argue that this visual component is a crucial aspect of that poem's parodic disruption of the scriptural authority of Genesis.

The opposition between liberated orality and the oppression of the written is not rigorously maintained by Blake. The daughter's acquisition of oral power in the Preludium to *America*, as I have already pointed out, is far from being a straightforward sign of liberation. Similarly, Blake operates with a notion of writing as containing both positive and negative potentialities. He seeks a writing that retains the fluidity of the voice; that seeks the status of 'poetic tales' rather than 'forms of worship'. That is why the written code of Urizen is always figured in terms of inflexible metal. Blake sought to

---

[37] See Blair, *A Critical Dissertation*, 12. For a discussion of the historiographical links made between writing and priestcraft, see p. 122 below.

achieve a means of literary production that was fluid and operated against the notion of the single authoritative Word 'by printing in the infernal method, by corrosives, which in Hell are salutary and medicinal, melting apparent surfaces away, and displaying the infinite which was hid' (E 39). The 'radical variability' of Blake's work prevented it from taking a fixed or final form. The doubled printing method of Blake's books, the fact that they were engraved in metal and then printed on paper, allowed him to insert differences at each stage of production. Changes were always available to Blake in transcribing copy-text to plate and in the process of transferring plate to paper. The printed copy itself could be coloured in different ways such that different aspects of the plate were either obscured or developed. His books always went beyond the state of Urizen's books of metals, that is, the copper-plate, and each of the final states varied one from the other so none could claim the status of scriptural authority. None of the different versions of *The Book of Urizen* can be claimed as Blake's definitive version of the Creation myth. Indeed the word 'version' itself is inadequate since no original as such exists, only different performances. For Blake the notion of a single, authoritative text of divine revelation was anathema, as his annotations to Bishop Watson's *Apology for the Bible* made clear:

The Bible or <Peculiar> Word of God, Exclusive of Conscience or the Word of God Universal, is that Abomination which like the Jewish ceremonies is for ever removed.   (E 615)

He preferred instead a flexible canon of universal and continuing inspiration which could incorporate his own work as well as ancient texts, like 'the Songs of Fingal', from outside the hegemonic Christian tradition.

Blake's hostility to the '<Peculiar> Word of God' moves close to an antagonism to any notion of a transcendent Deity embodied in a univocal Word in the conventional Christian sense. *The Marriage of Heaven and Hell*'s antinomian stress on the immanence of the divine is typical of Blake in the 1790s. It is only in the later prophecies, when Christ and much of the machinery of Christianity take on a more positive role in Blake's rhetoric, that he seems to move towards a more conventional perspective. Even in these poems the incarnational nature of the divine is stressed:

> I am not a God afar off, I am a brother and friend;
> Within your bosoms I reside, and you reside in me:
> Lo! we are One; forgiving all Evil; Not seeking recompense!
> Ye are my members.

(Jerusalem, E 146; Pl. 4, ll. 18–21)

The attraction of the primitive bardic culture of the Ossian poems for Blake might have been to do with the fact that it was not just represented by Macpherson as a place of original liberty but also as a society free from notions of a transcendent deity, a place in which, to use Mallet's phrase, the 'active principle' in humanity was still identified with the divine. Both Macpherson and Blair drew attention to the absence of a deity or 'supream being' in the world of Ossian. In so far as there is a supernatural dimension to the poems, it takes the form of the spirits of ancestors who regularly appear. The divine in the world of Ossian is very much to do with human imagination and memory. Blair stressed that the ubiquitous spirits were socialized into the human community and continued to perform human functions: 'The ghosts of departed bards continued to sing. The ghosts of departed heroes frequent the field of their former fame.' Not that Blair and Macpherson were entirely relaxed about the absence of the deity in the poems. The former claimed that the poems would have been more satisfactory had they reflected the existence of the deity. Macpherson argued that a society without any notion of the divinity was unthinkable and that, despite the omission in the poems he offered as translations, there must have been some notion of the deity in Ossian's society.[38]

At this point it is worth drawing attention to another ambivalence in the primitivism of such writers. They treated the simple, sublime values and honest emotions they valued in northern antiquity as unavoidably locked in the past. Such

---

[38] See Blair, *A Critical Dissertation*, 40 and 34, and Macpherson, 'Aera of Ossian', *Ossian*, ii. 219–21.

qualities were a cost of progress which could not be recovered; they belonged to those 'artless ages . . . before those refinements of society had taken place, which enlarge and diversify the transactions, but disguise the manners of mankind'. Thomas Gray's poetry offers a similarly ambiguous perspective on the past, which is represented as a site of primitive integrity and untrammelled inspiration irretrievably passed away. His 'Stanzas to Mr. Bentley', for instance, give a typically melancholy account of the decay of poetic genius:

> But not to one in this benighted age
> Is that diviner inspiration giv'n,
> That burns in Shakespear's or in Milton's page,
> That pomp and prodigality of heav'n.

> (ll. 17–20)

Blake's poem 'To the Muses', like others in his early collection *Poetical Sketches*, is to some extent an imitation of Gray:

> How have you left the antient love
> That bards of old enjoy'd in you!
> The languid strings do scarcely move!
> The sound is forc'd, the notes are few!

> (E 417; ll. 13-6)

Despite the obvious attraction that Gray's primitivism held for Blake, he tends to go beyond the nostalgia for a lost past characteristic of Gray's poetry. The primitive style that Blake developed in the 1790s, which moves away from the derivative forms of his *Poetical Sketches*, announced itself as a creative refoundation of the inspirational art of the past in his own time. It was a continuation of the bardic tradition which did not merely describe or translate the past but sought continually to reappropriate its power for the Revolution controversy. Just as radical enthusiasts claimed that the drama of the Bible continued in their visions, so Blake's poetry asserts its equivalence with the inspiration of the ancient bards.[39]

Blake's poetry and designs avoid the disabling nostalgia of

---

[39] See Blair, *A Critical Dissertation*, 1.

literary primitivists like Macpherson and Blair. His style is not locked into any single textual antecedent; nor his primitivism to any particular period in the past. It invokes notions of original liberty and equality without accepting that such a state cannot be reproduced. Blake's millenarian rhetoric always looks forward to a restoration of this freedom. It is interesting to consider his use of the word 'Eternity' from this perspective since it is a term which avoids definite temporal limits. Eternity is set up in *The Book of Urizen* as an original state from which Urizen falls, but it is always being evoked by Blake as available in the present and future. Neither described nor circumscribed, Eternity is fixed neither in the past nor any distant 'allegorical abode'. Blakian 'Eternity' could be characterized as a space in which the reader is invited to join in the re-creation of original vision: 'The true Man is the source he being the Poetic Genius' (E 2). Blake's primitivism is not nostalgic but fundamentally active; 'an Endeavour to Restore <what the Ancients calld> the Golden Age' (E 555). The nature of this endeavour becomes clearer if we keep in mind that Blake practised his primitivism in the Revolution controversy. Writers like Gray more often admired the primitive in its historical context. They saw the loss of the virtues of the Golden Age as an inevitable part of progress. Macpherson translated an ancient epic into a style he thought appropriate to its period of origin. Blake used a similarly primitive style for a product of the 1790s, a decision which becomes vulgar to polite taste in its rejection of 'civilized' norms and conventions.

The Welsh poet and antiquarian Edward Williams, who took the name Iolo Morganwg in the 1780s, offers an interesting perspective against which to describe Blake's primitivism. Williams, like Macpherson, has unfortunately attracted most attention for his activities as a forger of antiquarian documents. Yet, unlike his Scottish predecessor, Williams always presented himself as an active part of a bardic tradition, refounding what he claimed were original bardic institutions which continue to function even now. His work represents a creative engage-ment with his conception of the Welsh past which offered a practice for his contemporary culture. Indeed his efforts are one of the foundations of modern Welsh nationalism and

provided an identity which could assert itself against the hegemonic English culture: 'he was driven by historical myths, and
in turn he used historical myths to create new traditions which
had profound, far-reaching effects'. This characterization, by
the historian Prys Morgan, reflects a growing recognition
amongst Welsh scholars that Williams was much more than a
mere forger.[40]

There are a number of similarities between the whole range
of Williams's writing and Blake's poetry. Williams published a
two-volume collection of his own poems in 1794. Blake's
employer Joseph Johnson was listed at the head of the booksellers on the title-page as well as amongst the most prominent
subscribers. The reader familiar with Blake's work will find
many verbal echoes when coming to Williams's poems. In his
notes Williams contrasted the Celtic bardic culture he looked
back to with Gray's 'savage Scandinavian mythology', just as
Blake's rhetoric is built upon an opposition between a primitive
bardic utopia and a fallen druidic religion identified with Odin.
Where Williams and Blake differ is in the fact that Blake often
follows Mallet in identifying the druids with Odin in opposition
to the inspired bard, while Williams asserted the identity of the
bards and druids as distinct from Scandinavian barbarity. When
Blake did consistently identify the bards and the druids, in his
descriptions of his painting *The Ancient Britons*, he was being
commissioned by Williams's friend and collaborator William
Owen Pughe. Blake claimed that the painting was based on an
ancient Welsh triad. Williams published and translated collections of these triads in both his *Poems* and the great collection of
Welsh antiquities, *The Myvyrian Archaiology* (1803–7), he
worked on with Owen Pughe. Many of the triads published by
Williams were his own re-creations of bardic vision intended
'to fit the native view of past history into the frame provided
by classical writers in the accounts of Roman Britain'. He does,

[40] See Prys Morgan, 'From a View to a Death', in *The Invention of Tradition*
(Cambridge, 1983), 61. See also his *Iolo Morganwg* (Cardiff, 1975), and A.
Johnston, 'William Blake and "the Ancient Britons"', *National Library of Wales
Journal*, 22 (1981–2), 309–12.

however, seem to have translated in 1791 the original triad
which inspired Blake's painting.[41]

Williams presented the bardic tradition which produced the
triads as part of the original Patriarchal Religion discussed by
Stukeley. In doing so he was following trends in syncretizing
the biblical and Celtic antiquities in a way which identified the
Hebrew prophet with the northern bard, but taking this tendency to radical conclusions by contrasting contemporary Christianity with the purity of primitive religion. Williams's writing
is also permeated by a millenarian expectancy which eschewed
nostalgia in favour of a conviction that 'the primeval state of
Innocence, Peace, and Benevolence' could be restored. As with
Blake, Williams tied his primitivism to radical political ends.
Williams held republican views and listed Tom Paine and other
radical luminaries amongst the subscribers to his book. The
bardic role in the struggle against imperial ambition delineated
by Macpherson and Gibbon was taken up by both Blake and
Williams as part of the politics of their present:

> Proud ROME would fain, for ages long,
> Impose the victor's yoke;
> But CIMBRIC souls, in valour strong,
> The chain of slav'ry broke.
> The Saxon fierce could ne'er subdue
> The dauntless British mind;
> Our spirit high, to freedom true
> The world shall ever find.

The example of Williams and Blake offers a version of antiquarianism which looks beyond the nostalgia of Gray to the
rhetorical appeals of radicals like Paine to notions of primitive
liberty and equality. They are typical of a radical primitivist
trend which sought to reimport antique virtue into the material
circumstances of the 1790s.[42]

Antiquarianism in the eighteenth century did not just involve

---

[41] See Williams, *Poems*, 2 vols. (London, 1794), 195; and Johnston, 'William
Blake and "the Ancient Britons"', 309–10.
[42] See Williams, *Poems*, 167 n. and lines from 'Song sung by the Society of
Ancient Britons in London', p. 95.

the examination of texts from the distant past. The cultural tendency I have been identifying as primitivism also comprised an interest in popular culture, often motivated by a belief that the peasantry and inhabitants of remote districts had retained intact the primitive authenticity of ancient times. Macpherson, for instance, went to the Highlands to find the remnants of the canon of Ossian extant in ballads and old manuscripts preserved by traditional culture. Yet Macpherson's attitude to his sources exhibits another of the ambivalences of literary primitivism. He saw them as corruptions of originals which had been written by a single high-born bard. His translations were an attempt to rework these sources into the more respectable form of the epic. The original collection of Ossianic verse, *Fragments of Ancient Poetry*, was expanded into two epics *Fingal* and *Temora*. Despite his evident antagonism to priestly attempts to transcribe the oral tradition in the past, Macpherson himself was involved in transforming his highland heritage into a genre more acceptable to the polite literary tastes of metropolitan Edinburgh and London.[43]

Not all antiquarians, however, were so keen to distance themselves from the roughness of the popular culture. Francis Grose and John Brand, for instance, specialized in collections of folklore and what were known as popular antiquities. The latter was particularly interested in ballads and proverbs. Grose produced his *Classical Dictionary of the Vulgar Tongue* (1785) in direct competition with Johnson's *Dictionary*. Where the latter attempted to limit 'the language properly so-called' to literary sources and polite usage, Grose's dictionary was orientated towards the language as spoken by the people and included scurrilous and often indecent entries.[44] Sometimes such interests coincided with political commitments. The antiquarian collector Francis Douce, for instance, kept close contact with a variety

[43] On Macpherson's attitude to the corrupt manuscripts and ballads, see Stafford, *Sublime Savage*, 83, 97, 124.
[44] See Johnson, *A Dictionary of the English Language*, 2 vols. (London, 1755), 'Preface'. For a fuller discussion of the development of British antiquarianism see R. M. Dorson, *The British Folklorists* (London, 1968) and P. Burke, *Popular Culture in Early Modern Europe* (London, 1978), 1–18.

THE

FIRST   BOOK

of

URIZEN

LAMBETH. Printed by Will Blake 1794.

1. Title-page to *The Book of Urizen*, Copy D (1794)

2. *Europe*, Copy D, Plate 11 (1794)

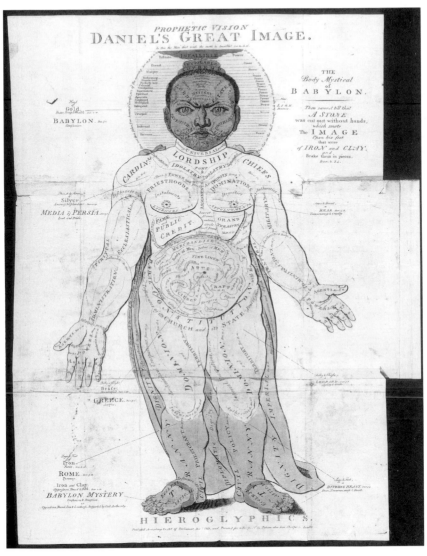

3. Garnet Terry, 'Daniel's Great Image' (1793)

4. James Gillray, *The Tree of Liberty—with the Devil Tempting John Bull*
(1798)

5. Frontispiece to *The Song of Los*, Copy A (1795)

6. *The Song of Los*, Copy A, Plate 8 (1795)

Fertilization of Egypt.

7. 'The Fertilization of Egypt', Plate engraved by Blake after Fuseli for Johnson's edition of Darwin (1791)

8. *The Book of Urizen*, Copy D, Plate 23 (1794)

of radicals from the 1790s onwards and his interest in the popular culture was clearly tied up with his republican views. He eventually became an owner of some of Blake's prophetic books, perhaps finding in them the same challenge to the hegemony of politeness he relished in the antiquities he collected. Douce was in contact with another radical antiquarian whose activities have been less well documented by modern scholarship. It is on Douce's friend, Joseph Ritson, and the similarities between his work and Blake's antiquarianism which I wish to concentrate in the remaining pages of this chapter.[45]

In the 1780s and 1790s Ritson was involved with the antiquarian Thomas Percy in a public controversy which had at its centre the question of the respect to be accorded the popular tradition. Ritson's researches into the origins of the ballad and popular song led him to draw a distinction between the popular entertainer who travelled 'about from place to place, singing and playing to the illiterate vulgar' and the more aristocratic minstrel who entertained in the houses of the great. Ritson represented the former as genuine successors of the ancient poets, not least because, like Gray's Welsh bards, they had been suppressed by a centralized English monarchy. Ritson's account of the popular travelling entertainer, 'often entirely destitute of education, and probably unable to read or write', was intended to refute Thomas Percy's theory of the ballad. Ritson believed that the street ballad of his day was part of a popular tradition,

---

[45] For evidence of Douce's radical commitments, see Bodleian Library, *The Douce Legacy* (Oxford, 1984), 8, and, J. W. Robinson, 'Regency Radicalism and Antiquarianism', *Leeds Studies in English*, NS 10 (1978), 133–4 and 138. Douce owned *The Book of Thel*, *The Marriage of Heaven and Hell*, and a copy of the *Descriptive Catalogue*: see Bodleian Library, *Catalogue of the Printed Books and Manuscripts Bequeathed by Francis Douce* (Oxford, 1840), 32. He also owned more or less everything published by Ritson, see *Catalogue*, 238. MS Douce e. 33, f. 34 in the Bodleian Library lists Ritson amongst others as one of the friends he valued. For further details of the relationship between Douce and Ritson, see B. H. Bronson, *Joseph Ritson*, 2 vols. (Berkeley, Calif., 1938), i. 243–8. Ritson, a consciously radical theorist and collector of popular culture, has been surprisingly neglected by cultural critics and historians, though Marilyn Butler's *Romantics, Rebels, and Reactionaries* does pay him some attention, pp. 35 and 149. Her *Burke, Paine, Godwin, and the Revolution Controversy* (Cambridge, 1984) discusses and reproduces portions of the preface of Ritson's important collection of Robin Hood ballads, pp. 203–5.

not the corruption of an aristocratic original. Percy presented
the traditional ballads he collected as the degraded remains of a
respectable medieval minstrelsy 'far superior to anything we
can conceive at present of the singers of old ballads'. Ritson
refused to compromise his material in this way and presented
his collections as part of a continuing popular tradition which
amounted to a complete alternative culture replete with its own
version of history enshrined in the ballads and folklore.[46]

The differences between Percy and Ritson are evident in their
editing techniques. Percy strove to present the songs and ballads
of his collections in a polite form. Ritson, on the other hand,
delighted in the 'vulgar' qualities of the material he published.
He celebrated the fact that the songs and ballads were 'extremely
incorrect' and ran into the 'utmost licence of meter'. Not
surprisingly the literary magazines preferred Percy's manicured
versions to Ritson's collections, which they felt were too close
to the state 'in which they may be found in any vulgar copy of
Robin Hood's Garland, dangling on the walls of the poor ballad
stationers'. The *Critical Review* dismissed his *Pieces of Ancient
Popular Poetry* (1791) as 'a collection of trash', while the *British
Critic* 'wanted something like an elegant or classical edition' of
his *Robin Hood* (1795).[47]

These critics were clearly aware of the political implications
of Ritson's theories. Ritson himself translated his radical antiquarianism into a democratic political commitment: 'I abomi-

[46] See J. Ritson, 'A Historical Essay on the Origin and Progress of National
Song' in *A Select Collection of English Songs*, 3 vols. (London, 1783), vol. i,
p. lii, and his 'Observations on the Ancient Minstrels' in *Ancient Songs*, 2 vols.
(London, 1792), vol. i, p. xvi, for his definition of the indigenous strolling
player. On the suppression of the bards and minstrels, see *A Select Collection*,
vol. i, pp. xxxv and liii. For Percy's disclaimer of the notion of a popular
origin for his ballads, see T. Percy, *Reliques of Ancient English Poetry*, 3 vols.
(London, 1765), vol. i, p. xix. Ritson gives his account on the role of the
popular ballad as an alternative national history in *A Select Collection*, vol. i,
p. lvii.

[47] The phrases quoted come from Percy's description of his ballad sources
in *Reliques*, vol. i, p. xxii. Ritson made his preference for 'the humble effusions
of unpolished nature' over 'artificial refinements' plain in *Pieces of Ancient
Popular Poetry* (London, 1791), pp. xii–xiii. The criticisms of Ritson are taken
from the *British Critic*, 9 (Jan. 1797), 19 and 21, and the *Critical Review*, 4 (Jan.
1792), 57–8.

nate all refinements and restrictions, and wish every one at full
liberty to adopt the language of Rabelais or Verville. In short I
detest every species of aristocracy, and would be *tout-à-fait sans
culottes.*' As these sentiments indicate, Ritson became an ardent
supporter of the French Revolution. He visited Paris in 1791
and returned full of praise for the new regime. In 1793 the
French calendar began to be used in his letters and he started to
address his friends as 'citizen' after the republican style. His
only twentieth-century biographer notes that Ritson was busier
with literary activities at this period than at any other in his life.
Many of the contacts he made at this time testify to the radical
complexion of his antiquarianism. He shared Edward Williams's politicized interest in bardism and corresponded on the
subject with the Welsh radical. Ritson's letters also reveal him
to have been an associate of others sympathetic to reform like
Godwin, Holcroft, and Thelwall. He even had contacts with
more unrespectable radicals like Eaton and Spence, using his
antiquarian knowledge to provide material for the former's
Politics for the People. Ritson's antiquarianism was clearly
involved in the radical attempt to undermine the hegemonic
culture. The same can be said of Blake and figures such as
Edward Williams. All three of these men had an association
with Joseph Johnson, whose circle seems to have been a
particular focus of radical antiquarianism. It was Johnson who
launched Ritson's controversy with Percy when he published *A
Select Collection of English Songs* in 1783. Blake worked as an
engraver on the book, producing nine plates after Stothard in a
simple and direct style in accord with the antagonism Ritson
felt towards refinement.[48]

Like Ritson's ballad collections, the writing and designs

---

[48] See *The Letters of Joseph Ritson*, 2 vols. (London, 1833), ii. 85. Evidence
of Ritson's radical affiliations are to be found throughout the letters. He
indicates his friendship with Spence, ii. 34. On his contributions to Eaton's
Politics for the People, see *Letters*, ii. 70. Visits from Godwin and Holcroft are
mentioned ii. 34, and elsewhere. Williams, 'the Welsh bard', is mentioned on
ii. 82. Bronson's *Joseph Ritson* mentions Ritson's association with Eaton and
Spence, ii. 154–6. For a discussion of Blake's plates after Stothard published in
A Select Collection of English Songs, see R. N. Essick, *William Blake, Printmaker*
(Princeton, NJ, 1980), 146 and 175.

produced by Blake in the 1790s make use of formal devices and traditions which were likely to be viewed as either 'vulgar' or 'primitive' by the cultural hegemony in a decade when labels like these had quite explicit political significance. My previous chapter argued that Blake's prophetic rhetoric should be counted as a challengingly vulgar aspect of his verse. David Punter has suggested that the ballad tradition which Ritson documented is a class-determined and submerged element in Blake's style. Given the conscious commitment to popular forms among radical antiquarians, a distinction between the conscious and submerged determinants on these aspects of Blake's rhetoric is difficult to maintain. Perhaps more sustainable is Punter's claim that the ethos of street ballads subsists in the violence and hyperbole of the imagery of *America*. Punter has also identified something of the versification of the ballad in the long line Blake used in *America* and *Europe*, though the influence of popular song is perhaps more apparent in some of the notebook verses and *Songs of Innocence and of Experience*. The ballad was typically based around an alternation of the trimeter and tetrameter which was sometimes written out long to approximate to the septenary. However, as Punter stresses, these metrical patterns were very casually used in authentic street literature, as opposed to the sanitized literary ballad of the sort promoted by Percy and imitated by numerous late eighteenth-century poets. Blake's long line has a similarly wayward relationship to the septenary and like the street ballad does not aspire to metrical regularity. The ballad element in Blake's versification may explain the incidence of the short line or tetrameter occasionally in *Europe*, which might be seen as the ballad line emerging more explicitly.[49]

The influence of the popular ballad on *Europe* is perhaps clearest, both in terms of style and content, in the problematic Plate iii of the poem. The Plate is centred on an encounter between the poet and a mocking fairy. The fairy's manner and its celebration of sensual 'joy' identifies him as the sprite of

---

[49] See Punter, 'Blake: Social Relations of Poetic Form', 187–91.

songs such as 'The Mad Merry Pranks of Robin Goodfellow' collected by Ritson:

> When lads and lasses merry be,
> With possets and with junkets fine,
> Unseen of all the company,
> I eat their cates, and sip their wine,
> And to make sport,
> I fart and snort;
> And out the candles I do blow;
> The maids I kiss;
> They shriek—who's this?
> I answer nought, but ho ho ho!

Plate iii was only intermittently retained as part of the format of the poem by Blake. It is present only in two of the extant copies of *Europe*, both of which seem to have been printed after 1800. Bentley, however, has shown that internal evidence points to a date for the etching of the Plate at around the same time as the rest of the prophecy. Certainly the fairy's celebration of sensual enjoyment chimes in with the antinomian celebration of energy in *The Marriage of Heaven and Hell*. The fairy's belief that 'every particle of dust breathes forth its joy' (E 60, l. 18) correlates with the Orcian conviction that 'every thing that lives is holy'. It is this sensual enjoyment which Enitharmon tries to stamp out, or at least appropriate for her children, in Plates 4, 5, and 8 of *Europe*.[50]

Plate iii closes with the claim that the prophecy *Europe* was dictated to the poet by the fairy, a claim which places the fairy in the role of the poet's muse. This aspect of the fairy's role is interesting in terms of the cultural politics of the prophecy. The traditional muse of Christian poetry is, of course, the Holy Spirit; the 'Heavenly Muse' that Milton invokes at the beginning of *Paradise Lost*. Milton also follows tradition in showing the Holy Spirit to be the moving force in the original Creation:

[50] See 'The Mad Merry Pranks of Robin Goodfellow' in Ritson, *A Select Collection*, ii. 160–4; and *Europe: A Prophecy*, ed. G. E. Bentley (Memphis, 1978).

> . . . thou from the first
> Wast present, and with mighty wings outspread
> Dove-like sat'st brooding on the vast abyss
> And mad'st it pregnant.
>
> (ll. 19–22)

Blake's rejection of this traditional muse is all the more apparent since the reader is prepared for the appearance of the Holy Spirit by *Europe*'s frontispiece, the now famous design commonly known as 'The Ancient of Days'. Michael Tolley, along with most other Blake scholars, takes this design to illustrate the following passage from *Paradise Lost*:

> . . . in his hand
> He took the golden compasses prepared
> In God's eternal store, to circumscribe
> This universe, and all created things.
> One foot he centred, and the other turned
> Round through the vast profundity obscure,
> And said, 'Thus far extend, thus far thy bounds,
> This be thy just circumference, O world!'
>
> (VII. 224–31)

Blake's design presents God the patriarchal setter of bounds and limits, exactly the God of circumscribing Reason parodied in *The Marriage of Heaven and Hell*. Soon after the lines alluded to in Blake's frontispiece, Milton's poem refers to the part in the Creation of the 'brooding wings' of the 'Spirit of God'. Yet the Holy Spirit of *Paradise Lost* never makes an appearance in Blake's *Europe*. Instead he pointedly prefers the riotous spirit of popular tradition to preside over his poem.[51]

Europe, or at least those versions containing Plate iii, bases its authority on an appeal to the transgressive spirit of popular tradition rather than the holy muse of conventional Christian verse. The history of Enitharmon's dominion and its imminent collapse is vouchsafed to Blake by a representative of what the *Gentleman's Magazine* called 'vulgar superstitions concerning fairies'. Presenting Burke's patriotic view of the benign devel-

---

[51] Tolley, '*Europe*: "To those ychain'd in sleep"', 117.

opment of British state religion as 'canting', *Europe* is an alternative history of Britain watched over by the fairy of popular tradition. Joseph Ritson claimed that the ballads he collected represented just such an alternative perspective; the product of a political consciousness which had continuously rejected the official version of history. Thomas Spence likewise believed that the stories of 'giants and their castles in romances' were really 'satires upon great lords' put about by the common people. For Ritson the official history was a politically motivated distortion 'consecrated to the crimes and follies of titled ruffians and sainted idiots'. Blake similarly had little time for the idea that the official history was honest: 'Nothing can be more contemptible than to suppose Public RECORDS to be True Read them & Judge. if you are not a Fool' (E 617). [52]

Perhaps, with his 'infernal method by corrosives . . . melting apparent surfaces away', Blake was able to read through Macpherson's attempts to present his collections as a respectable epic to find in them a manifestation of the alternative history traced by Ritson. The preface to Macpherson's *Fragments* had emphasized Ossian's hostility towards monkish attempts to transcribe his work and incorporate it into the official culture and its polite, written forms. Furthermore, Macpherson claimed to have collected the Ossian poems from a living tradition in Scotland. He emphasized that they had formed a popular oral tradition which had persisted over many centuries despite official hostility: 'it was impossible to eradicate, from amongst the bulk of the people, their own national traditions'. There were enough clues here to allow an 'infernal' reading of Macpherson's translations not only as primitive literature but as part of a living culture which recorded a perspective outside that given in the official public histories. [53] What is clear is that a hostility to the dominant English aristocratic culture was more explicitly part of Edward Williams's account of the primitive

[52] See the *Gentleman's Magazine*, 65 (1795), 553, and Ritson, *Robin Hood*, 2 vols. (London, 1795), vol. i, p. xii. Spence made his remarks in *A Further Account of Spensonia*: see *Pig's Meat*, ed. G. I. Gallop (Nottingham, 1982), 83.
[53] See Macpherson's comments in Ossian, *Fragments*, p. iv, and 'Poems of Ossian', *Ossian*, ii. 279.

liberties of the Welsh and the alternative history traced by Joseph Ritson in the ballad tradition. Both were rejoinders to Burke's legitimizing history of the origins of British institutions. They revealed that the population had not always willingly acquiesced in the process of history but had developed its own culture and traditions which were continually in conflict with the dominant culture. Ritson celebrated the incorrectness of the vulgar ballad as a facet of the popular rejection of received authority. Blake's determined use of 'primitive & original ways of Execution' (E 724) shares in the rejection of hegemonic standards of politeness which was at the centre of Ritson's radical antiquarianism. Like Edward Williams's bardic poetry, Blake's work is 'original' in so far as it lays claim to participate in a continuing process of keeping alive a vision of the ancient liberties of Britain. It is a version of primitive literature created afresh for the present.[54]

[54] See Barrell, *The Political Theory of Painting*, 225–31 and 245–53 for a discussion of Blake's two, distinct uses of the word 'original'.

3

'Forms of Dark Delusion':
Mythography and Politics

THE uses made of northern antiquity in Blake's radical rhetoric represent one aspect of a broader intervention in the discourse of speculative mythography. Studies in the origins of religion and myth in the eighteenth century offered not so much a parallel as a grounding to literary primitivism since mythography theorized the paradigms which figures like Gray and Macpherson developed. The conceptions of druidism, for instance, discussed in the previous chapter were made available by general theories of the evolution of priestcraft and particularly what was taken to be the seminal case of Egyptian religion.

Underlying such studies was a syncretic approach, seeking to demonstrate the grand unity of all myths, which was the dominant tendency in eighteenth-century mythography. Often this syncretism was used to shore up the Christian hegemony by representing all other religions as corrupted versions of what Stukeley called 'patriarchal religion', 'no other than Christianity'. There is nothing particularly original in noticing Blake's syncretism. What is often overlooked, however, is the distance between Blake and the Christian apologists, like William Warburton and Jacob Bryant, to whom he is frequently linked. Blake's mythography shares more of the radical impulses of those speculators like Erasmus Darwin and C. F. Volney (and, indeed, the earlier work of John Toland) whose syncretism was part of an attempt to break up the Christian hegemony in the 1790s. Yet, while mythographers like these tended to try to displace that hegemony with some kind of progressive rationalism, Blake's syncretism more often implied that this rationalism itself was in danger of being reified into a mystificatory cult. The enthusiastic traces discussed in Chapter

1 are the signs of Blake's difference from this rationalist tradition.[1]

Nowhere is Blake's interest in comparative religion more obvious than in *The Song of Los*, which I shall use as the focus of my discussion of his mythography in this chapter. The first section of the poem, 'Africa', develops the paradigms of Plate 11 of *The Marriage of Heaven and Hell* into a mythologized catalogue of the history of priestcraft. The frontispiece to the poem is a pictorial representation of the reified 'forms of worship' associated with priestly mystification in *The Marriage* (see Pl. 5). The design shows a hoary, white-robed druid prostrating himself before a sun covered with obscure hieroglyphics. The association of the druids with secret writings is part of a more general picture of pagan priestcraft operative in studies of comparative religion in the eighteenth century. Thomas Blackwell compared the druids to the Egyptians in his influential *An Enquiry into the Life and Writings of Homer* (1735), focusing the comparison on their common devotion to secret writings. William Stukeley had also related the druid temples to Egyptian hieroglyphics. On the frontispiece to *The Song of Los* the worship of a mystified Word is established as the symbolic definition of priestcraft.[2]

What follows in 'Africa' is similar to the opening plates of *Europe*. The latter recounted the establishment of Enitharmon's religion of obedience and repression. 'Africa' deals with the foundation of the same principles in a series of historical religions. The main difference is one of scope, as John Beer has noted: 'Where *America* and *Europe* contained sizeable segments of human history, this further book, though brief in compass, comes nearer to an account of human history as a whole.'

---

[1] See W. Stukeley, *Stonehenge* (London, 1740), p. Aiv.

[2] See T. Blackwell, *An Enquiry into the Life and Writings of Homer* (London, 1735), 163, and Stukeley, *Abury*, 56. Blake's antagonism to the operations of priestly mystification is announced pictorially on the poem's title-page, where the title takes up the dominant position held by the hieroglyphic sun on the frontispiece. The words of the title are forcing the druid priest into the ground. Dominated by the name of the bard-prophet, Los, the Plate as a whole signifies the poem's aspiration to replace the dead hand of druidic priestcraft with the liberating vision of prophecy.

Europe's plot, in part through the allusions to Milton's 'Nativity Ode', presents itself as a parabolic history of the corruptions of Christianity. 'Africa' represents the origins of all religions and includes Christianity within a longer historical and wider cultural framework.[3]

Blake presents this new parabolic history as a specimen of bardic poetry:

> I will sing you a song of Los. the Eternal Prophet:
> He sung it to four harps at the tables of Eternity.
>
> (E 67; Pl. 3, ll. 1–2)

Lowth, Blair, and Macpherson had all emphasized the role of primitive poets as historians of their peoples.[4] The international perspective of *The Song of Los* places both Blake and Los in the parallel but broader role of historians to humanity as a whole. However, if, as the singer of this critical history of religion, Los is the idealized bard still in touch with visions of Eternity, his children are the prime agents of the dissemination of false religions catalogued in the poem. Most of these children have the same names as Enitharmon's progeny in *Europe*, names which are inventions of Blake's and strange to the reader. Their puzzling opacity is indicative of the priestly mystification they disseminate.

But why is it the children of Los who promote the oppressive systems of Urizenic state religion? The explanation lies in a commonplace of eighteenth-century speculative mythography: the theory that the origins of priestcraft lay in the poetry of the ancient bards. Thomas Blackwell, for instance, described 'the Birth of the Gods, the Rise of Things, and the Creation of the World' as 'the common Theme of the first Poets and Lawgivers'. Blackwell went on to describe how the cosmogonies and theogonies of the ancient poets came to be appropriated by manipulative priests who presented poetic fictions as metaphys-

---

[3] See J. Beer, *Blake's Humanism* (Manchester, 1968), 133.

[4] See Lowth, *Lectures*, i. 96–7, Macpherson, 'Aera of Ossian', *Ossian*, ii. 225–8, and Blair, *Lectures*, ii. 317. See also Rubel, *Savage and Barbarian*, 66–7, for evidence of the pervasive nature of this idea among the 18th-cent. theorists of the primitive.

ical realities. 'The Ambition and Avarice of the Priests, and the Superstition of the credulous' led to a situation where the arbitrary nature of the sign was forgotten, 'the Representations' were mistaken 'for Things'.[5]

Blake's most explicit account of the process whereby the poetry of the ancients came to be corrupted into priestly 'forms of worship' is Plate 11 of *The Marriage of Heaven and Hell*. There are obvious parallels between that Plate and the theories advanced by Blackwell. The latter's claim that 'the Gods of the ancients' were originally poetic representations of 'the Parts and Powers of Nature' is echoed by Blake's belief that the ancient poets 'animated all sensible objects with Gods and Geniuses'. Both Blackwell and Blake held that it was the machinations of manipulative priests which led to the reification of these poetic tales into metaphysical realities, a process Blake described as 'attempting to realize the mental deities from their objects' and Blackwell as a substitution of 'Representations' for 'Things'.[6]

In the context of these parallel accounts of the origins of myth, the role of Los's children in 'Africa' becomes easier to explain. They are the descendants of the ancient bard, Los, to the same extent that the 'forms of worship' promoted by priestcraft were held to be the children of the earliest poets. Blake claimed that the appropriation of poetry by the priesthood led to a situation where humanity forgot that 'All deities reside in the human breast'. The opacity of the names of the children of Los may be Blake's way of suggesting that the reader is still implicated in this collective amnesia.[7]

The historical and geographical sweep of 'Africa' is typical of the boom in speculative mythography which gathered pace in

---

[5] See Blackwell, *An Enquiry into the Life and Writings of Homer*, 96, and *Letters Concerning Mythology*, 275 and 176.

[6] See ibid. 62–3, for Blackwell's definition of the origins of the gods of the ancients. Both Blake and Blackwell believed that a decline of metaphor into allegory was at the heart of the growth of priestcraft: see the discussion in my Introduction.

[7] The use of the children of Los as a trope in this way could be read as an aspect of Blake's primitive style, since the metonymic use of 'sons of', for instance, when describing arrows as 'sons of the bow', was typical of Macpherson's translations of Ossian.

the eighteenth century. Its global perspectives are redolent of the Enlightenment desire to know the whole history of humanity. Such enquiries never lost their heretical overtones and in *The Song of Los* Blake was presenting a syncretic enterprise in a decade particularly sensitive to religious enquiry. Of course, the sorts of radically syncretic vision presented by Blake had long since vied with conservative exercises in containment which sought to synthesize new knowledge about primitive religion with hegemonic conceptions of religion and history. Many of these more conservative studies, such as Newton's *The Chronology of the Ancient Kingdoms Amended* (1728) and Samuel Shuckford's *The Sacred and Prophane History of the World Connected* (1728–30), operated by attempting to correlate pagan religion with the Mosaic history to vindicate the Bible. Such vindications constituted a conservative syncretism which sought to use parallels between pagan and Christian material as proof of the primacy of the latter and, ultimately, the authority of the cultural status quo. The implications of Blake's syncretism do not work in this direction. His mythography represents a destabilization of the authority of the Christian hegemony.[8]

As the titles of Newton's and Shuckford's volumes indicate, eighteenth-century studies in comparative religion had an obsessive interest in chronology. The emphasis in Blake's 'Africa' is different. The opening lines of Blake's catalogue function as a mythic paradigm, centred on the unhistorical figure of Urizen, of which all the historical epiphanies are presented as incidents;

> Adam stood in the garden of Eden:
> And Noah on the mountains of Ararat;

[8] There is a survey of mythographical enquiry in F. E. Manuel's *The Eighteenth Century Confronts the Gods* (Cambridge, Mass., 1959). Also useful is the anthology of extracts together with introductory essays in B. Feldman and R. D. Richardson, *The Rise of Modern Mythology 1680–1860* (Bloomington, Ind., and London, 1972). Manuel, p. 50, claims that the relatively tolerant atmosphere enjoyed by deist enquirers into the origins of religion deteriorated as the century went on. See Feldman and Richardson, p. 71, on the conservative syncretism of Newton and Shuckford. Stukeley's work on the druids was clearly motivated by the same impulse.

They saw Urizen give his Laws to the Nations
By the hands of the children of Los.

(E 67; Pl. 3, ll. 6–9)

In contradiction of the biblical chronology, this paradigmatic event, if it can still be called an event, is witnessed by both Adam and Noah at the same time. Although this pairing seems to negate the Bible as history, it does not reject the Bible as poetic model since it conforms to the prophetic practice, described by Thomas Howes, of interrupting 'the right chronological order of the events referred to, by placing two or more distant events contiguous to each other, whenever these could supply proofs of some general assertion or conclusion'. There are two points to be made here. First, Blake's preference for the Bible as a poetic model rather than a public record fits in with his endeavour to recuperate poetic tales from forms of worship. Secondly, the 'general assertion' that Blake makes is that the various religions he mentions are all variants of Urizenic oppression. All his epiphanic moments are ironic revelations which have betrayed humanity into state religion.[9]

Blake's catalogue of religious origins has been related to the theories of William Warburton's *Divine Legation of Moses Demonstrated* (1738–41). Warburton believed that the Egyptians had invented state religion as a means by which the initiated few could delude and control the masses.[10] Some aspects of *The Song of Los* do seem to allude to details in Warburton's theory. The hieroglyphics on the frontispiece and the subtitle 'Africa' may both echo the dominant role Warburton gave Egypt in the history of priestcraft. Nevertheless to identify these features firmly with Warburton would be misleading since the centrality of Egyptian religion was a commonplace of speculative mythography throughout the century. Even the most influential

[9] See Howes, *Critical Observations*, ii. 149. Howes called his non-chronological ordering 'oratorical': see ii. 139.

[10] For a recent account of *The Song of Los* in the context of Warburton's book, see L. Tannenbaum, *Biblical Tradition in Blake's Early Prophecies* (Princeton, NJ, 1984), 187–8. For an example of the central role Warburton gave Egypt in the rise of priestcraft, see W. Warburton, *The Divine Legation of Moses Demonstrated*, 2 vols. (London, 1738–41), i. 174–7.

aspect of Warburton's thesis, his discussion of the role of hieroglyphics as instruments of mystification, was original more for its details than its account of the function of the symbols. There were important discussions of the role of the Egyptians as the initiators of state religion by both John Toland and Thomas Blackwell. Toland pointed out that it was 'in Egypt Men had first, long before others, arrived at the various beginnings of Religions . . . and that they preserv'd the first occasions of Sacred Rites conceal'd in their secret writings'. Blackwell claimed that the Egyptians exploited the human tendency to 'admire what they do not understand' and 'adapted their religious Belief and solemn Ceremonies, to this Disposition; made their Rites mysterious, and delivered their allegorical Doctrine under great Ties of profound and pious Secrecy'.[11]

What distinguishes Blake's 'Africa' from the theories of Toland, Blackwell, and Warburton is that he does not begin his catalogue of false religions with the Egyptians. The first recipient of Urizen's 'Abstract Philosophy' is 'Brama in the East'. This deviation from Warburton alone should alert us to the fact that it would be wrong to limit the influences on *The Song of Los* to any single text from the great body of eighteenth-century mythography. The catalogue of epiphanies indicates a wide knowledge of the subject, which Blake may have gained as an engraver of a variety of such works and, more diffusely, as someone involved in the publishing trade. The prominence of Brahma in Blake's list indicates an interest in the very latest research in comparative religion since it was not until the last decades of the eighteenth century that the religion, literature, and philosophy of ancient India came to wide public notice in Europe. This new material, presented by gentlemen-scholars like Charles Wilkins and Sir William Jones, made Europe aware of what was potentially an even more distant antiquity than the familiar classical and biblical eras. It represented a challenge to the primacy of the Judaeo-Christian tradition, a challenge which

[11] See J. Toland, *Letters to Serena* (London, 1704), 70, and Blackwell, *An Enquiry into the Life and Writings of Homer*, 50. There is a discussion of Warburton's theories and their influence on the French Enlightenment in Manuel, *The Eighteenth Century Confronts the Gods*, 121–2.

conservative reviewers of the work of Wilkins and Jones were quick to denounce.

Blake, on the contrary, was happy to number these works, along with the Bible and the poems of Ossian, amongst the inspired 'poetic tales' of the ancients which came to be distorted by priestcraft. They are part of the 'Word of God Universal'. Although not mentioned in the brief list of such texts in the annotations to Watson, the *Descriptive Catalogue* makes clear their status as examples of the inspired art of the ancient cultures. 'Apotheoses of Persian, Hindoo, and Egyptian Antiquity' had represented the 'stupendous originals' from which Greek mythology had derived (E 530). One of the pieces Blake exhibited in his 1809 show, 'The Bramins—A Drawing', was an 'ideal design' which showed 'Mr Wilkin translating the Geeta' (E 548). In 'Africa', of course, we see a negative moment in the history of the 'Geeta'; that is, the point at which it is transformed from a poetic tale into a sacred text. What is clear though is that Blake regarded the 'Geeta' as having the same claim to being a 'stupendous original' as the sacred texts of the Christian and the familiar classical traditions. A similar point is made in relation to the Koran later in the poem, where it is described as 'a loose Bible'. The capital letter implies that the scriptures received by Mahomet have the same status as the Christian Bible. In terms of their appearance in 'Africa' both the Bible and the Koran are represented negatively as reified and corrupted versions of stupendous originals.[12]

The account of the history of religions given in 'Africa' after the mention of Brahma is much more in line with others like Warburton's. Blake represents the Egyptian religion as the antecedent of Greek mythology and philosophy in the persons of Pythagoras, Socrates, and Plato. Blackwell had identified the

[12] For an account of the process by which the material of eastern religions affected European mythography, see Feldman and Richardson, *Rise of Modern Mythology*, 267–9, and G. Cannon, 'The Construction of the European Image of the Orient', *Comparative Criticism*, 8 (1986), 167–88. There are hostile reviews of Wilkins's translation of *The Bhagavad-Gita* in the *Monthly Review*, 76 (Mar. 1787), 198–210, and (Apr. 1787), 295–301.

origins of Greek religion in Egyptian allegories, while Warburton had claimed that Plato had travelled to Egypt to be initiated into the mysteries of the priesthood. Blake figures all these epiphanic foundations as the acceptance of an 'abstract Law' (E 67; Pl. 3, l. 18), a fettering of the liberating energies identified with Orc in *America* and *Europe*: 'time after time | Orc on Mount Atlas howld, chain'd down with the Chain of Jealousy' (ll. 20–1).[13]

Blake's description of the chaining of Orc brings the catalogue of false religions in *The Song of Los* up to the starting-point of *Europe*. In the latter the Incarnation was represented as a false dawn which saw the promise of a gospel of liberation swamped in the reinstitution of Urizenic religion. *The Song of Los* again presents Christ as the founding figure of the latest in a long list of oppressive religions:

> Then Oothoon hoverd over Judah & Jerusalem
> And Jesus heard her voice (a man of sorrows) he receivd
> A Gospel from wretched Theotormon.
>
> (ll. 22–4)

Theotormon and Oothoon first appear in *Visions of the Daughters of Albion* and *Europe*. In both instances they are linked together as in *The Song of Los*. The most extensive treatment of their relationship comes in *Visions*, where the focus is on the sexual awakening of Oothoon disrupted in turn by the violence of Bromion and Theotormon's moral condemnation. Oothoon becomes the spokeswoman for a doctrine of liberation and forgiveness. Theotormon remains a stern guardian of the moral law who seeks 'the places of religion, the rewards of continence | The self enjoyings of self denial' (E 50; Pl. 7, ll. 8–9). The basis of this relationship is maintained in *Europe* though its circumstances are altered. Both Theotormon and Oothoon appear towards the close of the poem as the fires of Orcian revolt are beginning to burn away Enitharmon's version of the moral law. Oothoon is ready to 'give up woman's secrecy', the

---

[13] See Blackwell, *An Enquiry into the Life and Writings of Homer*, 83–98, and Warburton, *Divine Legation*, i. 350 and 405.

doctrine of repression espoused in Plate 5 by Enitharmon. At the prospect of the destruction of the moral law Theotormon is 'robb'd of joy' and weeps (E 66; Pl. 14, l. 24). This joy is presumably the perverse delight in repression that Theotormon shows in *Visions*. It is to the founding site of this perverse joy that *The Song of Los* returns. Jesus ignores Oothoon's liberated vision and accepts the repressed condemnation of desire which is at the heart of Theotormon's gospel. Jesus is not the antinomian prophet he is in *The Marriage of Heaven and Hell*. 'Africa' represents him as the misguided patriarch of Christian state religion.

At this point in 'Africa' Blake modulates into a description of the fate of the human race left in the thrall of false religion:

> The human race began to wither, for the healthy built
> Secluded places, fearing the joys of Love
> And the disease'd only propagated.

> (ll. 25–7)

These lines mark a return to the attack on dualism Blake had mounted in the early plates of *The Marriage of Heaven and Hell*. There Blake rejected the distinction between the soul and the body together with the assumption that the former was more virtuous than the latter. The infernal method of *The Marriage* revealed that 'All Bibles or sacred codes' had propagated the 'Error' that 'God will torment Man in Eternity for following his Energies' (E 34; Pl. 4). Blake confidently stated, in the voice of the Devil, that 'Energy is Eternal Delight'. 'Africa' expands the brief account of the role of sacred codes in *The Marriage* to offer a catalogue of their origins and a brief account of the disastrous effects of the acceptance of the religious devotion to an abstract soul over the body. The 'disease'd' come to dominate human energies in the world of religious dualism; desire cannot be eradicated only restrained and deformed. In *The Marriage* Blake described restrained desire as 'only the shadow of desire' (E 34; Pl. 5). *The Song of Los* gives a more graphic representation of the monstrous consequences of repression. 'Africa' presents these shadows of desire as lust and violence:

the 'loose Bible' of Mahomet and Odin's 'code of war' (E 67;
Pl. 3, ll. 29–30).[14]

Blake often treats the process whereby repressed desire
returns in monstrous forms in terms of a withering of the
human faculties. The digressive narrative of Har and Heva
which interrupts the history of false religions in *The Song of Los*
is typical:

> These were the Churches: Hospitals: Castles: Palaces:
> Like nets & gins & traps to catch the joys of Eternity
> And all the rest a desert;
> Till like a dream Eternity was obliterated & erased.
> Since that dread day when Har and Heva fled.
> Because their brethren & sisters liv'd in War & Lust;
> And as they fled they shrunk
> Into two narrow doleful forms:
> Creeping in reptile flesh upon
> The bosom of the ground:
> And all the vast of Nature shrunk
> Before their shrunken eyes.
>
> (E 67–8; Pl. 4, ll. 1–12)

Elsewhere the trope of the shrinking of humanity is associated
with the effects of a catastrophic deluge. Earlier in *The Song of
Los*, for instance, the covenant between God and Noah is
figured in exactly these negative terms:

> Noah shrunk, beneath the waters;
> Abram fled in fires from Chaldea;
> Moses beheld upon Mount Sinai forms of dark delusion.
>
> (E 67; Pl. 3, ll. 15–17)

I shall return to the implications of this aspect of Blake's
imagery for his attitude to the biblical Flood in my next chapter;
what I want to concentrate on here is the mythographical
context for his use of the trope.[15]

---

[14] For a discussion of the druidic significance of Odin here see Ch. 2, n. 29.

[15] Blake's use of the trope of a deluge leading to a shrinking of human
possibility may have a biblical origin since Gen. 6: 4 mentions that giants
populated the earth before the Flood. For a further discussion of the significance
of Blake's use of the trope in a biblical context, see below, pp. 188–90. The
same image also occurs on Plate 10 of *Europe*, discussed above, pp. 92–4.

The Flood was often identified by mythographers as the catastrophic point at which an original, patriarchal Christianity was lost, only to be dimly remembered in the degraded forms of pagan worship. One text which put forward this thesis was Jacob Bryant's *A New System* (1774), on which Blake worked as an engraver. Bryant claimed that all pagan mythologies had been erected around the trauma of the Flood described in the Bible. In the privileged position he gives to the biblical account, Bryant was typical of the perspective on the ancient world shared by conservatives like Newton, Shuckford, and Stukeley. He believed that pagan mythology was a degraded version of the biblical history. The Flood had cut humanity off from the primitive Christianity of the patriarchs. In its place, Bryant claimed, humanity resorted to sun worship, itself a dim recollection of the monotheism of the primary religion. Ancient sun worship, of course, is represented on the frontispiece to *The Song of Los*, but where Bryant suggested that sun worship was a corruption of primitive monotheism Blake adjusts the relationship to suggest the continuing identity of the two religions. Volney had taken a similarly radical move when he claimed that Christianity was really the worship of the sun. Blake's history of religion rejects Bryant's assumption of Christianity's primacy. He implies that any religion which worships a deity outside of the human is in danger of forgetting that 'All deities reside in the human breast'.[16]

Blake did acknowledge the influence of Bryant on his syncretic mythologizing in the *Descriptive Catalogue*:

The antiquities of every Nation under Heaven, is no less sacred than that of the Jews. They are the same thing as Jacob Bryant, and all antiquaries have proved. How other antiquities came to be neglected and disbelieved, while those of the Jews are collected and arranged, is an enquiry, worthy of both the Antiquarian and the Divine. All had originally one language, and one religion, this was the religion of Jesus, the everlasting Gospel.   (E 543)

---

[16] See the Preface to Bryant's *A New System*, 3 vols., 2nd edn. (London, 1775). Essick discusses Blake's engraving for Bryant's book in *William Blake, Printmaker*, 31.

By 1809, when this was written, Blake seems to have been less generally hostile to certain aspects of received Christianity than he was in the 1790s. He is prepared in these comments to except Jesus from the catalogue of religious imposture in which he is included in *The Song of Los*, though the phrase 'everlasting Gospel', which was dear to antinomian enthusiasts, suggests that this Jesus is the transgressive prophet of *The Marriage of Heaven and Hell* rather than the patriarch of established Christianity. There is also something paradoxical about the reference to Bryant in the *Descriptive Catalogue*, a paradox which is consistent with Blake's infernal method of appropriating hegemonic texts so that they work against themselves. Bryant would have been deeply shocked to find his work cited as evidence that 'The antiquities of every Nation under Heaven, is no less sacred than that of the Jews' since his theories were designed to show that the pagan mythologies were degraded versions of the biblical story, not that they were 'the same thing'. Bryant would have felt it perfectly proper that pagan antiquities should be 'disbelieved'. He believed the Jewish antiquities to be true while their pagan counterparts were only distorted corroborations: 'it will be found from repeated evidence, that everything, which the divine historian [Moses] has transmitted, is most assuredly true. And though the nations, who preserved memorials of the Deluge, have not perhaps stated accurately the time of that event; yet it will be found the grand epocha, to which they referred.' For Blake both the biblical account and the antiquities of other cultures were equally original visions of Eternity, 'poetic tales' which were distorted when 'collected and arranged' into scripture. The events Blake describes in *The Song of Los* are the correlatives of Bryant's Flood; each is a catastrophe which leads to the loss of the original vision. Blake differs from Bryant in two crucial ways however. First, Blake included established Christianity in the catalogue of false religions produced in the Flood. Second, Blake's own use of the Flood as a trope in poems like *The Book of Urizen* differs from Bryant's in being rhetorical rather than historical. It is not a single event which had universal effects but something which recurs each time the human origin of the divine is denied.[17]

L. H. Tannenbaum's *Biblical Tradition in Blake's Early Prophecies* contains an interesting discussion of Blake's use of the Flood as a trope for the fall into organized religion which includes an explanation for the role of the continents in the titles of *America*, *Europe*, and the 'Africa' and 'Asia' subsections of *The Song of Los*. Tannenbaum bases his reading on a biblical tradition that Noah had given each of his sons one of the continents to control. America, where an antediluvian liberty was held to prevail, was isolated by the submersion of a connecting stretch of land in a subsequent disaster. Blake seems to make use of this last detail in his reference to the submerged 'Atlantean hills' in Plate 10 of *America*. More generally, he does use America as a site of primitive liberty lost to the other continents. The Orcian spirit of revolt rises there before spreading to Europe, Africa, and Asia.[18]

Tannenbaum, however, has overlooked a more immediate source for this configuration of the continents. The trope of liberty as a light transmitted to Europe from America was a commonplace of radical writing in the 1790s, which typically represented the American and French Revolutions as part of a continuum of enlightenment. Perhaps the single most famous example is to be found in the sermon Richard Price published as *A Discourse on the Love of our Country*: 'Behold the light you have struck out, after setting AMERICA free, reflected to FRANCE, and there kindled into a blaze that lays despotism in ashes, and warms and illuminates EUROPE!' The trope is given an even more extended treatment in the introduction to the second part of Paine's *Rights of Man*:

So deeply rooted were all the governments of the old world, and so effactually had the tyranny and antiquity of habit established itself over the mind, that no beginning could be made in Asia, Africa, or Europe, to reform the political condition of man. Freedom had been

---

[17] See Bryant, *A New System*, vol. i, pp. xi–xii.
[18] See Tannenbaum, *Biblical Tradition*, 191–3.

hunted around the globe; reason was considered as rebellion; and the slavery of fear had made men afraid to think.

But such is the irresistible nature of truth, that all it asks, and all it wants, is the liberty of appearing. The sun needs no inscription to distinguish him from darkness; and no sooner did the American governments display themselves to the world, than despotism felt a shock, and man began to contemplate redress.

Much of the rhetoric of this passage is a familiar part of texts on the radical side of the Revolution controversy.[19] The representation of tyranny as a deeply rooted tree of mystery and of liberty as enlightenment are commonplaces. The description of the progress of liberty across the continents occurs in the writings of Price and Blake and many other radical texts. A more precise rhetorical link with Blake's *The Song of Los* can be found in the phrase 'The sun needs no inscription to distinguish him from darkness'. The frontispiece of *The Song of Los* represents the religion installed by Urizen as the worship of a sun covered with obscure inscriptions. The poem ends with Orc exploding Urizen's order in an apocalyptic denouement and a full-page design which seems to have been conceived of as the dialectical contrary of the frontispiece (see Pl. 6). The design shows a naked human figure resting on a hammer and contemplating a fiery sun free from any inscriptions. Whereas the human figure in the frontispiece was dominated by the sun, here the human figure is in harmony with it. The total effect of the piece suggests that the figure is leaning on the sun in repose after labouring on it with the hammer. *The Book of Urizen* and *The Book of Los* both contain passages where Los is described working, with limited success, to create the sun at his forge. The endplate of *The Song of Los* represents a successful outcome to these labours. Los has created a sun free from hieroglyphic inscriptions which no longer dominates the human form. Blake returned to the relationship between a human figure and the sun many times in his writing and designs. He seems to have

[19] See R. Price, *A Discourse on the Love of our Country*, 2nd edn. (London, 1789), 50, and Paine, *CWP*, i. 354. Cf. Paine's earlier use of the same trope in *Common Sense*, *CWP*, i. 30–1.

been especially fascinated with the artistic potential in the relationship between 1793 and 1795. The design known as *The Dance of Albion* or *Glad Day*, though invented by Blake in 1780, was engraved sometime between 1794 and 1796. The print shows a naked human figure bursting free of clouds and backlit by the sun's rays. Radiating light and energy, the figure has humanized the power of the sun. The design might be regarded as another version of the endpiece of *The Song of Los* where Los has transformed the sun by human labour. A more negative version of the relationship, where an obscured sun dominates human desire, is to be found in several of the designs of *The Book of Urizen* and on the final plate of *The Book of Los*. The frontispiece of *Europe* might also be regarded as a representation of the installation of the hieroglyphic sun by Urizen.

What I want to stress here, however, is the way Blake's various configurations of the sun in these designs develop Paine's image of the sun of liberty standing free from the inscriptions of received authority. The similarity of the imagery is especially striking if we bear in mind that both Blake and Paine place it in the broader metaphorical context of the light of liberty spreading across the continents. Let me make it clear that I am not trying to construct Paine as a source for Blake, nor vice versa, though I do feel they are too little discussed together. Others, like Thomas Spence, also made use of the notion of the bright, clear sun of freedom: 'The Meridian Sun of Liberty bursts forth upon the astonished world dispelling the accumulated mists of dreary ages.' This sentence could stand as an exact description of Blake's *Glad Day* print, where the central figure bursts forth from dreary clouds. The last plate of *The Book of Los*, in contrast, shows the 'accumulated mists of dreary ages' obscuring the sun of liberty. What these various configurations of a basic trope should remind us is the deep involvement of Blake's rhetorical resources, both visual and written, in the Revolution controversy.[20]

Much the same point could be made at a more general level about the whole mythographic dimension of Blake's writing and designs in the 1790s. *The Song of Los*, for instance,

---

[20] See Spence, *The Rights of Infants* (1797), in *PWS*, 50.

participates in the attempt to undermine orthodox histories of religion by those radicals inclined to infidelity. Hegemonic histories usually presented Christianity as the original religion which had become degraded and perverted in the mythology and worship of the Gentile world. Blake's version of the history of religion in *The Song of Los* deviated from this thesis by including Christianity amongst the degraded religions. Before turning to discuss the most notable radical proponents of this same point in the 1790s, Paine and Volney, it is worth noting that it was a recurrent feature of rationalist critiques of Christianity earlier in the century. Deists such as John Toland paralleled Christian religions with paganism so as to promote a rational monotheism. Toland called on his readers to 'consider how in very many and considerable Regions, the plain institution of Jesus Christ cou'd degenerate into the most absurd Doctrins, unintelligible jargon, ridiculous practices, and inexplicable Mysterys'. Blake emulated Toland, as I showed in my previous chapter, by making use of druidism as a primary signifier of such mystificatory priestcraft.[21]

W. H. Reid claimed that Toland was one of the important influences on the infidels of the 1790s. Rationalist critiques of the manipulative compact between Church and State, and its origins in paganism, were an important feature of radical writing in that decade. Paine, for instance, in *The Age of Reason* claimed that 'all national institutions of churches, whether Jewish, Christian or Turkish, appear to me to be no other than human inventions set up to terrify and enslave mankind and monopolize power and profit'. This opinion restates Toland's claim that 'there was not wanting sometimes a mutual compact between the Prince and the Priest, whereby the former oblig'd himself to secure all these Advantages to the latter, if he in return would preach up his absolute Power over the People'. The anticlericalism of Paine and other radicals in the 1790s was also probably influenced by more recent attacks on the corruptions of Christianity staged by Rational Dissenters on into the

[21] See Toland's *Letters to Serena*, 129, and Feldman and Richardson, *Rise of Modern Mythology*, 25–6.

Revolution controversy itself. Joseph Priestley's *History of the Corruptions of Christianity* was perhaps the most important text in this pre-Revolution controversy movement. Priestley's *History* echoed Toland in so far as it claimed that 'the first corruptions of Christianity were derived from heathenism', though Priestley was more concerned to defend the integrity of what he saw as proper Christianity. Of particular interest in relation to Blake's attack on dualism in *The Marriage of Heaven and Hell* is Priestley's claim that 'the doctrine of a soul as a substance distinct from the body . . . was borrowed from pagan philosophy'. The proximity of the language to Blake's on Plate 4 of *The Marriage* suggests that Priestley may well have been a direct source in this instance. What is clear is that Priestley was an important if more diffuse general influence on the convictions of those who like Paine believed that 'the Christian theory is little else than the idolatry of the ancient Mythologists accommodated to the purposes of power and revenue'.[22]

Paine's *The Age of Reason* was an important contribution to this strand of British radicalism, but it was probably less influential than the various translations of Constantin Volney's *The Ruins*, the first of which was published in 1792 by Joseph Johnson with extracts regularly reprinted in places like Spence's *Pig's Meat* and Eaton's *Politics for the People*.[23] Volney's book, like Paine's *The Age of Reason*, mounted a powerful critique of religion as 'a political expedient by which to rule the credulous vulgar', but the Frenchman's polemic differed from Paine's in the global perspective offered on religion. Volney treated in some detail most of the known faiths and identified in each the process, described by earlier theorists like Blackwell, whereby poetic systems had been reified into metaphysical realities.

[22] See Reid, *The Rise and Dissolution*, 85, Paine, *CWP*, i. 464 and 467, Toland, *Letters to Serena*, 104, and Priestley, *History of the Corruptions of Christianity*, 2 vols. (Birmingham, 1782), ii. 207, and i. 345. On the differences between Priestley and the more infidel anticlericalism of Paine and Volney, see B. Rigby, 'Volney's Rationalist Apocalypse', in *1789 Reading Writing Revolution*, ed. F. Barker *et al.* (Colchester, 1982), 26–7.

[23] On Volney's influence see Thompson, *The Making of the English Working Class*, 107–8, McCalman's *Radical Underworld*, 24, 65–6, and 81, and Rigby's 'Volney's Rationalist Apocalypse'.

Volney also followed Blackwell in tracing the origins of religion to the worship of the creative power of nature. What outraged Christians, including radical Dissenters like Priestley, was that Volney claimed that Christianity was the allegorical worship of the sun. Volney's influential book has a number of features in common with Blake's mythography in the 1790s. The catalogue of false religions, for instance, in 'Africa' participates in Volney's global perspective. Most of Blake's international cast of founding fathers are also to be found amongst Volney's 'bold and energetic spirits' who 'formed vast projects of ambition' in their religious systems. It is even possible that Volney's identification of sun worship with Christianity informs the frontispiece of *The Song of Los* and the various other configurations of the image discussed above. *The Ruins* would especially have appealed to Blake as a model since, unlike Paine's book, it has some mythological aspects itself. Volney set his theories in a narrative wherein he gains his global perspective at the hands of a genie who takes him up to the heavens to look down on earth. Blake's transportation of his reader to the tables of Eternity at the beginning of 'Africa' is a parallel rhetorical strategy through which he gains a universal historical and geographical vantage-point on the origins of religion.[24]

Despite these similarities in their radical mythography, it is clear that, as Marilyn Butler has put it, 'Blake mythologizes in a far less rational spirit' than Volney. Blake's catalogue of false religions has a twist in its tail that distinguishes it sharply from the rationalism of Paine and Volney. Among the founding fathers of mystery are included those doyens of eighteenth-century rationalism, Newton and Locke. Blake's catalogue of false religions concludes with the 'Philosophy of Five Senses' (E 68; Pl. 4, l. 16). The Enlightenment cult of Reason is represented as the latest in a long series of mystificatory religions. From Blake's point of view, a reified Reason set prescriptive limits to human desire as much as the sacred codes of traditional religion.[25]

[24] See Volney's *Ruins*, 278 and 279–80.
[25] See Butler, *Romantics, Rebels, and Reactionaries*, 45.

One particular reason why Blake included the rationalist tradition in his catalogue may have been the ambivalent way in which some deists presented their version of the imposture theory of state religion. Despite his persistent and sharp anti-clericalism, John Toland, for instance, sometimes suggested that the invention of a state religion was a necessary instrument of social control: 'Without question, when wise and good Men perceiv'd that the People wou'd needs have a plurality of Gods, and temples dedicated to them, they, to comply with their weakness and at the same time to bring 'em as much as they cou'd to better and nobler Thoughts, deify'd such things.' Toland's conception of the origins of religion, with its picture of a small informed group of thinkers seeking to educate a superstitious, irrational mob, has been seen as the projection back into prehistory of his position as an eighteenth-century intellectual. Indeed in his *Pantheisticon* (1720, English translation 1751) Toland urged his fellow thinkers to separate themselves from the vulgar and to keep their advanced ideas to themselves, a point unlikely to impress the Blake who wanted to scatter religion abroad.[26]

This strain of élitism in rationalist writing was not necessarily normative, though it is also evident in the perspectives of Hume and Voltaire amongst others. A more pervasive aspect of Enlightenment theories of religious origins, shared both with some conservative theorists and the literary primitivists discussed in the previous chapter, was the idea that the religion of the world had originally been a simple, rational monotheism. Both Toland and Paine presented the original religion as the direct worship of the Creator and his Creation which had become distorted in later religious systems, including Christianity. Toland claimed that 'the most antient Egyptians, Persians, and Romans, the first Patriarchs of the Hebrews, with several other Nations and Sects had no sacred Images or Statues, no peculiar Places or costly Fashions of Worship, the plain

---

[26] See Toland, *Letters to Serena*, 89, and 'To the Reader', *Pantheisticon*, English trans. (London, 1751). See also Manuel, *The Eighteenth Century Confronts the Gods*, 66–7.

Easiness of their Religion being most agreeable to the Simplicity of the Divine Nature'. Paine put it more directly: 'Adam, if ever there was such a man, was created a Deist.'[27]

Typically this rationalist tendency ended up installing Reason as a transcendent monad. Paine, for instance, wrote approvingly of the French having 'brought their titles to the altar, and made of them a burnt-offering to Reason'. Normally altars and burnt-offerings would have been scorned by Paine as the paraphernalia of superstition. Brian Rigby has made a similar point in relation to Volney: 'after desacralizing and demystifying traditional religions, Volney simply goes on to invest reason with similar characteristics of the sacred'.[28] It is quite clear that the notion of a primitive religion, free of the corruptions of Christianity, was as operative in Blake's rhetoric as that of Priestley, Paine, and Volney. His validation of bardic culture, for instance, seems to draw on Macpherson's description of the society of Ossian as free from any form of institutionalized religion. But the society described by Macpherson and invoked by Blake was also without any notion of a transcendent deity, whether the Christian God or Reason, a fact which Blair and Macpherson seem to have been nervous about. What does appear in the Ossian poems is a socialized interaction with the spirits of the dead and a respect for what Blackwell called 'the Parts and Powers of Nature'. This representation of primitive religion (or lack of it) differs from the rationalism of Toland and Paine, but has something in common with Blake's conception of 'Divine Vision'.[29]

Much of Blake's writing in the 1790s is fundamentally averse to any notion of a transcendent principle outside the human totality, including the rational monotheism towards which the deist tradition tended. *The Song of Los*, for instance, represents Moses' central perception of the single godhead on Sinai as an encounter with 'forms of dark delusion'. The emphasis in

[27] See Toland, *Letters to Serena*, 71, and Paine, *CWP*, i. 512.

[28] See Paine, *CWP*, i. 287, and Rigby, 'Volney's Rationalist Apocalypse', 31.

[29] See Blair, *A Critical Dissertation*, 34 and 40, and Macpherson, 'Aera of Ossian', *Ossian*, ii. 219–21.

'Africa' is on the identity of all the epiphanic moments
described; they all mark the denial of the divine in the human
and the acceptance of a deity beyond human experience. Blake's
portrayal of Urizen throughout the 1790s is linked closely to
the sort of 'mysticism' which Priestley condemned as 'an
abstraction of the mind from all corporeal things' and a corruption of true Christianity. Where Blake goes beyond rationalist
Christians like Priestley and deists like Paine is in suspecting
their cult of Reason to be another such abstraction. In Plate iii
of *Europe*, for instance, Blake dispenses with the Holy Spirit,
the abstract muse of traditional Christian poetry, and replaces it
with the mocking and antinomian imp of popular culture. Blake
sanctions a human and democratic conception of creativity
which seeks to go beyond the critical power of Reason celebrated by Paine and Volney.[30]

Although Blake's rejection of rational monotheism is at odds
with much radical speculation on religion in the 1790s, it does
have something in common with other progressive theories in
the decade which traced the origins of religion to the celebration
of the active or procreative principle in humankind and nature.
Something of these links can be illustrated by a discussion of
the closing lines of *The Song of Los*:

> Forth from the dead dust rattling bones to bones
> Join: shaking convuls'd, the shivring clay breathes
> And all flesh naked stands: Fathers and Friends;
> Mothers & Infants; Kings & Warriors:
>
> The Grave shrieks with delight, & shakes
> Her hollow womb, & clasps the solid stem:
> Her bosom swells with wild desire:
> And milk & blood & glandous wine
> In rivers rush & shout & dance,
> On mountain, dale and plain.

(E 69–70; Pl. 7, ll. 31–40)

This passage is perhaps the most direct expression of the Blakian
Apocalypse from the 1790s. It stands in stark contrast to the

---

[30] See Priestley, *History*, ii. 216.

Newtonian Apocalypse described in *Europe*. The latter witnessed the dissolution of the angelic host of the moral order,
rattling their bones as they fell to their graves. The Blakian
Apocalypse is, conversely, a reconstitution of the human form,
the reversal of the process of shrinking and division documented
in 'Africa', *Europe*, and *The Book of Urizen*. So thoroughgoing
is this process of renewal that the grave itself comes to life and
is transmuted into the womb. Earlier in the closing Plate (l. 8)
Blake describes the Urizenic system as leading from 'the gates
of the Grave'. This deathly regime is changed for one of furious
activity and celebration which calls to mind Godwin's perfecti-
bilitarian belief that progress might see the end of death. For
both Blake and Godwin all social distinctions are to be washed
away in this renewal.

What critics often overlook about this denouement is its
stridently sexual nature. Throughout his writing of the 1790s
Blake presents the Apocalypse not as the end of history but as
the onset of its radical transformation through the liberation of
human energies. The final lines of *The Song of Los* take this
revision of the Bible to an extreme. The orthodox climax of
history, the intervention of the judgemental deity, is replaced
by a cosmic act of copulation. Typically for Blake, a reified
concept is replaced by a concrete instance, a literal sexual
climax. From a conservative perspective the moral order of
state religion is profaned at the very moment it is supposed to
enjoy its ultimate triumph. Moreover, the vision of cosmic
copulation is strikingly different from the configurations of
revolution and sexuality presented in the Preludium to *America*.
There the daughter of Urthona was violated by male desire in a
moment when liberated passion turns into patriarchal
oppression:

> I know thee, I have found thee, & I will not let thee go;
> Thou art the image of God who dwells in darkness of Africa;
> And thou art fall'n to give me life in regions of dark death.
> On my American plains I feel the struggling afflictions
> Endur'd by roots that writhe their arms into the nether deep:
> I see a serpent in Canada, who courts me to his love;
> In Mexico an Eagle, and a Lion in Peru;

> I see a Whale in the South-sea, drinking my soul away.
> O what limb rending pains I feel. thy fire & my frost
> Mingle in howling pains, in furrows by thy lightnings rent;
> This is eternal death; and this the torment long foretold.
>
> (E 52; Pl. 2, ll. 7–17)

These lines are much more ambivalent than those critics who read them as a straightforward celebration of the liberation of desire allow. They offer an almost Burkian image of revolt itself being reified into monstrous tyranny which stands as a rider to the millenarian optimism of the account of the American Revolution in the poem proper. It is a dystopia against which the utopianism of the main narrative can be judged. This rider does not mean that Blake was committed to an 'Orc-cycle' which read political revolt as necessarily defeated in its origins. It reveals rather that even in his earliest radical commitments Blake was aware of the dual potential of victory and defeat in the millenarian moment. Such duality runs throughout his depiction of Los as well as Orc. The prophet-bard is always liable to become the druid–priest. The denouement of *America*, where the citizens of the colonies rush to defend their evolution, represents it as a question of commitment rather than predetermined Providence whether liberated desire will prosper or not. At the close of *The Song of Los* the liberated womb is similarly involved in the process of its own emancipation. The 'hollow womb' actively 'clasps the solid stem'.

Blake's writing and designs in the 1790s return again and again to the theme of sexual freedom. The desire for freedom from moral repression is a recurrent issue in the lyrics of *Songs of Innocence and of Experience*, while in *America*, *Visions of the Daughters of Albion*, and *The Song of Los* it is treated as part and parcel of political liberation. This link between sexual and political liberation was fairly common in radical writing. The close of *America* offers a vision of liberated female sexuality which stands as a counterpoint to the Preludium and echoes Thomas Spence's belief that 'it is supposed the chains of hymen would be among the first that would be broken, in case of revolution'. Writers like Blake and Spence, however, reflect a perennial tendency among male prophets of women's liberation to limit that liberation to the sexual sphere. Blake's vision of 'females naked and glowing with the lusts of youth' (E 57; Pl. 15, l. 22) fails to allow women the role of active virtue and social participation Mary Wollstonecraft had claimed was their potential and right in her *Vindication of the Rights of Woman*. A central theme of Wollstonecraft's polemic was that women frequently accepted the illusory power of 'insignificant objects of desire' in place of active virtue and real social participation. She emphasized the need for women to 'unfold their own faculties'. Blake avoids the passive ideal of what Wollstonecraft termed the male 'sensualist', but retains the sexual as the primary sphere of women's activity.[31]

The radicalism of Blake's vision at the close of *The Song of Los* is more indebted to new theories of the sexual basis of religion which emerged at the end of the eighteenth century than to Wollstonecraft's rational feminism. Blake's Apocalypse reveals the true end of religion to be a celebration of human energies. The graphically sexual nature of much of his language stresses the importance of the erotic aspect of these energies. In France Hancarville had been a central figure in disseminating the notion that phallicism was integral to the ancient religions. His theories were picked up and developed in England by the wealthy antiquarian Richard Payne Knight. Knight wrote a treatise entitled 'A Discourse on the Worship of Priapus' which he published privately, together with a letter from Sir William Hamilton on Priapic remains in Italy, in a pamphlet entitled *An Account of the Remains of the Worship of Priapus* (1786). Although the pamphlet was distributed only to various members of the Society of Dilettanti and other interested parties, its contents became widely known in intellectual circles and were attacked by conservatives on into the 1790s, when Thomas Mathias characterized its contents as typical of progressive morality.[32]

[31] See Spence, *The Restorer of Society to its Natural State* (1801) in *PWS*, 76, and Wollstonecraft, *Vindication of the Rights of Woman*, 83, 109, and 107.

[32] By the 1780s, perhaps under the influence of finds at Herculaneum, ideas about the sexual nature of religion were becoming increasingly common. The material from India introduced by scholars such as Jones also drew attention to

Knight's thesis was that phallic and vaginal symbols and their traces in a whole range of religions were not 'ludicrous or licentious' but icons of 'some fundamental principle of their faith'. Knight believed that 'the power of procreation' had been worshipped in the ancient world. To some extent, his ideas were only an extension of the fairly common idea that, before being corrupted by priestcraft, primitive religion had worshipped the parts and powers of nature. Knight identified a whole range of images as symbolic of this procreative power; the bull, the egg, the sun, the moon, the serpent, and many others. The last two may carry something of this sexual connotation in Blake's visual vocabulary. The fiery serpent of the frontispiece to *Europe* certainly seems to represent a creative force in opposition to the moral law of the Urizenic system.[33]

Knight's theories, like most of the studies of comparative religion mentioned in this chapter, operated with the notion of a fall from the purity of an original religion into a corrupt and corrupting priestcraft. For Knight this fall was not centred around any primal catastrophe but the substitution of the symbols for the procreative powers they represented as the object of worship. In other words, his thesis provides further examples of the process described in Plate 11 of *The Marriage* whereby representations come to be reified into deities.[34] The most controversial aspect of Knight's theory, however, lay in his claim that all religions were essentially alike:

Men think they know because they are sure they feel; and are firmly convinced, because strongly agitated. Hence proceeds that haste and violence with which devout persons of all religions condemn the rites

---

a religious tradition which delighted in carnal love. Knight's 'Discourse' acknowledged a debt to Hancarville, p. 25. For details of publication of Knight's 'Discourse' and the subsequent attacks on him, see F. J. Messman, *Richard Payne Knight* (The Hague, 1974), 44, and N. Penny, 'Richard Payne Knight: A Brief Life', in *The Arrogant Connoisseur*, ed. M. Clarke and N. Penny (Manchester, 1982), 5. For Mathias's fierce attack, see *The Pursuits of Literature*, 3 parts, 3rd edn. (London, 1797), i. 134 n.

[33] See Knight's 'Discourse', 25–6 and 28–9.

[34] Warburton similarly believed that the Egyptians came to worship the hieroglyphics themselves rather than the knowledge which they represented.

and doctrines of others, and furious zeal and bigotry with which they maintain their own; while perhaps, if both were equally well understood, both would be found to have the same meaning, and only to differ in the modes of conveying it.

The implication was that the procreative principle was the basis of all religions, including Christianity. One of his notes makes the latter point explicitly: 'It is the avowed intention of the learned and excellent work of Grotius to prove that there was nothing new in Christianity. What I have here adduced, may serve to confirm and illustrate the discoveries of that great and good man.' In this context Christianity becomes a distorted and corrupted version of an earlier and explicit religion of procreation. Here was a syncretism which directly controverted the Christian apologetics which dominated eighteenth-century mythography from Shuckford to Bryant. Knight's syncretism conceded the common basis of all religions, but replaced the position of Christianity and even deist monotheism with the worship of procreative energy. It was all the more shocking in that it argued that true religion was intimately involved with sexuality.[35]

Knight's theories probably informed the much more popular publications of Erasmus Darwin, who fused mythological theories with the latest biological knowledge in the two parts of his *The Botanic Garden*, 'The Loves of the Plants' and 'The Economy of Vegetation'. Darwin's publisher was Joseph Johnson and Blake was involved with engraving a design of Fuseli's as well as his own drawings of the Portland vase for 'The Economy of Vegetation'. Darwin's mythologized account of natural history was widely read and Blake's writing and designs show a deep knowledge and complex engagement with *The Botanic Garden*.[36]

---

[35] See Knight's 'Discourse', 23, 64 n., and 193–4.

[36] Darwin's poem had a complicated publication procedure since what was to be the second part of the complete poem, 'The Loves of the Plants', was published first in 1789. Part I, 'The Economy of Vegetation', was published with the first complete edition of *The Botanic Garden* in 1791. For similarities between Knight and Darwin, see Marilyn Butler, *Romantics, Rebels and Reactionaries*, 130. Recent discussions of Darwin's influence on Blake include

Darwin's poems are often dismissed as a careless and even risible attempt to disseminate scientific knowledge through poetic personification and the pathetic fallacy. His additional use of the machinery of classical mythology to represent the loves of the plants is usually seen as compounding the problem. What this view ignores is that Darwin's poetic methodology was far from being a tired reflex. His decision to use myth and personifications to describe the processes of nature was derived from the theories of the origins of mythology discussed in this chapter. Darwin believed that classical mythology was an anthropomorphic representation of natural processes: 'The Rosicrucian doctrine of Gnomes, Sylphs, Nymphs, and Salamanders, was thought to afford a proper machinery for a Botanic poem; as it is probable, that they were originally the names of hieroglyphic figures representing the elements.' This idea was common to studies of comparative religion from Blackwell and even earlier onwards. What was radical about Darwin's poem was that it presented the generative powers of nature as a respectable object of worship. In the context of the Revolution controversy this was bound to be read as part of an attempt to destabilize the authority of Genesis.[37]

At one point in 'The Economy of Vegetation' Darwin does rewrite the biblical Creation in terms of the operations of nature's procreative power:

> NYMPHS OF PRIMEVAL FIRE! Your vestal train
> Hung with gold tresses o'er the vast inane,
> Pierced with your silver shafts the throne of Night,
> And charm'd young Nature's opening eyes with light;
> When LOVE DIVINE, with brooding wings unfurl'd,
> Call'd from the rude abyss the living world.
> "LET THERE BE LIGHT!", proclaimed the ALMIGHTY LORD,
> Astonish'd Chaos heard the potent word,—

D. Worrall, 'William Blake and Erasmus Darwin's *Botanic Garden*', *Bulletin of the New York Public Library*, 78 (1974–5), 397–417; D. C. Leonard, 'Erasmus Darwin and William Blake', *Eighteenth-Century Life*, 4 (1978), 79–81; D. King-Hele, *Erasmus Darwin and the Romantic Poets* (London, 1986), 35–46; and M. McNeil, *Under the Banner of Science* (Manchester, 1987), esp. 37–41.

[37] See Darwin, *The Botanic Garden*, 'EV', p. vii.

Through all his realms the kindling Ether runs,
And the mass starts into a million suns;
Earths round each sun with quick explosions burst,
And second planets issue from the first;
Bend, as they journey with projectile force,
In bright ellipses their reluctant course;
Orbs wheel in orbs, round centres centres roll
And form, self-balanc'd, one revolving Whole.

('EV'; Canto I, ll. 96–111)

Though it gestures towards the conventional account of the Holy Spirit as a dove hovering over the abyss, the passage goes on to identify 'Love Divine' with the generative power of nature. Darwin's poem represents Creation as an evolutionary process and draws on Buffon's theory that the earth originated in a series of eruptions from the sun. The note appended to these lines by Darwin is even more emphatic in its shift away from Genesis:

From having observed the gradual evolution of the young animal or plant from its egg or seed; and afterwards its successive advances to its more perfect state, or maturity; philosophers of all ages seem to have imagined, that the great world itself had likewise its infancy and its gradual progress to maturity; thus seems to have given origin to the very and ancient and sublime allegory of Eros, or Divine Love, producing the world from the egg of Night as it floated in Chaos.   ('EV'; Canto I, l. 101 n.)

In his prose treatise *Zoonomia* (1794) Darwin returned to the issue and developed the notion that the world itself 'might have been generated rather than created, . . . increasingly by the activity of its own inherent principles'. Although his work was initially greeted as a novel contribution to the Enlightenment, opinions such as these soon made Darwin suspect as the atmosphere of the 1790s became increasingly reactionary. He became one of the chief bogy-men of anti-Jacobinism. A fierce attack by the *British Critic*, for instance, claimed that he had discarded 'all the authority of Revelation' in favour of 'the sports of his own imagination'. Much the same charge, as I shall show in the next chapter, was brought against other associates of Joseph Johnson who more directly questioned the authority of the Bible.[38]

Recent scholarly discussions of the significance of Darwin's achievement for Blake have tended to qualify their attributions of influence by stressing Blake's repugnance for anything that smacked of natural religion. Maureen McNeil has made important points about the class basis of the differences between Darwin and Blake. The former was very much a spokesman of the progressive bourgeoisie, a rationalist defender of the factory system and the process of industrialization. From the sort of artisan perspective which Blake shared, these were not positive developments. Blake celebrated less the parts and powers of nature than human creative energies, energies which he feared were undervalued both by the *ancien régime* and the bourgeois rationalism which sought to supersede it. Even so, Blake's antagonism to 'Generation' and the 'Vegetative Powers' should not be exaggerated in the context of his debt to Darwin. First, their deadening influence only becomes a dominant motif in the rewritings of *The Four Zoas* some time after 1796–7. Secondly, it should be noted that Darwin's anthropomorphic representation of the loves of the plants was by implication as much a celebration of human sexuality as of natural procreation.[39]

There is a striking instance of this sort of double signification in Darwin's account of the plant Adonis, where 'many males and many females live together in the same flower' ('LP'; Canto IV, l. 388 n.):

> As round the shrine the gaudy circles bow,
> And seal with muttering lips the faithless vow,
> Licentious Hymen joins their mingled hands,

[38] See Darwin, *Zoonomia*, 2 vols. (London, 1794), i. 509. For details of the increasingly hostile response to Darwin, see N. Garfinkle, 'Science and Religion in England, 1790–1800', *Journal of the History of Ideas* (1955), 378 and 381–5. The attack on *Zoonomia* can be found in the *British Critic*, 5 (1795), 120.

[39] See McNeil, *Under the Banner of Science*, 38. Regarding the implications of Darwin's poem on human sexuality, King-Hele has noted that 'one can hardly read the poem's repeated revelations of plant polygamy, practised by pseudohumans, without suspecting that Darwin was trying to subvert the custom of monogamy by implying that it was usual in nature'. See his *Erasmus Darwin* (London, 1963), 144.

And loosely twines the meretricious bands,—
Thus where pleased VENUS, in the southern main,
Shed all her smiles on Othaleite's plain,
Wide o'er the role her silken net she draws,
And the Loves laugh at all, but Nature's laws.

('LP'; Canto IV, ll. 399–406)

His notes explain that the last four lines refer to a human
example of polygamy among the people of the Othaleite
islands, where 'about 100 males and 100 females form one
promiscuous marriage' (l. 388. n.). The positive nature of
Darwin's attitude to human sexuality is even more explicit in
Zoonomia, where it is described as 'the purest source of human
felicity, the cordial drop in the otherwise vapid cup of life'.[40]
Marilyn Butler has suggested that Darwin's permissiveness is
epitomized by his treatment of the Psyche story since he
significantly rejects the influential Platonic reading of the myth
as an account of the travails of the soul in the material world.
For Darwin Psyche is clearly to be seen as a personification of
sexual fulfilment:

Fair PSYCHE, kneeling at the ethereal throne;
Won with coy smiles the admiring court of Jove,
And warm'd the bosom of unconquer'd LOVE—
Beneath a moving shade of fruits and flowers
Onward they march to HYMEN's sacred bowers;
With lifted torch he lights the festive train,—
Sublime, and leads them in his golden chain,
Joins the fond pair, indulgent to their vows,
And hides with mystic veil their blushing brows.
Round their fair forms their mingling arms they fling,
Meet with warm lip, and clasp with rustling wing.—
—Hence plastic Nature, as oblivion whelms
Her fading forms, repeoples all her realms;
Soft joys disport on purple plumes unfurl'd;
And Love and Beauty rule the willing world.

('EV'; Canto IV, ll. 48–62)

[40] See *Zoonomia*, i. 146–7.

Darwin's revision of the Psyche myth as an allegory of the generative power of 'plastic Nature' implies, as does Priestley's *History* and Blake's *The Marriage of Heaven and Hell*, that the notion of a soul distinct from the energies of nature is a misreading of ancient poetry. It was precisely Darwin's failure to mention the soul in his evolutionary account of the natural world in *Zoonomia* which attracted the critical fire of the *British Critic*. The reviewer castigated him for 'dismissing all consideration of any soul, in the usual acceptation of the word' and substituting 'what he calls a spirit of animation'. Blake's poetry of the 1790s is also broadly concerned with the celebration of 'a spirit of animation', most impressively in the antinomianism of *The Marriage of Heaven and Hell*. Both Darwin and Blake were seeking to undermine the authority of orthodox Christianity. Where they differed was, perhaps, in that Blake replaced Christian monotheism with a sense of human divinity, while Darwin moved towards a materialism which Blake would have felt reified nature over the human.[41]

Whether he completely agreed with it or not, what is clear is that Blake did make extensive use of Darwin's mythologized account of the loves of the plants. It could be said that he usually reverses the operation of Darwin's imagery since Blake represents human sexuality in terms of floral procreation rather than vice versa. Erdman's *Illuminated Blake* indicates many potential allusions to Darwin in the designs to the books Blake published in the 1790s and even earlier. The title-page to *The Book of Thel* (1789), for instance, shows the sexual activities of pistils and stamens, which dominate 'The Loves of the Plants' published in the same year. David Worrall has suggested that the plate depicts the sexual freedom celebrated in Darwin's verse which within Blake's poem Thel struggles and fails to achieve. Throughout *The Book of Thel* any number of the personifications of flowers which appear in Darwin's book recur. The lily is among the first mentioned in 'The Loves of the Plants', where it amongst Darwin's more shy and retiring

---

[41] See Butler, *Romantics, Rebels and Reactionaries*, 133, and the *British Critic* (1795), 114.

creations: 'With secret sighs the Virgin Lily droops' (Canto I,
l. 15). Blake has a similarly modest lily which is described as a
'little virgin of the peaceful valley' (E 4; Pl. 2, l. 3). More
generally, there is a tendency within both poems to evoke a
tremulous world of fragile natural processes:

> Say on each leaf how tiny Graces dwell;
> How laugh the Pleasures in a blossom's bell;
> How insect-Loves arise on a cob-web wings,
> Aim their light shafts, and point their little stings.

('LP'; Canto I, ll. 35–8)

It was passages such as these that were parodied in Mathias's
Pursuits of Literature:

> In filmy, gawzy, gossamery lines,
> With lucid language, and most dark designs
> In sweet tetrandryan, monogyrian strains
> Pant for a pystill in botanic pains;
> On the luxurious lap of Flora thrown,
> On beds of yielding vegetable down,
> Raise lust in pinks; and with unhallow'd fire
> Bid the soft virgin violet expire.

(ll. 85–92)

Although ridicule is the dominant note of Mathias's parody, he
does identify 'dark designs' behind the verse. His notes accuse
Darwin of having sacrificed 'propriety and just imagery to the
rage of mere novelty'. He clearly identified in Darwin that
feminization of culture which so alarmed critics after the French
Revolution and which publications like Mathias's were designed
to destroy.[42]

Doubtless Mathias would have also found a similar overload
of sensibility in passages such as these from *The Book of Thel*:

> Nothing remains; O maid I tell thee, when I pass away,
> It is to tenfold life, to love, to peace, and raptures holy:
> Unseen descending, weigh my light wings upon balmy flowers;
> And court the fair eyed dew. to take me to her shining tent;

---

[42] See D. V. Erdman, *The Illuminated Blake* (Oxford, 1975), 33–4; Worrall,
'William Blake', 400.

The weeping virgin, trembling kneels before the risen sun,
Till we arise link'd in a golden band, and never part;
But walk united, bearing food to all our tender flowers.

(E 4; Pl. 3, ll. 10–16)

Blake's use of such gossamer imagery is not confined to *The Book of Thel*. He made frequent use of flowers in discursive treatments of sexuality. They occur, for instance, in the fairy's song in *Europe*. Poems like 'My Pretty Rose Tree', 'The Lilly', and 'Sick Rose' in *Songs of Innocence and of Experience* also explore the sexual symbolism of flowers. The trope of the worm devouring the bud in 'Sick Rose', though something of a literary commonplace, may be a development of the special role in *The Botanic Garden* of the worm which sabotages the sexual energy of the flowers. *Visions of the Daughters of Albion*, like *The Book of Thel* another poem of the struggle for sexual self-expression, is equally involved in developing Darwin's botanic imagery. The marigold, for instance, which accompanies the poem's 'Argument' emits rays of light, a phenomenon which Darwin touched on several times. Within the poem itself it is flowers that Oothoon seeks to comfort her in the face of doubts about her sexual desires:

And thus she spoke to the bright Marygold of Leutha's vale
Art thou a flower! art thou a nymph! I see thee now a flower;
Now a nymph! I dare not pluck thee from thy dewy bed!
The Golden nymph replied; pluck thou my flower Oothoon the
    mild
Another flower shall spring, because the soul of sweet delight
Can never pass away. she ceas'd & closd her golden shrine.

(E 45–6; Pl. 1, ll. 5–10)

The freedom from sexual jealousy which Oothoon manages to maintain in the face of male violence and moral censure can itself be seen as analogous to the polygamous energies of the botanic world celebrated by Darwin.[43]

---

[43] For a general discussion of the flower imagery in *Songs of Innocence and of Experience* in the context of Darwin's poem, see D. King-Hele, *Erasmus Darwin and the Romantic Poets*, 45–50. Worrall discusses *The Book of Thel* and *Visions* in his 'William Blake', 398–405. Darwin discussed plants which emit light in 'LP'; Canto IV, l. 45 n. In a supplementary note (p. 183) he states: 'The light was most brilliant on Marigolds, of an orange or flame colour.'

One poem which the assiduous researches of David Worrall and others have overlooked in relation to Blake's Darwinian debts is *The Song of Los*. Although obviously a phallic image, 'the solid stem' clasped by the grave at the denouement of the poem may also retain the botanic connotations of 'stem'. Certainly many of Darwin's descriptions of the loves of the plants give as active a role to the female participants as does Blake's apocalyptic finale. *The Song of Los*, of course, represents this sexual liberation as part of the political liberation associated with the French Revolution. 'The Economy of Vegetation' also offered an account of the French Revolution which, given the context of the rest of the poem, implied that the Revolution was part of the burgeoning power of nature. Paine himself, batting back Burke's representation of the Revolution as a monstrous deformation of the natural order, had figured events in America and France as a new flowering of the human spirit: 'What pace the political summer may keep with the natural, no human foresight can determine. It is, however, not difficult to determine spring is begun.' The same trope is picked up by Orc in *America* when he declares that his destruction of received authority will make 'the desarts blossom'. Blake extended the figure to include its antithesis when he represented the dead hand of the *ancien régime* as a blight on nature later in the poem.[44]

Darwin's poem figured the Revolution as the awakening of a primitive giant, a sort of huge spirit of nature:

> Long had the Giant-form on GALLIA's plains
> Inglorious slept, unconscious of his chains;
> Round his large limbs were wound a thousand strings
> By the weak hands of Confessors and Kings;
> O'er his closed eyes a triple veil was bound,
> And steely rivets lock'd him to the ground;

---

[44] See Paine, *CWP*, i. 273. Ronald Paulson, *Representations of Revolution*, 73–5, has suggested that the idea of a political spring in the French Revolution was a commonplace of radical rhetoric. It is obviously involved with the discourse surrounding the Trees of Mystery and Liberty discussed above. Darwin's lines on the French Revolution reviving nature were popular enough to be reprinted in *Politics for the People*, vol. i, Part 1, p. 165.

> While stern Bastile with iron cage inthralls
> His folded limbs, and hems in marble walls.
> —Touch'd by the patriot-flame, he rent amazed
> The flimsy bonds, and round and round him gazed;
> Starts up from the earth, above the admiring throng
> Lifts his colossal form, and towers along;
> High o'er his foes his hundred arms He rears,
> Plowshares his swords, and pruning hooks his spears;
> Calls to the Good and Brave with voice, that rolls;
> Like Heaven's own thunder round the echoing poles;
> Gives to the winds his banner broad unfurl'd,
> And gathers in its shade the living world.
>
> ('EV'; Canto II, ll. 377–94)

The similarities between Blake's Orc and Darwin's 'Giant-form' are both obvious in general and numerous in particularities. Worrall has given a brief account of the specific verbal parallels. He notes, for instance, that 'bonds' and 'veils' are frequently 'rent' by Orc in poems like *America* and *Europe*. It can be added that Orc's voice echoes that of Darwin's giant in its ability to rouse 'the living world'. Worrall has also drawn attention to Darwin's reprint in his notes of Helen Maria Williams's account of the Bastille: 'We saw the hooks of those chains, by which the prisoners were fastened by their necks to the walls of their cells . . . Some skeletons were found . . . with irons still fastened to their decayed bones' ('EV'; Canto II, l. 383 n.). Worrall compares this to Blake's 'den nam'd Horror' in *The French Revolution*, where there is a prisoner 'Chain'd hand and foot, round his neck an iron band, bound to the impregnable wall'. There are other examples of the importance of similar images in Blake's work which could be added to Worrall's account. The most notable is Plate 12 of *Europe*, where Blake imagines the 'citizens' of Enitharmon's dominion 'With bands of iron round their necks fasten'd into the walls' (l. 29). The image is given graphic representation in the design on the next Plate which shows a prisoner fastened to the wall by a leg-iron.[45]

---

[45] See Worrall, 'William Blake', 406–12.

The more general similarities between Darwin's giant and Blake's Orc are interesting in relation to several of the features of *The Song of Los* discussed above. The giant in Darwin's poem, who has 'Long . . . Inglorious slept', can be compared to the expanded form of the human frame which Orc struggles to reawaken and Los works to rebuild against the Urizenic processes of diminution and fragmentation. Furthermore, Darwin's personification of the Revolution implies its popular nature; it becomes an aggregation of human energies. Blake similarly stresses the role of human agency in his apocalyptic version of revolution. The Orc of the main part of *America* is a 'Human fire'. Later in the poem Orc's promise is only fulfilled when the citizens of America themselves rush to lend their support. Darwin's giant must likewise gather to himself 'the Good and Brave'. Both Darwin and Blake represent the ideal of revolution as the aggregation of human energies, not just the fulfilment of a natural process or the intervention of a divine Providence.

I want to return now to considering Blake and Darwin from the perspective of mythographical theory. Before discussing more generally what Darwin's example may have meant for Blake as a model of practice, I should briefly mention the significance of one of the plates Blake engraved after Fuseli for Johnson's edition of Darwin's poem (see Pl. 7).[46] The Plate, called 'The Fertilization of Egypt', illustrates the following lines;

[46] Sometimes critics are apt to forget that the inscription on the Plate credits Fuseli as the inventor and Blake only as the engraver so Blakian does the design seem. Although collaboration between draughtsmen and engravers is common, it seems unnecessary to credit Blake with actually having invented the design to justify discussing it in relation to him. What the design does is touch on a number of themes common to mythographic studies in the 18th cent. It could even be claimed that it relates to themes of particular interest to those associated with or published by Joseph Johnson. Johnson's edition of Volney's *Ruins* was full of discussions of the origins of priestcraft in the worship of natural forces and included Egypt as an important example; see, for instance, pp. 231–5. It seems likely that Darwin, Fuseli, and Blake all had similar interests. It is probably most useful to think of the origins of the design as lying in the shared mythographical interests of the Johnson circle.

> Sailing in air, when MONSOON inshrouds
> His tropic mountains in night of clouds;
> Or drawn by whirlwinds from the LINE returns,
> And showers o'er Afric all his thousand urns;
> High o'er his head the beams of Sirius glow,
> And, Dog of Nile, ANUBIS barks below.

> ('EV'; Canto III, ll. 129–34)

The design shows the dog-headed priest of Anubis welcoming the flooding of the Nile which is personified as a faintly etched deity hovering above the waters. It is the latter figure which most critics have dwelt on, since it offers a prototype for Blake's subsequent portrayals of Urizen. He too is a God 'seat'd on waters' and associated with Egyptian priestcraft. Indeed Darwin's lines describe a situation very similar to that at the end of *The Book of Urizen* where Urizen institutes his 'Net of Religion':

> And the thirty cities remaind
> Surrounded by salt floods, now call'd
> Africa: its name was then Egypt.

> (E 83; Pl. 28, ll. 8–10)

The difference is that Darwin represents the flooding of the Nile as a positive event: 'And towns and temples laugh amid the deep' (l. 144). Blake's thirty cities 'surrounded by salt floods' in *The Book of Urizen* have been betrayed into an Egyptian slavery. Interestingly Fuseli's design participates more in the darker perspective of Blake's poem than the lines by Darwin which it illustrates. Both Blake's poem and Fuseli's design share Volney's negative emphasis on the manipulative practices of priestcraft. *The Ruins* identified Egypt as the source of such practices and specifically identified the flooding of the Nile as the natural event allegorized in the original pagan religion. Indeed Fuseli's design actually illustrates the precise moment when this process begins. The priest of Anubis is turning his attention away from the river to praise the bearded figure which hovers above it. In terms of Plate 11 of *The Marriage of Heaven and Hell*, we are witnessing the abstraction of 'a mental deity' from the 'Genius' of the Nile. To be even more specific, the design is an illustration of the moment described in *The Song of Los* when the Egyptian patriarch Trismegistus accepts an 'abstract Law'.[47]

Whatever the different perspectives of Blake and Darwin on Egyptian priestcraft, it is evident that they shared a deep interest in the origins of religion and myth. Most critical accounts of this shared interest have sought to stress as an essential difference the priority of Blake's awareness that the celebration of the parts and powers of nature which Darwin tried to emulate could itself become the worship of an 'abstract Law'. This difference has led Nelson Hilton to describe Darwin as only 'spectrally present' in Blake's texts, limiting the former's importance to 'the compendium of scientific imagery he offered, rather than . . . massive direct influence'. While there is little doubt that Blake's poetic debts do not amount to anything like an acceptance of a Darwinian philosophy, Hilton overlooks what Darwin offered Blake as a positive model of a radically orientated mythological practice. Unlike many of the speculative mythographers mentioned above, Darwin had a very positive attitude to myth. He complained that it was not sufficiently used as an artistic medium: 'why should not painting as well as poetry express itself in metaphor, or in indistinct allegory?' ('EV', Canto I, l. 358 n.) Hilton has drawn attention to a very similar passage in Blake's *Descriptive Catalogue* (E 541): 'Poetry consists in these conceptions; and shall Painting be confined to the sordid drudgery of fac-simile representations of merely mortal and perishing substances, and not be as poetry and music are, elevated into its own proper sphere of invention and visionary conception?' Rationalist sceptics like Volney criticized myth as irrational and corrupt. Other mythographers criticized it as a degraded version of an earlier primitive Christianity or deism, sometimes qualifying this criticism by admitting its utility as a religious means of social control. Darwin, however, was a mythologist and not only a mythographer. He sought to renew mythology through his poetry, to

---

[47] See Volney, *Ruins*, 239.

replace the corrupt with a revised version fitted to modern scientific knowledge. A similar revisionary aesthetic is also obviously part of Blake's poetic enterprise. Blake's attempt to create his own mythology is an attempt to 'burn away the apparent surfaces' of received allegories and replace them with a revivified version of ancient poetry: 'The Nature of my Work is Visionary or Imaginative; it is an endeavour to Restore what the Ancients call'd the Golden Age.' Blake's conception of the Bible as a poetic text is concomitant with this endeavour and helps explain where he departs from the scepticism of someone like Paine. Blake and Paine both sought to undermine the authority of the Bible as a public record and legal authority. Paine believed that if the Bible's historical basis was undermined it was worthless, although he did acknowledge the beauty of the Hebrew poetry bound up with the 'trash'. Blake was much more fully involved in trying to recover the Bible and ancient literature in general as poetry. Discredited as scripture, revealed as a corrupted form of worship, it could be revalued as a poetic tale. As I shall show in my next chapter, a large part of Blake's work in the 1790s is involved in refashioning the Bible with such an end in mind.[48]

[48] See N. Hilton, 'The Spectre of Darwin', *BIQ* 15 (1981), 39.

4

Blake, the Bible, and its Critics in the 1790s

THE preceding two chapters have revealed the ways in which the authority of the hegemonic Christian tradition is decentred in Blake's writing and designs of the 1790s. What emerges is his sense of Christianity's incubation of the errors of pagan priestcraft, a perception which equally informs the attacks on state religion staged by radical writers like Eaton, Paine, and Volney. I shall pursue this theme more directly in this chapter by examining Blake's use of the Bible in the 1790s, the relationship of his writing to developments in late eighteenth-century biblical criticism, and the part such criticism had to play in the Revolution controversy. Whereas the prophetic celebration of liberation and desire seems to represent the positive dimension of Blake's rhetoric in the 1790s, the under-mining of scriptural authority is its negative or critical contrary. This dual approach can be related back to 'the poetic tales'/ 'forms of worship' paradigm derived from mythographic the-ories. Blake values the Bible as poetic myth, but seeks to free this positive dimension by undermining the 'apparent surface' of the scriptural authority which masks it.

The revisionary freedom of Blake's use of the Bible may have been partially determined by his social origins and lack of formal education. Notions of fidelity to an authoritative text tended to exert less pressure on those educated informally than on readers produced within an academic system. This relative freedom often made for a fluid approach to texts in general and the Bible in particular. There are many examples of readers from the vulgar culture first encountering the Bible as a powerful reservoir of stories and images which they continued to draw on in the same way later in their lives. This approach to the Bible was not concerned with textual propriety or notions of a single, proper reading. Thomas Spence's work offers an example of how someone who encountered the Bible as a primer could both retain and transform its influence as an intimate part of personal style. Although his political writings are full of denunciations of organized religion, they are also shot through with the language and cadences of the Bible.[1] A similar conception of a popular, fluid Bible was also available to Blake in a historicized and theorized form in some of the scriptural criticism of the time. Alexander Geddes, for instance, traced the origins of the Bible to the national antiquities and oral culture of the ancient Hebrews. The seeming convergence in Blake's text of a popular practice and emergent polite theory is familiar from previous chapters. What it marks is the unstable origins of Blake's texts, the texts of a bricoleur operating between two (or more) cultures.

Among Blake's publications of the 1790s those most directly involved with a critique of the Bible are *The Book of Urizen*, *The Book of Ahania*, and *The Book of Los*. It is these poems of 1794–5 which most closely mimic the layout of the Authorized Version, double columns divided into chapter and verse, as well as shadowing quite closely particular sections of biblical narrative. Taken as a group, the three poems might be said to stand in the same relation to Blake's prophecies of liberation, like *America* and *Europe*, as Paine's *The Age of Reason* does to his *Rights of Man*. The former represent a critique of the Bible; the latter, a manifesto of revolutionary possibility. The opening pages of *The Age of Reason* make it clear that Paine believed the two were necessary complements; a revolution in religion was the natural corollary, even prerequisite, of a fully successful political revolution. His book was an attempt to challenge the Bible, the pre-eminent example in his culture of that 'manu-

---

[1] H. T. Dickinson has pointed out Spence's indebtedness to the Bible. See *PWS*, p. vii. David Vincent's *Literacy and Popular Culture: England 1750–1914* (Cambridge, 1989) has some useful insights into the role of the Bible and religious material generally in popular literacy. See, for instance, pp. 85, 176–7, and 183. By the late 18th cent. the popular oral tradition had already been long penetrated by printed forms. The Bible was a crucial aspect of that penetration but one which was itself transformed by the popular culture it invaded.

script assumed authority of the dead' he first confronted in
Rights of Man.[2]

There are two basic ways in which *The Book of Urizen*, *The
Book of Ahania*, and *The Book of Los* contest the cultural
hegemony of the received Bible. First, they refute any notion
of 'manuscript assumed authority' through their own structural
indeterminacy. Secondly, this general feature of Blake's work
interacts strongly with the particularities of the treatment of the
Bible itself in the three poems, which shadow quite closely
distinct sections of the Bible in order to parody or subvert
them. The parodic relationship, for instance, between *The Book
of Urizen* and Genesis is by now a familiar tenet of Blake
scholarship. Harold Bloom presented the poem as 'an ironic
explanation of how both man and nature fell into their presently
botched condition'. More recently Leslie Tannenbaum claimed
that a 'principle of ironic inversion' is the structural key to the
poem. Both follow the general tendency of Blake criticism in
reading this ironic principle as a break with the political
commitments of poems like *The Marriage of Heaven and Hell*
and *America*. They fail to offer a sense of the political impera-
tives of the ironic principle in the poems and its relationship to
radical discourse in the 1790s.[3]

I shall deal with the general point about Blake's structural
indeterminacy before turning to a consideration of his treatment
of the Bible in the three poems. As I pointed out in my
Introduction, Blake denied *The Book of Urizen* any definitive
form. All seven extant copies are different. Some versions
contain plates which are absent in others, while all seven

[2] Paine described the relationship between religious and political change in
The Age of Reason in the following way: 'I saw the exceeding probability that a
revolution in the system of government would be followed by a revolution in
the system of religion. The adulterous connection of church and state . . . has
so effectually prohibited by pains and penalties every discussion upon established creeds, and upon first principles of religion, that until the system of
government should be changed, those subjects could not be brought fairly and
openly into the world; but that wherever this should be done, a revolution in
the system of religion would follow' (*CWP*, i. 465).
[3] See H. Bloom, *Blake's Apocalypse* (London, 1963), 170 and Tannenbaum,
Biblical Tradition in Blake's Early Prophecies, 141.

versions of the poem have a different ordering of the plates. Internally not one of these arrangements of the plates provides a consistent narrative. All, for instance, contain two conflicting accounts of the origins of Urizen. He forms himself by breaking away from Eternity in the opening chapter of the poem, but his body is also created in the process of Los's attempts to bind him later in the narrative. Such problems are legion in the poem. Perhaps the most blatant example is Blake's decision to incorporate two headings introducing 'Chap. IV' in six versions of the poem. The majority of the copies of *The Book of Urizen* effectively have a duplicate chapter four.[4]

Although there are internal narratological difficulties and disjunctions in *The Book of Ahania* and *The Book of Los*, none is as obvious as those in *The Book of Urizen*. Nor are there variations between different copies to discuss, since only one copy of each is extant. J. J. McGann has suggested, however, that the relationship between these two poems and *The Book of Urizen* displays an indeterminacy which also throws light on Blake's attitude to the textual authority of the Bible. Both *The Book of Ahania* and *The Book of Los* seem to rework sections of the narrative of *The Book of Urizen* in ways which offer not only a different perspective on the events described but substantive and even contradictory differences of detail. These differences undermine the deep-rooted critical notion that there is some kind of prior Blakian myth articulated in each of his poetic performances. Blake's poetic practice is predicated on a freedom from any notion of fidelity to the authority of a single, antecedent text, a predication which operates in *The Book of Urizen*, *The Book of Ahania*, and *The Book of Los* directly against the received cultural authority of the Bible.[5]

J. J. McGann has described the 'textual indeterminacy' of the three poems as 'part of a deliberate effort to critique the received Bible and its traditional exegetes'. He traces the historical origins of Blake's textual indeterminacy to 'the latest

---

[4] For a detailed account of the variations see G. E. Bentley, *Blake's Books* (Oxford, 1977), 171–3, and (ed.), *William Blake's Writings*, 2 vols. (Oxford 1978), i. 238–59. See also McGann's *Social Values and Poetic Acts*, 153–8.

[5] See McGann, *Social Values*, 170–2.

research findings of the new historical philology' and, in particular, the work of Alexander Geddes. Geddes was another of the intellectuals who associated with the publisher Joseph Johnson. He was the chief theological reviewer for Johnson's *Analytical Review* from 1788 to 1793 and regularly to be found in attendance at the famous literary suppers held by the publisher. It does seem likely therefore that Blake would have at least encountered Geddes's work at Johnson's shop, if not the man himself.[6]

Geddes's most significant publication was a new translation of the Bible. He produced the first volume, containing the Pentateuch, in 1792. The second and last volume was published in 1797. This new translation, together with a number of related pamphlets, drew attention to repetitions, gaps, and contradictions in the biblical narrative. Geddes was far from being the first biblical scholar to be aware of these features of the text. Nor was this awareness confined to rarefied circles of scholarship. Samuel Fisher's Quaker textbook, *The Testimony of Truth Exalted* (1679), for instance, had described the Bible as a 'huge heap of uncertainty'. What was relatively original about Geddes's work was that he put forward the so-called 'Fragment Hypothesis' to account for the state of the Bible. This theory placed the explanation for the defective condition of the text in the nature of its origins. Geddes believed the Bible to be a heterogeneous compilation based on the oral traditions of the Hebrews. Building on this theory, Geddes went on to offer a reading of the text as poetry rather than history. He claimed that the Fall, for instance, was to be understood as 'an excellent mythologue' designed to explain the origin of evil to a primitive people. Similarly, he saw the seven-day Creation as 'a beautiful mythos or philosophical fiction' contrived to meet 'the shallow intellects of a rude and barbarous nation'. These attitudes coincide with Blake's conception of sacred texts as originally having been 'poetic tales'. Both men seem to have made the

---

[6] See McGann, *Social Values*, 172. Details of the relationship between Johnson and Geddes and Johnson and Blake over this period are given in G. P. Tyson's *Joseph Johnson* (Iowa, 1979), 102 and 109–29.

radical move of applying generally available theories of the origins of myth to the Bible.[7]

Geddes's discussions of the origins of the Pentateuch imply something more than the metaphorical or poetic nature of the Bible. Geddes claimed that the Hebrews had no written records prior to Moses. He described Genesis as a collation 'derived from monumental indexes, or traditional tales'. An important source for the compilers of the written text was 'the oral testimony, transmitted, from generation to generation, in simple narratives, or rustic songs'. Volney similarly believed that 'Genesis in particular was never the work of Moses, but a compilation digested after the return from the Babylonian captivity'. Both suggested that the received Bible had its origins in a collection of popular antiquities appropriated to the ends of state religion. Such a view of the Bible seems to combine the mythographic paradigm of poetic tales being usurped by priest-craft with the sort of radical antiquarian theories advanced by Joseph Ritson. The received Bible is revealed to be caught up in the transcription and distortion of oral tradition and becomes part of that official record which Ritson revealed to be 'conse-crated to the crimes and follies of titled ruffians and sainted idiots'.[8]

It is revealing, bearing the above in mind, that Blake's scornful dismissal of the notion that public records could be true takes place in the context of a discussion of the Bible. Other aspects of his annotations to Watson's *Apology for the Bible*, perhaps influenced by the currency of such ideas in the circle around Joseph Johnson, also seem to chime in with the attitudes sketched in the previous paragraph. That Blake believed the unperverted Bible to have its basis in Hebrew popular antiquities, for instance, is suggested by his comparison

---

[7] See Fisher's *Testimony*, 396, and on the longevity of the text's influence, Hill, *The World Turned Upside Down*, 268. For Geddes's comments, see his *Holy Bible*, 2 vols. (London, 1792–7), vol. i, pp. xix, xi, and *Critical Remarks on the Hebrew Scriptures* (London, 1790), 25–6. Geddes also made it clear that he did not consider the judgemental God of the Old Testament to be a true representation of the Deity, but a metaphorical device fitted to the mentalities of 'a stupid carnal people', *Holy Bible*, vol. i, p. xii.

[8] See Geddes, *Bible*, vol. i, p. xix, and Volney, *Ruins*, 196.

of the scriptures with 'the Songs of Fingal' and other ancient
texts from a variety of cultures. He also implies that Moses was
not the author of the Pentateuch: 'If Moses did not write the
history of his acts. it takes away the authority altogether it
ceases to be history & becomes a Poem of probable impossibil-
ities fabricated for pleasure as moderns say but I say by
Inspiration' (E 616). Revealing though the annotations are,
however, nowhere is Blake's sense of the difference between
the official Bible and the original antiquities of the Hebrews as
clearly expressed as in the couplet:

> The Hebrew Nation did not write it
> Avarice & Chastity did shite it.

Blake's own creative revisions of the Bible in his poetry and
designs are in part to be seen as an attempt to re-create the
'Inspiration' of the Hebrew popular antiquities suppressed in
the perverted Bible of state religion.[9]

To an extent, this dimension of Blake's poetic enterprise
represents an intensification of the way the Bible was treated in
the popular culture of his own time. Blake's description of the
Bible as a 'book of Examples' (E 618) rather than an authoritative history, for instance, was already in place in a culture where

---

[9] What Geddes called the 'monumental indexes' of Hebrew antiquity were
discussed by Blake in his *Descriptive Catalogue*: 'The Artist having been taken
in vision into the ancient republics, monarchies, and patriarchates of Asia, has
seen those wonderful originals called in the Sacred Scriptures Cherubim, which
were sculptured and painted on walls of Temples, Towers, Cities, Palaces, and
erected in the highly cultivated states of Egypt, Moab, Edom, Aram, among
the Rivers of Paradise' (E 531). Most commentaries on this passage concentrate
on Blake's subsequent claim that the classical pantheon comprised only copies
of Hebrew originals. What this overlooks is that Blake describes the 'Cherubim' as themselves versions of 'wonderful originals', only 'called' by their
biblical name in the 'Sacred Scriptures'. Though the Hebrew antiquities are
clearly more exalted for Blake, in 1809 at least, than their classical successors,
they themselves are placed in the context of originals erected in other ancient
Asian states. What Blake seems to share with Geddes is a notion of the
derivative nature of the scriptures. State religion, as Blake's annotations to
Watson make clear, is involved in covering up these complex origins in its
presentation of the Bible as the '<Peculiar> Word of God'. See the discussion
in Morton D. Paley's '"Wonderful Originals"—Blake and Ancient Sculpture',
in *Blake in his Time*, ed. Essick and Pearce, 170–97.

the Bible had to serve as primer, story-book, and moral guide. The writings of extreme religious enthusiasts often reveal a conscious extension of these attitudes, a willingness to treat the Bible as a stock of inspiration which could be added to and altered by each visionary performer or reader. Some, like Richard Brothers, were prepared to claim that whatever they were taught by inspiration had the same validity as scripture. In the 1790s such attitudes could often take an avowedly political edge. William Bryan, for instance, indicated that 'kings, princes, bishops, parliaments, and judges' had deliberately promoted error through 'a multitude of books'. His own writing was an attempt to break through this body of orthodox error with his own inspired visions to reveal the truth of the Bible. Much of Blake's writing in the 1790s similarly seeks to liberate the Bible and its readers from the forms of worship sponsored by state religion.[10]

Both Blake and Geddes seem to be part of a varied but discernible dimension of the Revolution controversy which sought to destabilize the authority of the received Bible. W. H. Reid's *Rise and Dissolution of the Infidel Societies* identified religious enthusiasts as an auxiliary force in this process of subverting state religion. At the centre of the broader challenge Reid placed books like Paine's *The Age of Reason*. Paine makes frequent references to the Bible's 'traditionary' basis and its distortion by an exploitative priestcraft. He claimed that Genesis was based on 'oral traditions' and that Moses was not its author. Similarly the Psalms were originally 'a collection, as song books are nowadays, from different song writers, who lived at different times'. Of particular interest in relation to Blake's work are Paine's remarks on prophecy. Paine believed the biblical prophecies were 'the work of the Jewish poets and itinerant preachers, who mixed poetry, anecdote and devotion'. He clearly followed Lowth's bardic conception of the prophets, though Paine's description of the Hebrew bard is closer to Ritson's travelling entertainer of the people than Lowth's sublime public poet. It

---

[10] See Bryan, *Testimony*, I and II, and the discussion of this matter above, pp. 35–6. See also S. Tucker, *Enthusiasm* (Cambridge, 1972), 27.

followed from Paine's conception of the bard that the idea that prophecy had a predictive function was 'a modern invention', a phrase which may lie behind Blake's claim that prophets in 'the modern sense' had never existed (E 617). The invention of modern conceptions of prophecy was part of a political conspiracy for Paine. Ancient poetry had been manufactured into scripture to serve the ends of a manipulative priestcraft. Just as Ritson claimed that Thomas Percy distorted popular ballads into aristocratic poetry, so Paine believed that the traditional tales of the Hebrew prophets had been 'erected into prophecies and made to bend to explanations'. Both Geddes and Paine presented the Bible less as the text of divine revelation than as a rather dubious compilation copied from popular sources. It is something like this copying process which seems to be illustrated on the frontispiece of *The Book of Urizen*, where Urizen blindly transcribes from one book to another the holy laws of obedience and repression promulgated in the poem (see Pl. 1). Ultimately it matters little whether Geddes or Paine (or even Samuel Fisher) was the prime influence on Blake's attitude to the Bible. What is more important to establish is that the Bible was included among the targets of a contemporary radical critique aimed at the way the cultural hegemony appropriated and distorted tradition. Blake's work seems very much involved with this critique, which seems to have been particularly strong amongst writers either associated with or published by Joseph Johnson.[11]

That the status of the Bible was a politically sensitive issue in the 1790s can be gauged by the hostile response to Geddes's translations. As early as 1790 the *Monthly Review* cautioned Geddes against 'wanton innovation' in his proposed translation of the Bible. Once the translation appeared it was attacked as part of a 'dangerous tendency' by the *British Critic*. This tendency presumably included Darwin's revision of the Genesis story in his *Botanic Garden* and the evolutionary theories of his

---

[11] See Paine's *The Age of Reason*, *CWP*, ii. 474, 524, 549, and 510. Dutton's *A Vindication of the Age of Reason* repeats Paine's claim that the Bible is a 'miscellaneous collection' (p. 50).

Zoonomia which were fiercely attacked by the same journal the
following year. Geddes tried to defend himself against charges
that he was a 'Paineist' or 'Jacobine' in his *Address to the Public*
(1793), though he did admit to being a moderate supporter of
some of the principles of the French Revolution. He presented
himself as a 'true Whig'; 'a sworn enemy to implicit faith, as
well as implicit obedience'. Yet even this moderate position
was an affront to the loyalist devotion to the traditional
authority of Church and King. Obviously Geddes's writings
on the Bible were felt to be part of the innovating tendency
which threatened the establishment. They were operating in
one of the key domains of that establishment. The Bible was
the ultimate sacred text of the state, it was as essential a part
of the hegemony of the ruling classes as the vaunted constitutional liberties of the free-born Englishman. 'Wanton innovation' in relation to the Bible threatened the status quo at its
very core.[12]

Radical writers were obviously aware of the centrality of the
Bible to the cultural hegemony. I have already drawn attention
to the importance Paine gave his critique of the Bible in relation
to his broader political design. Geddes's approach to the Bible
is similarly bound up with his politics. His conviction that 'the
laity have as good a right to know the true state of the Bible-
Text as any clerk of us all' is of a piece with his belief that 'the
free choice or the acquiescence of the people' is the only
reasonable basis for the constitution. Both Geddes and Paine
pointed out the cruelty of the Old Testament God. Geddes, for
instance, described the God of Moses as 'a jealous God, . . . an
irascible and avenging God . . . He is even said to harden
sometimes the hearts of wicked men, that he may take more
flagrant vengeance on them.' Paine typically used stronger
language, claiming that if the reader took account of 'the
obscene stories, the voluptuous debaucheries, the cruel and

---

[12] See the *Monthly Review*, 1 (Jan. 1790), 66, and the *British Critic*, 4 (Aug.
1794), 156. For Geddes's defence of himself, see his *Dr. Geddes's Address to the
Public* (London, 1793), 17 and 1. E. S. Shaffer claims that Bible criticism 'fell
under the general ban of radical opinion' in the 1790s: *'Kubla Khan' and 'The
Fall of Jerusalem'* (Cambridge, 1975), 22.

tortuous executions, and unrelenting vindictiveness' which filled the Old Testament, it seemed more 'the work of a demon, than the work of God'. The implication which lay behind such views was that the *ancien régime* had chosen to worship a version of the deity which reflected its own brutishness.[13] If anything, the extreme nature of Blake's revisions of Genesis in *The Book of Urizen* has more in common with the iconoclastic Paine than the relatively moderate Geddes. The satanic aspects of Blake's Urizen, for instance, fit in with Paine's claim that the Bible seemed the work of a demon. The defence of Paine in the annotations to Watson's *Apology* similarly reiterate the deist's sense of horror at the biblical atrocities committed in the name of God: 'The destruction of the Canaanites by Joshua was the unnatural design of wicked men.' Blake concluded that this political manipulation of religion would be a 'lasting witness against' the Hebrews, 'the same it will . . . against Christians' (E 615). Although there are important differences between them, there are enough similarities to undermine Northrop Frye's influential claim that Blake's 'own ideas of the Bible were unaffected by Paine's iconoclasm'. At the very least both participated on the radical side of a debate on the Bible which was at the centre of the Revolution controversy.[14]

I want to turn now to the detail of Blake's treatment of the Bible in *The Book of Urizen*, *The Book of Ahania*, and *The Book of Los* and their relation to developments in radical criticism of the Bible. I shall discuss *The Book of Urizen* and its parodic relationship with Genesis first. Far from being a 'retreat into metaphysics', as it is often characterized, the concern with the Creation in *The Book of Urizen* seems to be of a piece with the prophetic enterprise discussed in preceding chapters.[15] This

---

[13] See *Dr. Geddes's General Answer* (London, 1790), 10, his *Address to the Public*, 15, and *Bible*, vol. i, p. xii. For Paine's conception of the Deity, see *CWP*, ii. 474.

[14] See N. Frye, *Fearful Symmetry* (Princeton, NJ, 1947), 109.

[15] See, for instance, A. Ostriker, *Vision and Verse in William Blake* (Madison, Wis., 1965), 163. Equally representative is the view put forward in Mitchell's *Blake's Composite Art*, 107; 'The political prophecies, *America*, *Europe*, and *The Song of Los*, all . . . promise an imminent end to the era of empire and priesthood. In the later Lambeth books (*Urizen*, *Ahania*, and *The Book of Los*),

continuity is not simply a biblical matter. *The Book of Urizen* is also a product of Blake's attempt to take up the role of the ancient bard. Thomas Blackwell claimed that one of the primary functions of the ancient poets had been the production of a 'Theogeny or History of the Creation'. *The Book of Urizen* is Blake's theogony, but, instead of seeking to provide a 'poetic tale' which could function as the basis of a 'form of worship', it is fundamentally ironic. The poem is mainly concerned with undermining scriptural authority. Its return to Genesis is Blake's response to Paine's claim that 'the error of those who reason by precedents drawn from antiquity, respecting the right of man, is, that they do not go far enough into antiquity. They do not go the whole way.' Where Paine described the beginnings of the British monarchy in the usurpation of an earlier state of liberty, Blake shows Urizen rising against the community of the Eternals to impose his world of hierarchy and obedience.[16]

Although *The Book of Urizen*, unlike *America* or *Europe*, is not offered to the reader as a prophecy, the division into chapters and verses gives it a more obviously biblical format than either of those poems. In addition, the title in some copies is given as *The First Book of Urizen*, which reinforces the internal links with Genesis, alternatively known as *The First Book of Moses*. Within the poem various events and motifs from Genesis seem to be replayed with the principle difference that the actors are taken from Blake's personal mythology. This difference in itself implies a freedom to remake the received form of the Bible. Chapter 1 argued that Blake's freedom in this respect was informed by an antinomian tradition. The presence of this enthusiastic strain in Blake's rhetoric should not obscure the similarities with the principle of conjectural emendation on which Geddes, to the disgust of conservative reviewers, based his translations.[17]

---

however, Blake seems to be moving into a new thematic and stylistic period, characterized superficially by increasing irony and pessimism and with poetic forms which end not with a promise of resolution but with a note of apparent despair.

[16] See Blackwell, *An Enquiry*, 91, and Paine, *CWP*, i. 273.
[17] Geddes described his method of 'conjectural criticism' for the first time in

The Book of Urizen opens with a short preludium which makes clear Blake's distaste for state religion:

> Of the primeval Priests assum'd power,
> When Eternals spurn'd back his religion;
> And gave him a place in the north,
> Obscure, shadowy, void, solitary.
>
> Eternals I hear your call gladly,
> Dictate swift winged words, & fear not
> To unfold your dark visions of torment.
>
> (E 70; Pl. 2)

These lines recall the invocation of the muse at the outset of *Paradise Lost*, another poetic rendering of Genesis. The key difference is that, whereas Milton appeals to the muse to help him 'justify the way of God to men', Blake's poem is involved with revealing 'dark visions of torment'. *The Book of Urizen* as a whole seeks to uncover the destructive nature of the authoritarian God of Genesis, not to validate his providential plan. The use of the word 'assum'd' immediately ties the poem in with contemporary radical discourse which frequently characterized its opponent as 'assumed' authority. Paine had argued, for instance, that 'all power exercised over a nation, must have some beginning. It must be either delegated, or assumed. There are no other sources, and all assumed power is usurpation.' The book of laws that Urizen transcribes on the frontispiece, which the poem as a whole implies is the received Bible, equates to Paine's 'manuscript assumed authority of the dead'.[18]

Urizen's cosmogony begins with a 'void' (E 70; Pl. 3, l. 4). Genesis, of course, also opens when 'the earth was without form, and void', but in Blake's version it is a 'void' which is created. Blake rewrites Genesis so as to suggest that its cosmo-

---

his *Prospectus* (Glasgow, 1786), 55. The *Monthly Review*, 1 (Jan. 1790), 52, commented that 'if ever conjectural criticism be admissible (concerning which we must confess we still have some serious doubt) it ought not to be admitted till every other resource has been tried in vain'. The conjectural nature of enthusiastic treatments of biblical texts was, of course, precisely what alarmed polite critics of popular preachers.

[18] Paine, *CWP*, ii. 376 and 252.

gony was preceded by another. Prior to Urizen's travesty of the biblical Creation, there exists 'Eternity', peopled by an uncircumscribed community described as the 'Eternals'. This revision of the Bible undermines the claim made by state religion to possess an authoritative narrative of origins in Genesis. A scepticism about origins runs through the poem and correlates to the more directly political rejection, in the annotations to Watson, of the idea that 'Public Records' offer the exclusive truth of history. Urizen and the Eternals are described in sharp opposition. Blake's Urizen is defined through a vocabulary of mystery and isolation. He is 'unknown, abstracted I Brooding secret' (E 70; Pl. 3, ll. 7–8), definitively singular where the Eternals are undifferentiatedly plural. The Eternals represent an idealized alternative or antecedent to the hierarchical order consistently identified with Urizen. Their plurality may be related to the influential historiographical theory, invoked in Chapter 2, that the original state of humanity was essentially communitarian. Paine contrasted the 'mutual dependence and reciprocal interest' of the earliest times with the usurping practices of government, which he believed defended privilege and divided society. The latter was 'a thing made up of mysteries which only themselves understood', a sentence that calls to mind the mysteries of Urizen's solipsistic Creation.[19]

Other details of Blake's description tap more specifically into criticism of the Bible available in the 1790s. Urizen is described as 'brooding' twice in the opening chapter of the poem (E 70–1; Pl. 3, ll. 7 and 25). Geddes had drawn attention to the same term in his objections to the notion that the Holy Spirit hatched Creation in the form of a dove. He cited Milton's description of the Holy Spirit 'brooding on the vast abyss' (PL l. 21) as an influential example of the mistake. Geddes located the origins of the misconception in the traditional translation of Genesis 1: 2. He believed that generations of translators had wrongly rendered the Hebrew conception of 'the vital principle . . . that

[19] See Paine, CWP, ii. 358, and 361. On the historiographical background to the concept of a primeval unity, see Rubel, Savage and Barbarian, 43 and 26–7, and above, pp. 86–9.

makes matter capable of vegetation, increase, sensation' as the abstraction 'soul' or 'spirit'. Blake's *The Book of Urizen* concurs with Geddes to the extent that the original state of Eternity has the fluidity of Geddes's vital principle, while Urizen's usurpation is characterized as the product of abstract brooding.[20]

Geddes's translation nicely illustrates the preference among rationalist intellectuals for notions of generation and natural evolution over the biblical version of Creation. Darwin's work, discussed in the previous chapter, provides another example of this tendency. Geddes's evident hostility to the traditional conception of the Holy Spirit is also typical of the fierce anti-Trinitarianism abroad in radical circles in the 1790s. On a less rarefied level than Geddes's Bible criticism, publications like Eaton's *Politics for the People* repeatedly attacked the Trinity as a corner-stone of the 'cursed superstition' exploited by state religion. 'A New Creed', one of the many parodies of religious forms published by Eaton, made the investment of the established order in such mystification blatantly clear:

Whosoever will get a place, it is necessary, before all things, that he hold the true political faith.
Which faith, except every one do keep whole and undefiled, he shall everlastingly be deemed a Jacobin.
And the true political faith is, that we worship one government in trinity, and trinity in unity.
Neither confounding the orders, nor dividing the power
For there is one order of the king, another order of the lords, and another order of the commons.
But the power of the kings, lords, and commons, is all one, the immaculacy equal, the supremacy co-existing.

It was in response to such attacks that the Bishop of Lincoln identified the repudiation of the Trinity as a central element in radical ideology.[21]

[20] See Geddes, *A Letter to the Right Reverend Lord Bishop of London* (London, 1787), 50–3.
[21] See 'The Unity in Trinity and the Trinity in Unity, or a Moment's Reflection on the Creed of St. Athanasius' and 'A New Creed, used on Christmas Day in all Churches and Chapels throughout his Majesties Dominions instead of the Creed of St. Athanasius' in *Politics for the People*, ii. 213–16 and 353–6. The Bishop of Lincoln's views on this matter are quoted in full in my Introduction.

In so far as such a repudiation did become a part of the radical platform in the 1790s, it was anticipated in Joseph Priestley's *History of the Corruptions of Christianity*.[22] Priestley's book included the traditional conception of the Trinity among the many misunderstandings of the rhetorical use of personification in the Bible motivated by a residual pagan dualism. Geddes, who was directly influenced by Priestley, ascribed the idea of 'the third person of the Trinity hatching creation into life, as a bird does her eggs' to a similar misapprehension of the poetry of the Hebrews. The various theories of mythology discussed in the previous chapter, of course, placed the literalism of such misreadings at the root of the development of pagan religion. Usually it was the reification of Egyptian hieroglyphics which was put forward as the original instance. Priestley was applying this theory to the Bible in a manner which unintentionally paved the way for those like Volney and Paine who wished to argue that there were fundamental continuities between Christianity and pagan mystification. Typically Paine made a much more pungent statement of Priestley's point about personification when he derisively referred to the representation of the Holy Ghost in Matthew 3: 16 as a 'flying pigeon'.[23]

The approach to the Bible shared by Priestley and Geddes suggested that it needed to be read as a poetic document in the light of the reader's active judgement rather than a rigid, sacred authority. Their promotion of an active role for the reader in producing the meaning of the text has similarities with Blake's general desire to 'rouze the faculties to act' and with his more particular hostility to the 'Peculiar Word of God'. It is a response

---

[22] Certainly Priestley was in direct contact with Darwin and Geddes as well as being an important influence on the intellectual milieu around Joseph Johnson's bookshop more generally. He was recognized as an important figure in other radical circles as well. 'An Address by the Society of the United Irishmen of Dublin', published in Eaton's *Politics for the People*, ii. 24–8, mourned his emigration to America as the loss of the foremost philosopher of the age.

[23] See Priestley's *History*, i. 88, Geddes, *Letter*, 50–2, and Paine, *CWP*, ii. 601. Dutton's *A Vindication of the Age of Reason* celebrates Paine's iconoclasm and defends it against the strictures of the more cautious Dissenters, Priestley and Gilbert Wakefield, who he believed maintained an illogical 'partial belief', p. 50, in the divine authority of the Bible.

which suggests that the corruption of the Bible is not just a matter of the way it has been transmitted but also of the way it has been read. Blake's ambivalent attitude to the Bible moves between a disgust at a corrupted document, 'Avarice and Chastity did write it', and the celebration of a text which was still available to be read as poetry. His own poetic practice could be seen as both an attempt to induce a way of reading, through textual practices which demand the active participation of the reader, and an effort to revise sacred texts so they could be read in this way. Not only could 'forms of worship' be returned to the status of poetic tales by rewriting them, they could also be reread in a way which appreciated them as poetry. Blake's faith in a redemptive reading of the Bible differentiates his work from that of Volney and Paine, who offered instead the prospect of demolishing its influence and replacing it with the transparent truth of Reason. The rationalist dream of the transparent text is very much alive in the writing of Paine and Volney.[24]

Blake also participated in the debate about dualism central to both Priestley's and Geddes's discussions of the Bible. Geddes's view of the Bible was almost certainly influenced by the repeated attacks on the notion of a soul abstracted from the body in Priestley's *History*. Priestley believed such abstractions derived from heathen and Platonic traditions. At the root of this derivation Priestley perceived a tendency in Christianity towards a 'mysticism' which understood virtue as 'an abstraction of the mind from all corporeal things'. Similar attitudes are also part of the populist opposition to book-learning discussed in Chapter 1. Terry's introduction to his edition of Cobbler How charged the learned with importing heathen corruptions into the original simplicity of the Christian faith. Blake's antagonism to the notion of a soul abstracted from the body is evident throughout his writing of the 1790s, perhaps most distinctly in *The Marriage of Heaven and Hell*. In Plate iii of *Europe* Blake dispensed with the Holy Spirit, the muse of

[24] In terms of Lévi-Strauss's opposition between the bricoleur and engineer, I am suggesting Blake is much more of a bricoleur in this respect than either Paine or Volney, who are engineers to the extent that they aspire to a transparent language of truth.

traditional Christian poetry, and replaced it with the mocking imp of popular culture. The imp seems the very embodiment of the 'vital principle' which Geddes believed to be the true character of the creative agent in the universe, though its unruliness is perhaps evidence of more popular origins distinct from the respectable rationalism of Geddes and Priestley. What is clear, however, is that in *The Book of Urizen* Blake offers an account of the stultifying power of the abstract mystification vilified by Priestley which subverts orthodox accounts of the Creation.[25]

At the very heart of this subversion is the way Blake profanes scripture by identifying its God with his arch adversary Satan. Urizen's Creation is simultaneously his Fall from Eternity. Recognition of this mixed role is reinforced by a number of references which link Urizen to Milton's Satan.[26] Blake's mixed representation of Urizen, as Old Testament God and his adversary Satan, produces a protagonist who is both the originator and punisher of sin. Radical polemicists often adopted this paradox as an expression of the oppressive nature of the legal system: 'The snares of temptation are everywhere set about them. Governments, like the author of evil, first make the criminal and then punish the crime.'[27] The critique of the perverse effects of laws was often extended to include the moral doctrines of Christianity. Antinomian enthusiasts, like Blake's fellow engraver Garnet Terry, were especially keen to show that the notion of God as 'an accuser' was put about by hirelings to 'keep up their trade'. Blake also wrote scathingly of 'The Accuser who is The God of this World' and inscribed a late state (1809–10) of the engraving known as *Our End is Come* with the words 'The Accusers of Theft Adultery Murder . . . Satans' holy Trinity The Accuser The Judge & The Executioner'

[25] See Priestley, *History*, i. 345.
[26] For allusions to Milton's Satan in the configuration of Urizen, see Stevenson, p. 251, and Mitchell, *Blake's Composite Art*, 124.
[27] The quotation is taken from Gerrald's *A Convention*, 77. Perhaps Godwin's *Caleb Williams* is the clearest literary statement of what was a very widespread belief (namely, that the law was the author of the crimes it punished) in radical circles in the 1790s.

belief That Christian ... ...
... .al law by virtue ... .

(E 672). The iconoclastic move of identifying the Accuser with Satan is central to the rhetoric of Blake's *The Book of Urizen*, where the figure of Urizen is built up out of allusions to Satan, the Old Testament God, and Moses. For Blake in these works, as for Terry, sin is coeval with law; 'All Penal Laws court Transgression & therefore are cruelty & Murder' (E 618).[28]

The enthusiasm of much of Blake's rhetoric suggests that his attitude to God the lawgiver is the product of a popular antinomianism similar to Terry's, but in this chapter I shall show that his texts are far from innocent of the influence of the Bible's rationalist critics. Terry himself, after all, was accused of distributing Painite propaganda. Similarly, quite apart from the connections with Geddes, Paine, and Priestley sketched above, some specific contacts can be traced between Volney's *Ruins* and Blake's *The Book of Urizen*. Given the pervasive influence of Volney's book and the fact that the first English translation was published by Johnson, it would be surprising if the work had not reached Blake in some form. Among Volney's descriptions of the false religions of history was an account of the original cosmogony produced by the Egyptians. This cosmogony had at its centre a Creator 'absorbed in the contemplation of his own reflections'. Isolated brooding is likewise essential to Blake's representations of Urizen. Volney's Egyptian deity produces 'the vault or globe of the heavens in which the world is enclosed' from his state of solipsism. Similarly in Chapter III Blake's Urizen produces a 'roof vast, petrific' which is 'like a black globe' (E 73; Pl. 5, ll. 28 and 33). A further parallel comes in Volney's description of the Egyptian conception of their god as 'a legislator, by so much the more formidable as, while his judgement was final and his degrees without appeal, he was unapproachable to his subjects'. Once he has emerged from his solipsistic brooding, it is the role of moral legislator which Blake's Urizen also moves to take on.[29]

Before turning to discuss this role more fully, it is worth noting that the distinction between the singularity of Urizen

[28] See [Terry], *Letters*, i. 102.
[29] See *The Ruins*, 205 (and 325 n.) and 263–4.

and the plurality of the Eternals has some points in common with Geddes's account of the Genesis narrative. It was fairly well known by the end of the eighteenth century that the Bible seemed to be made up of two independent accounts of the Creation. Each used a different title for the Deity, that is, Elohim and Yahveh. Geddes described the latter as a proper name applied by the Hebrews to their God; the former was believed to be a generic term and a plural. The distinction could be mapped on to Blake's differentiation between the Eternals and Urizen. The Eternals are plural like Elohim, while the role of Yahveh as the one God of the Hebrews is caught by the representation of Urizen as a mysterious and isolated being. Tannenbaum, however, has pointed out that the Elohist narrative is typified by its precise, repetitive, and abstract language, qualities also typical of Blake's description of Urizen's Creation. These similarities have led Tannenbaum to identify the Elohim with Urizen and read the Yahveh account as the basis of the description of Los's labours later in *The Book of Urizen*. Yahveh is more fully anthropomorphized than the Elohim and Los's struggles are certainly more physically human than Urizen's abstract brooding. Tannenbaum relates Los's labours to a Blakian reading of the Yahveh account as an attempt to humanize the order instituted by the Elohim. Appealing though this neat explanation is, it leaves out the Eternals from Blake's cosmogony. The fact is that, far from resolving the contradictions of the Bible in *The Book of Urizen*, Blake exaggerates them. In place of the transcendent God of established religion, he reveals three different versions of divine creativity: Eternals, Urizen, and Los. His use of biblical material is eclectic and in line with his perception of the Bible as a book of examples which can be drawn on freely. It is a usage which exacerbates rather than covers up any awareness of the Bible as the fragmentary text of Geddes's hypothesis.[30]

Urizen is a representative of the opposing tendency which wishes to cover up the contingent nature of its origins. He

---

[30] See Geddes, *Critical Remarks*, I n. 1b, and Tannenbaum, *Biblical Tradition*, 203–4.

wants to impose a unified hierarchy with himself as its omnipotent and unique divinity in place of the variety and fluidity of
the Eternals. Once he has torn himself from Eternity, Urizen
proclaims his new regime in what seems to be a parody of the
announcement of the Mosaic law on Sinai:

> Shrill the trumpet: & myriads of Eternity,
> Muster around the bleak desarts
> Now fill'd with clouds, darkness & waters
> That roll'd perplex'd labring & utter'd
> Words articulate, bursting in thunders
> That roll'd on the top of his mountains.

(E 71; Pl. 3, l. 54–Pl. 4, l. 5)

Central to Urizen's intentions is a desire to fix human faculties
within the boundaries of his authority. His search for 'a solid
without fluctuation' (Pl. 4, l. 11) begins the process of the
diminution of human possibility which is Blake's familiar trope
for the progress of state religion.

Urizen shares the desire of the God of the Bible to establish
himself as the one and only true Deity. The flexible community
of the Eternals is to be replaced by a system based on his
transcendent authority. It is a univocal system, a state religion,
whose laws are the articulation of its founder's will:

> Lo! I unfold my darkness: and on
> This rock, place with strong hand the Book
> Of eternal brass, written in my solitude.
>
> Laws of peace, of love, of unity:
> Of pity, compassion, forgiveness.
> Let each chuse one habitation:
> His ancient infinite mansion:
> One command, one joy, one desire,
> One curse, one weight, one measure
> One King, one God, one Law.

(E 72; Pl. 4, ll. 31–40)

The final line of his proclamation initiates the Trinity of loyalist
propaganda in the 1790s and reveals the continuation of Urizen's authority in the reactionary English compact of Church

and King. A patriotic song printed by John Reeves's Association for Preserving Liberty and Property against Republicans and Levellers ends with strikingly similar lines:

> In peace then and honour may Britons still sing
> And bless their Good God, their old Laws, their Old King.

Though it lacks the explicit references to contemporary history of *The French Revolution* and *America*, allusions to the language of political discourse like these indicate *The Book of Urizen*'s involvement in the Revolution controversy. But it is the poem's critical engagement with the Bible which is the more fundamental link between Blake's text and the writings of figures like Geddes, Paine, and Volney.[31]

Integral to the indeterminate procedures of *The Book of Urizen* are the multiple configurations of what seem to be single events in the Bible. Beneath Urizen's declaration of his own omnipotence on Plate 4 is a design showing a naked figure running through heavy rainfall (though it also suggests a prisoner behind bars). The design implies that Urizen's usurpation of Eternity is a manifestation of the catastrophic Flood. The trope of a universal deluge is also invoked in the written text:

> . . . but condensing, in torrents
> They fall & fall; strong I repell'd
> The vast waves, & arose on the waters
> A wide world of solid obstruction.
>
> (E 72; Pl. 4, ll. 20–3)

The institution of Urizen's oppressive monotheism is a Flood as well as a variant of the Creation narrative of Genesis. Two separate events in the Bible (others such as the Fall and the announcement of the Decalogue could be added) become aspects of a single event in Blake's narrative. This multiplicity has a twofold corrosive effect on the scriptural authority of the Bible. First, it practises a freedom to use the sacred text as

---

[31] See Assoc. for Preserving Liberty and Property against Republicans and Levellers, *Liberty and Property Preserved* (London, 1792–3), no. 4, p. 16.

metaphor rather than history which implies a reading of the
Bible as poetic tale rather than scriptural authority. Secondly,
Blake's poetic transformation of the Bible contests the orthodox
interpretation of the events in the biblical original. To represent
the Creation as the Flood is also to represent it as the primal
catastrophe. What is a beneficent act of creativity in the Bible
becomes an act of terrible destruction in *The Book of Urizen*.

Although *The Book of Urizen* is largely devoted to an ironic
account of the genesis of state religion, Blake never suggests
Urizen's control is total: 'Eternity roll'd wide apart' (E 73;
Pl. 5, l. 5), but its potential is not obliterated. The Eternals
continue to exist in Urizen's world as 'ruinous fragments of life'
(l. 9). They also watch over the Urizenic world through the
person of Los:

> And Los round the dark globe of Urizen,
> Kept watch for Eternals to confine,
> The obscure separation alone.

> (E 73; Pl. 5, ll. 38–40)

Los remains in tentative contact with the Eternals just as the
bard-prophets of Gray and Macpherson provide a link with a
fading age of liberty. Blake's poetry in the 1790s insists on the
possibility of a renewal of prophetic inspiration whether in
individuals or communities. His belief that 'Every Honest man
is a Prophet' implies that fragments of Eternity remain univer-
sally available. The introduction of Los into the narrative of
The Book of Urizen marks another of the poem's internal
contradictions. Urizen is described as being rent from the side
of Los (E 74; Pl. 6, l. 4), when the first two chapters of the
poem have given a completely different account of Urizen's
origins. In the latter Urizen was placed in the paradigms of the
Creation and Flood; now his origins are related to the birth of
Eve as described in Genesis 2: 21–3. Common to both descriptions is the emphasis on division. Urizen is always involved in
a division or diminution of the human form. Los's labours at
his forge, although far from successful, begin a process of
reconstitution. Like Orc at the close of *The Song of Los*, Los
himself is importantly involved in reforming the human whole.

The transformation of Los from a peripheral figure, in poems like *Europe* and *The Song of Los*, to the central protagonist in the struggle against Urizen has been interpreted as part of a retreat from the political commitment of the Orc-centred poems. This formula ignores the similarities in the roles of Orc and Los. Both are obviously involved in reconstituting the human form. Moreover, the furnace where Los works at this task is also associated with Orc as early as *America*:

> Fires inwrap the earthly globe, yet man is not consumd;
> Amidst the lustful fires he walks: his feet become like brass,
> His knees and thighs like silver, & his breast and head like gold.

> (E 54; Pl. 8, ll. 15–17)

Los is often appropriated to a more aesthetic set of concerns than Orc by critics. He is seen, for instance, by Paul Cantor as part of a shift of emphasis which has Blake converted to a belief in the saving function of art. I do not deny that Los is conceived as a bardic figure, but would argue that it is a conception which maintains the widespread eighteenth-century notion that the primitive poets had a public and political role. The bards of Gray and Macpherson were centrally involved with the struggle against tyranny. The same is true of Blake's Los.[32] There is even a sense in which Los's labours more satisfactorily connect Blake's political rhetoric with human struggles than the Orcian Apocalypse. Orc's fiery energy, though explicitly defined as 'Human' in *America* and allied to the American populace, is superhuman or miraculous in the way it transforms the Urizenic order. In part this is an inescapable consequence of the millenarian representation of Orc. Although the rhetoric primarily functions to counter conservative versions of the Apocalypse, it depends on Orc retaining many of the qualities of their miraculous Christ of the Second Coming. Los's struggles, in contrast, are more fully humanized. He is a manual labourer at his forge

---

[32] See P. A. Cantor, *Creature and Creator* (Cambridge, 1984), 60. Given that it was commonly held that the French Revolution had been profoundly influenced by intellectual and artistic movements in France prior to 1789, something which even Burke and Paine agreed on, Blake may also have had a more immediate reason to believe in the political function of art.

whose struggle to overcome Urizen is protracted and sometimes even counter-productive. The distinction between Orc
and Los might be referred to different kinds of millenarianism.
Los is post-millennialist in conception, given the stress on the
exercise of human agency in his labours. Orc is more in tune
with the more populist pre-millennialist belief in a sudden and
total transformation of the world. I have already suggested that
a mixture of the two is to be found in Spence's work, which
never loses its radical commitment. There is no reason to
believe that the increasing centrality of Los in Blake's writing
and designs is allied to a retreat from political signification.
Los's labours are sometimes misdirected as when he attempts to
restrain the fiery energy of Orc in *The Book of Urizen*, but he is
always looking to push his struggle against Urizen forward.

My discussion of *The Book of Los* below will suggest that a
pattern of perpetually revived struggle is the basic plot structure
of that poem. Its denouement is a reworking of the description
of Los's labours on Plates 8, 10, 11, and 13 of *The Book of
Urizen*, which figure Los's attempts to limit the damage caused
by Urizen's fall from Eternity as a labour of seven ages.[33]
Mitchell points out that this section of *The Book of Urizen*
expands the events of one day of the seven-day Creation of
Genesis, the creation of the human body, into a vast historical
process. The implication is a point Geddes made explicitly: the
seven-day Creation is a mythos or poetic description rather than
historical fact. Some of the detail of the description of Los's
labours in *The Book of Urizen* further undermine the biblical
account. Whereas the God of Genesis saw his Creation as good,
Los recoils in horror when he sees what he has produced:

> In terrors Los shrunk from his task:
> His great hammer fell from his hand:

---

[33] The arrangement of these plates is variable. They are interrupted by
different full-page designs in different copies, but even if this complication is
removed it is still difficult to identify an authoritative narrative order since
Plate 8 is missing in one copy and where it does appear it comes after Plate 10
in half the copies and before it in the other three. Both Plate 8 and Plate 10
have the title 'Chap. 4' on them so where they both appear the chapter seems
to begin twice.

> His fires beheld, and sickening,
> Hid their strong limbs in smoke.
>
> (E 77; Pl. 13, ll. 20–3)

The vision of antediluvian liberty he struggles to keep alive is obscured by the Urizenic body created in the process:

> A nerveless silence, his prophetic voice
> Siez'd: a cold solitude & dark void
> The Eternal Prophet & Urizen clos'd.
>
> (ll. 38–40)[34]

Los's horror at these developments leads to the next of the series of divisions which move the poem forward. Enitharmon or 'Pity' emerges from the body of Los. Enitharmon's birth is a particularly strong signal of Blake's conception of the Bible as a book of examples. He reworks the story of Eve so that it becomes an occluded fable of the origins of a human emotion, 'Pity', the name applied to Enitharmon by the Eternals. Geddes similarly regarded the events in Eden as a poetic attempt to explain the world, though he claims it was meant to offer an explanation for 'the origin of human evil, and of man's antipathy to the reptile race'.[35] The identification of Enitharmon with 'Pity' is one of several important acts of naming in *The Book of Urizen*. The same interest in names and their origins is, of course, central to Genesis. God's naming of Creation is involved in his recognition of its goodness: 'And God saw the light, that it was good and God divided the light from the darkness. And God called the light Day, and the darkness he called Night' (Genesis 1: 4–5). But each naming in *Urizen*

---

[34] See Mitchell, *Blake's Composite Art*, 127.

[35] Pity divides because it marks the prophetic commitment to liberating transformation degenerating into a disabling grief for the Urizenic world, a point Blake made with explicitly political force in these deleted lines on events in the French Revolution from the notebook *c.*1793: 'Fayette Fayette thourt bought & sold | For well I see thy tears | Of Pity are exchanged for those | Of selfish slavish fears.' The virtue is often treated with ironic suspicion in Blake's work of the 1790s. See Glen, *Vision and Disenchantment*, 148–70, for a discussion of Blake's treatment of the received moral vocabulary and the context of radical polemic. For Geddes's explanation of the Eden story, see his *Bible*, vol. i, p. xi.

proclaims a further separation from the fluid community of the Eternals: 'They call'd her Pity, and fled' (E 78; Pl. 19, l. 1). Los looks at the world and does not see that it is good. The naming of its parts is an account of its errors not of its beauties.

The division into sexuality, Los and Enitharmon, begins another current in Blake's poem. It opens up the possibility of sexual (re)union as a part of the process of reforming the human totality. Los and Enitharmon create a child. This is Orc, who, although he remains relatively unimportant in *The Book of Urizen*, does at least set in train the re-formation of the Urizenic order that he actually achieves at the end of *The Song of Los*:

> The dead heard the voice of the child
> And began to awake from sleep
> All things heard the voice of the child
> And began to awake to life.
>
> (E 80; Pl. 20, ll. 26–9)

Nor are these stirrings the only positive current in the poem. Mitchell's discussion of the role of the designs has shown that Blake does not represent Urizen's hegemony as final. Even in those designs which show Urizen in his purest form of self-absorption and contraction, there are asymmetrical forms and patterns which work against his desire for 'a solid without fluctuation'. The most obvious aspect of this visual current are the flames evident in Plates 5, 11, 16, and 22. Mitchell calls these flames 'a metonym for all sorts of sinuous energetic forms'. Though they never become the poem's dominant motif, which remains Urizen's building of a world of division and hierarchy, they do show that his authority is not absolute. Blake is committed to the notion that Eternity is retrievable.[36]

The focus of the poem returns to Urizen at the beginning of Chapter VIII when he wakes up ready to explore his Creation (E 81; Pl. 22, l. 46). He sees with dismay that his 'iron laws' have not brought about the hierarchical perfection he sought but 'vast enormities' (Pl. 23, l. 2). Yet his response leads only to the refoundation of his iron laws in the form of 'The Net of

---

[36] See Mitchell, *Blake's Composite Art*, 142–5 and 157–8.

Religion' (E 82; Pl. 25, l. 22). Blake emphasizes that Urizen merely propagates what he sought to replace by figuring the effects of 'The Net of Religion' in the same terms that he had used for the original creation of the 'iron laws' at the beginning of the poem. Both, for instance, are represented as the products of a catastrophic deluge. Blake described Urizen's original proclamation of his system amongst 'torrents' and 'vast waves' on a plate augmented by a design showing a human figure trapped by driving rain. At the end of *The Book of Urizen*, on Plate 28, the Net of Religion leaves the population of the earth 'surrounded by salt floods' (E 83; l. 9).

Blake's description of Urizen's failure to reform his system stands in a complex critical relationship to the Bible. On one level it may include a specific reference to Volney's account of the Christian propagation of pagan forms of worship. Plate 23 of *The Book of Urizen* shows a druid-like figure carrying a lamp in the form of the sun which illustrates Urizen's exploration of his world (see Pl. 8). Although this sun is not mentioned in the text, it may represent the introduction of 'The Net of Religion' in the form of the hieroglyphic sun worshipped in the druidic religion shown on the frontispiece to *The Song of Los*. Section XIII of *The Ruins* had claimed that Christianity was the allegorical worship of the sun. Far from representing it as a major religious reform, Volney saw Christianity as a perpetua-tion of the state religion which had originated in Egypt. Urizen's sun is similarly a false enlightenment. His recognition of the deformity that his 'iron laws' have caused leads not to their reform but to their reintroduction in another guise. As with *Europe* and *The Song of Los*, the narrative of *The Book of Urizen* offers confirmation of the claim, made by Volney and Paine alike, that Christianity had been a perpetuation of the state religion it was meant to replace.[37]

The more obvious allusion, since it provides the basic trope for Blake's description of Urizen's reforms, is to the biblical Flood. Blake puts a crucial twist on the biblical history. Whereas the Bible represents the Flood as a righteous punishment for the

[37] See Volney, *The Ruins*, 243–4 and 286–92.

transgression of holy laws, he presents the holy laws themselves as the root of the problem. From this perspective the Flood becomes an aspect of the 'unrelenting vindictiveness' Paine found in the Bible. Urizen punishes his people for something he has caused. The point is driven home in the final plate of the poem, where Urizen's people attempt to reform themselves after the catastrophe by conforming to the new laws of the Net of Religion:

> And their children wept, & built
> Tombs in the desolate places,
> And form'd laws of prudence, and call'd them
> The eternal laws of God.
>
> (E 83; Pl. 28, ll. 4–7)

Instead of being rewarded for this obedience to Urizen's new system they find themselves sold into an Egyptian slavery:

> And the thirty cities remaind
> Surrounded by salt floods, now call'd
> Africa: its name was then Egypt.
>
> The remaining sons of Urizen
> Beheld their brethren shrink together
> Beneath the Net of Urizen;
> Perswasion was in vain;
> For the ears of the inhabitants,
> Were wither'd, & deafen'd, & cold:
> And their eyes could not discern,
> Their brethren of other cities.   (ll. 8–18)

The fate of the 'thirty cities' betrays the origins of the Net of Religion in the state religion of Egypt, a religion which promises future rewards for obedience but delivers only bondage.

The conclusion of *The Book of Urizen* is an ironic inversion of the providential view of history offered by the received Bible. The irony is richer because the opening lines of the poem, 'Lo, a shadow of horror is risen | In Eternity', allude to a key biblical account of the divine plan. The allusion is to Abram's dream of Genesis 15: 'And when the sun was going down, a deep sleep fell upon Abram; and lo, a horror of great darkness fell upon him.' The biblical explanation of this dream prophesies that Abram's descendants will become slaves in Egypt until liberated by Moses and led to the Promised Land. *The Book of Urizen* ends with a parodic fulfilment of this prophecy and its promise of deliverance; those who try to obey Urizen's laws of prudence are delivered only to an Egyptian bondage. The religious axiom that faith and obedience will bring salvation, an axiom being powerfully reiterated by loyalist propaganda in the 1790s, is revealed as a fraud.[38]

The poem ends on a muted note of promise with the introduction of Fuzon. Whereas Urizen takes on many of the qualities of Moses the lawgiver, Fuzon accedes to the biblical character's role of national liberator. Such a redistribution of the qualities of a single biblical character or event into multiple locations typifies Blake's poetical revision of the Bible. The freedom to refashion its language which this method implies finds a correlative in the narrative when Fuzon asserts his independence at the close. In a final parody of the orthodox reading of the Bible, the Exodus led by Fuzon is not a reward for the chosen people of the Creator. It is those who have rejected the Net of Religion that move towards liberation.

The story of Fuzon's rebellion is picked up and developed by *The Book of Ahania*, considered by most critics to be a continuation of *The Book of Urizen*.[39] The former shadows the other books of the Pentateuch, where the parodic force of the latter is primarily directed at Genesis. The central concern of *The Book of Ahania* is with the emergence of Moses as a biblical hero and the corruption of this reforming hero into the moral lawgiver. The familiar pattern of rebellion returning to religious oppression is at the centre of the narrative. Some critics choose to read this as a symbolic comment on political reform, a statement of disillusion with the very possibility of radical change. The classic statement of this position comes in Northrop Frye's

[38] See Tannenbaum, *Biblical Tradition*, 211, for a discussion of this allusion to Genesis.
[39] See, for instance, Frye, *Fearful Symmetry*, 186, P. F. Fisher, *The Valley of Vision* (Toronto, 1961), 195, and Tannenbaum, *Biblical Tradition*, 225.

Fearful Symmetry. Frye reads Fuzon as a revised version of Orc and represents the latter's fiery energy as necessarily involved in a cycle of corruption in which rebellion is always already compromised. Frye's eagerness to dissociate Blake from the radical politics of the 1790s leads him to overlook crucial differences between Orc and Fuzon and identify both figures as versions of an essential 'element of fire'. Yet Frye himself admits that, unlike Orc, Fuzon is clearly described as Urizen's son. Blake took special care to distinguish the Fuzon narrative from Orcian revolt. In *America* the reader effectively encounters two versions of Orc. One, in the Preludium, is the central protagonist of a plot close to the Fuzon narrative in that his rebellious energy becomes distorted into a dictatorship of power. In the main narrative, however, Orc is the guiding spirit of what is represented as a primarily benign process of revolutionary change. It is this latter Orc which appears in *Europe, The Song of Los*, and more briefly *The Book of Urizen*. Although *America* does not explicitly promote either version of Orc over the other, there is obviously the potential for reading one as being in a necessary relationship with the other. Frye read the Preludium's Orc as the dominant version, a mythical paradigm which inevitably contains the historical revolutions described within the prophecy. I prefer to see the competing narratives as part of the indeterminacy of the poem. It is the reader's choice, just as the success of the American Revolution in the poem proper is dependent on the commitment of the American citizens. I would suggest that by giving one of the strands of the two competing Orc narratives a separate identity, Fuzon, Blake more effectively separates the two patterns from any necessary relationship.[40]

All this is not to deny that Blake may have had ambivalent feelings about developments in the French Revolution and about particular currents in British radicalism. Erdman has actually identified references to Robespierre, as well as to Christ and Moses, in the figure of Fuzon. What I would argue, however, is that the context of the poem is primarily biblical

---

[40] See Frye, *Fearful Symmetry*, 214.

and any reference to Robespierre is muted in comparison to its anticlerical focus. The poem's representation of Urizen as a druidic practitioner of human sacrifice anticipates Paine's claim that 'there are things done in the Bible at the express command of God as shocking as anything done by Robespierre'. Paine's comment should also make it clear that criticism of Robespierre is not equivalent to a disavowal of radicalism. Even if we insist on identifying Robespierre and Fuzon in *The Book of Ahania*, Fuzon's failure is contingent on a failure of revolutionary commitment. He struggles against Urizen to install himself as an omnipotent godhead. Orc's successful revolution in *America* is more radically democratic in its commitment to 'scatter religion abroad'. Any implied criticism of Robespierre in the poem can similarly be read as a criticism of his betrayal of democratic principles and a perceived return to the authoritarian practices of Urizen. Nearly all Blake's narratives contain some account of a process in which prophetic potential is reified into state religion. *The Book of Ahania* is principally involved in a critique of this process and the role of the Bible in its perpetuation. This kind of critique was a recurrent aspect of the radicalism of the 1790s from Volney's powerful and comprehensive history of religious deception in *The Ruins* to the more varied and acerbic anticlericalism published in Eaton's *Politics for the People*.[41]

The Book of Ahania opens with Fuzon, on a 'chariot iron-wing'd' (E 84; Pl. 2, l. 1), burning with indignation at Urizen. The detail of the chariot marks one of the important differences between Orc and Fuzon. Fire and iron tend to function as antitheses in Blake's poetry. Orc is typically a fiery demon, whereas Urizen's promulgation of iron laws signals his fall from the fiery community of the Eternals in *The Book of Urizen*. Although Fuzon does have the fiery energy of Orc, he is already compromised by association with the 'solid obstruction' of

---

[41] Erdman, *Prophet Against Empire*, 314-15. Erdman also draws attention to a comparison made between Robespierre and Moses in Paine's *Examination of the Prophecies* (1802). See, Paine, *CWP*, ii. 876. Paine's comparison between Robespierre and the God of the Old Testament is made at the beginning of the second part of *The Age of Reason* (*CWP*, ii. 518).

Urizen's system.[42] Another detail which points in the same direction is the fact that Fuzon's fiery wrath hardens into a 'thunder-stone' (l. 8). Not only does this have the quality of intractable hardness associated with the law of Urizen, it is also a version of the traditional weapon of patriarchal deities like the God of the Old Testament and Zeus. These details culminate in the revelation that Fuzon is the 'Son of Urizen's silent burnings' (l. 9). He is as much the product of Urizen's brooding as the iron code proclaimed in *The Book of Urizen*. At the root of this brooding was Urizen's desire to proclaim himself an omnipotent power. Later in *The Book of Ahania*, Fuzon reveals that a similar motivation lies at the heart of his revolt.

At the outset of the poem, though, these details receive less emphasis than Fuzon's antagonism to Urizen. He accuses Urizen of being an 'abstract non-entity' (l. 11), a transcendent signifier of holiness devoid of human content. Fuzon describes Urizen as a 'cloudy God seated on waters' (l. 12), which plays on two important biblical accounts of the Deity: the Creator that 'moved upon the face of the waters' in Genesis 1: 2 and the 'cloudy God', the lawgiver, who appears to Moses on Sinai. It is the latter which is the most significant for *The Book of Ahania* since the whole confrontation of Fuzon and Urizen is worked out in terms of the events on Sinai. If Urizen is again partially represented as the God of the Old Testament, Fuzon is a reworking of Moses who shares the patriarch's desire to see his nebulous God face to face (Exodus 33: 18). Blake subversively transforms the biblical account by restaging this desire as a violent rebellion against the omnipotent power of God. Just as the Exodus became an ironic liberation from Providence at the close of *The Book of Urizen*, so in *The Book of Ahania* the revelation of God to Moses is worked up into a violent confrontation.

Not that the poem presents Fuzon's rebellion as a successful break with the state religion of Urizen. Although he initially

---

[42] Iron as a signifier of legalism and rigid hierarchy in Blake's rhetoric may mark a debt to Rousseau's historiography, which identified the introduction of iron as a key moment in the decline from the state of primitive egalitarianism into a society based on property. See *A Discourse*, 119–22.

succeeds in deposing Urizen, Fuzon's victory only marks a continuation of the Urizenic world order. I have already shown how the reader is prepared for this by Blake's subtle identification of Urizen and Fuzon. Their similarity becomes even more obvious once Fuzon achieves his tenuous ascendancy. First, when he succeeds in 'the cold loins of Urizen dividing' (l. 29), Fuzon only perpetuates the series of divisions described in *The Book of Urizen*. Ahania appears from the 'parted soul' (l. 32) of Urizen just as Enitharmon separated from Los. Once this division is complete Fuzon mimics Urizen's will to power and proclaims his own omnipotence at the head of his divided universe: 'I am God. said he, eldest of things!' (E 86; Pl. 3, l. 38.) In terms of Fuzon's Mosaic conception, this moment might be described as the triumph of the lawgiver on Sinai over the leader who liberated his people from the Egyptian slavery.

Fuzon effectively reinstitutes the religion of Urizen. The difference between the rebellions of Orc and Fuzon might usefully be related to Paine's distinction between the revolutions in America and France, that he claimed were 'a renovation of the natural order of things', and what 'were formerly called revolutions' which he believed to have been 'little more than a change of persons, or an alteration of local circumstances'. Fuzon's revolt in *The Book of Ahania* is a court revolution which brings about only a change of persons. In *America* Orc makes the deserts blossom in what is clearly a representation of the radical aspiration for a fundamental change in the order of things. Perhaps the clearest indication that Fuzon's desire to represent himself as an absolute god is a continuation of the Urizenic order comes in the fact that as soon as he utters his claim to omnipotence Urizen reappears and strikes him down. By proclaiming his omnipotence, Fuzon breathes new life into the Urizenic system.[43]

Tannenbaum has suggested that Fuzon's replication of Urizen's ambition implies that Moses fell back into the Egyptian practices from which he tried to free his people. Once again he traces the source of this notion to Warburton's *The Divine*

---

[43] See Paine, *CWP*, ii. 341–2.

Legation. The central thesis of Warburton's book concerned the doctrine of future rewards and punishments. Warburton played the rhetorical trick of accepting the deist case that the doctrine was invented by pagan priests as a means of social control but arguing that, since the Mosaic system never made any reference to the doctrine, Moses' religion must have come directly from God.[44] What Warburton did concede to his free-thinking opponents was that Moses had made use of his knowledge of Egyptian religion by introducing certain rites into his religion which would turn his people's 'Fondness for the forbidden Practice into an innocent Channel'.[45] A more contemporary source where Blake might have come across such ideas would have been Alexander Geddes's translation of the Bible, which acknowledged Warburton's point about Moses' use of Egyptian rites to placate the Hebrews' religious tastes. Geddes's political orientation became clear when he claimed that the Mosaic regime was a republican theocracy in which 'all magistrates, judges, and public offices, were to be chosen by the people'. The same idea is a powerful thread in the lectures delivered by Coleridge in 1795. Coleridge claimed that Moses had been 'informed by divine authority that it was unlawful to acknowledge any human superior'. The theocracy founded on this basis thrived until Samuel's time, when the Hebrews made what was for Coleridge the mistake of choosing to live under a monarchy.[46]

Blake's narrative in *The Book of Ahania* is obviously at odds with the conception of Moses as the founder of a virtuous Hebrew commonwealth. His narrative contradicts Warburton's theories and suggests the Mosaic system actively propagated

[44] Warburton outlines his aims and methods, *Divine Legation*, i. 6–7. On the influence of this work, see Feldman and Richardson, *Rise of Modern Mythology*, 112–13.

[45] Warburton, *Divine Legation*, ii. 323.

[46] See Geddes, *Bible*, vol. i, pp. xiii and xv, and Coleridge, *Works*, i. 126. Their view of the Mosaic theocracy has something in common with Spence's. All three are probably influenced by the republican traditions of civic humanism and, in particular, Harrington's view of the Hebrew republic. See M. Chase, *The People's Farm* (Oxford, 1988), 55, who traces the Spencian concept of the Jubilee to Harrington via James Murray. For Harrington's view of Moses, see J. G. A. Pocock's discussion in *The Political Works of James Harrington* (Cambridge, 1977), 39–92.

Egyptian state religion. This contradiction needs to be related both to the Revolution controversy and the earlier substantial body of deist thought against which Warburton wrote. Blake's account of Fuzon is deeply indebted to the tradition which emphasized the continuities between pagan religion and established Christianity. Deists like John Toland tended to see both Christian belief and pagan ritual as distortions of natural religion. Related to this critique was the Christian Dissenting emphasis on the need to return to a pure form of Christianity free of pagan custom and ritual. These currents became an important component in the radical polemics of the 1790s, exemplified by Paine's claim that Christianity had 'sprung out of the tail of the heathen mythology'. Paine was less concerned than either Geddes or Coleridge to construct a liberal version of Moses. Blake's hostile treatment of Moses in *The Book of Ahania*, perhaps surprisingly, has more in common with the scepticism of Paine and Volney than the Christian apologists among rationalist radicals.[47]

Paine explicitly dealt with the character and role of Moses in *The Age of Reason*. He presented Moses as the perpetrator of some of the worst atrocities described in the Bible:

The character of Moses . . . is the most horrid that can be imagined. If those accounts be true, he was the wretch that first began and carried on wars on that score or on that pretense; and under that mask, or that infatuation, committed the most unexampled atrocities that are to be found in the history of any nation.

Volney's book returned in more detail to the theory that Moses had perpetuated pagan religious practices. *The Ruins* explicitly states what Blake's *The Book of Ahania* implies, that is, that the Mosaic dispensation was a continuation of Egyptian religious practices: 'in vain did he proscribe the worship of symbols, the reigning religion, at that time, in lower Egypt and Phenicia: his

---

[47] See Paine, *CWP*, ii. 467. Ironically the scepticism of Paine and Volney has more in common with popular enthusiasm in its antagonism to Moses than with the Harringtonian perspectives of those radicals from more respectable Dissenting backgrounds. Perhaps this is one of the threads which explains why unrespectable enthusiasts like Terry and many others took so warmly to Paine and Volney.

God was not on that account the less an Egyptian God, or the invention of those priests whose disciple Moses had been'. Volney also described Moses as an ambitious egotist, one of the 'bold and energetic spirits' who had formed 'vast projects of ambition' in order to build a 'distinct and exclusive empire'. It is precisely this aspect of Moses which Blake maintains in his account of Fuzon. *The Song of Los*, of course, includes Moses in its own catalogue of those 'bold and energetic spirits' who founded the varieties of state religion described in Volney's book.[48]

It is not only through its treatment of Moses that *The Book of Ahania* is implicated in the radical critique of received religion. To the extent that the relationship between Urizen and Fuzon is also worked out in terms of God the Father and the Son, it engages with much more fundamental aspects of established Christianity. I have already indicated that Urizen is a Blakian version of the God of state religion. Some of the allusions to Christ in the representation of Fuzon were mentioned in Chapter 2. Not the least of these is the fact that he is the 'Son of Urizen's silent burnings'. The Christ-like aspects of Blake's representation of Fuzon become dominant when Urizen takes his body and nails it to the 'accursed Tree of Mystery' (E 87; Pl. 4, l. 6), a development which is a gruesome parody of the Atonement.[49]

The identification of Moses and Christ in the figure of Fuzon marks another similarity between *The Book of Ahania* and the critical perspectives of Paine and Volney. The latter presented both Moses and Christ as religious reformers who managed

---

[48] For their views on Moses, see Volney, *Ruins*, 279–80, and Paine, *CWP*, i. 528. Interestingly, Geddes's *Critical Remarks*, published in 1800, moved closer to the sort of view of Moses shared by Paine and Volney. Geddes attacked the totalitarian nature of Moses' theocracy and also followed Paine in blaming Moses for the various acts of cruelty described in Exodus. See the discussion of these opinions in J. M. Good, *Memoirs of the Life and Writings of Geddes* (London, 1823), 366 and 369. Thomas Dutton's *Vindication of the Age of Reason*, 113, closely follows Volney's line on Moses, who is described as a man of 'ambitious views' pursuing 'the establishment of Universal Hierarchy'. Dutton also stresses Moses' debts to Egyptian priestcraft, pp. 36 and 91.

[49] See Tannenbaum, *Biblical Tradition*, 227–8. For a discussion of the representation of Fuzon in terms of Christ, see pp. 99–100 above.

only to perpetuate the systems they sought to replace. Paine more specifically identified both as the patriarchs of oppressive systems of state religion: 'Every national church or religion has established itself by pretending some special mission from God communicated to certain individuals. The Jews have their Moses; the Christians their Jesus Christ, their apostles and saints; and the Turks their Mahomet, as if the way to God was not open to every man alike.' When Fuzon declares 'I am God . . . eldest of things', he aspires to the status of just such a founding patriarch.[50] There is an ambivalence about Blake's treatment of Christ in the 1790s. *Europe* treats the Incarnation as a false dawn. 'Africa' similarly represents Christ as the founder of one of a series of mystificatory religions. *The Marriage of Heaven and Hell* presents Christ more positively as an active reformer opposed to the repressive religious structures erected in his name. The ambivalence is extended in *The Book of Ahania*, where Fuzon is both a potential liberator sacrificed on Urizen's Tree of Mystery and himself an ambitious aspirant to the status of transcendent divinity. Paine often also inclined to the former view of Christ. He believed Jesus to have been 'a virtuous and amiable man' who 'preached most excellent morality and the equality of man; but he preached also against the corruptions and avarice of the jewish priests, and this brought upon him the hatred and the vengeance of the whole order of priesthood'. Blake put forward something like this view in his annotations to Watson: 'Was not Christ murdered because he taught that God loved all Men & was their father and forbad all contention for Worldly prosperity in opposition to the Jewish Scriptures' (E 614). What Blake in general shares with Paine in his allusions to Christ is a conviction that the religion erected in his name brought only a perpetuation of the practices of state religion, a perspective common to a wide range of radical opinion in the 1790s. James Bicheno epitomized a view shared by radicals of deist, dissenting, and enthusiastic tendencies alike when he wrote: 'Christianity has been converted into a system of commerce, and those called the ministers of Christ, have

---

[50] See Paine, *CWP*, ii. 465.

been a corporation of traders, in the souls and liberties of mankind.'[51]

Perhaps chief among the errors which critics like Bicheno believed had corrupted religion into a trade was the doctrine of the Atonement. Many in the 1790s concurred with Blake that God was 'not seeking recompense' (*Jerusalem*, E 146; Pl. 4, l. 20). Conservatives in the Church of England took such opinions to be at the heart of radical ideology, the essential creed of those 'who, denying, the necessity of a propitiatory sacrifice, presumptuously lay claim to eternal happiness upon the ground of their own merit'. Loyalist polemicists frequently countered the reformist rhetoric of radicals by claiming that the only real liberation of humanity was that made possible by the sacrifice of Christ at the Crucifixion. It is a position vigorously put forward in W. B. Cadogan's *Liberty and Equality*. Cadogan claimed that 'no people are "free" save those who are made so by Jesus Christ'. His sermons rehearse the view that Christ liberated humanity from the curse of sin under the Mosaic law by offering himself as a 'propitiatory sacrifice'. Of course Cadogan's version of Christianity did not follow this idea to antinomian conclusions. He did not believe that sin had been abolished at the Crucifixion. The moral law was still in place as an index of whether the sinner was worthy to be saved when Christ's mission was completed at the Second Coming, an event deferred to the very distant future by most churchmen. Cadogan's sermon sought to reinforce the moral law as the basis of the established social order. His first sermon begins with the rhetoric of liberation through Christ and ends with an exhortation to obey the status quo: 'pray for kings and all that are in authority, that you may lead quiet and peaceable lives in all godliness and honesty'. Blake's Fuzon narrative implies the sort of continuity of the Mosaic law in Christ evident in Cadogan's sermon. Fuzon's revolt ends in the reinstatement of the Urizenic principle as inevitably as Cadogan's sermon ends in a prayer for the preservation of the social order.[52]

---

[51] See Paine, *CWP*, ii. 466–7, and Bicheno, *Signs of the Times*, 1.
[52] See Pretyman-Tomline, *A Charge*, 15, and Cadogan, *Liberty and Equality*, 1, 32, and 35.

More specifically, *The Book of Ahania* represents the Crucifixion as the vengeful sacrifice of Fuzon, the Son, to Urizen, God the Father. As such it implies the barbarity at the heart of the version of the Atonement promoted by churchmen like Cadogan. Priestley similarly believed the idea that the Crucifixion was a 'propitiatory sacrifice' to be a slur on divine mercy, a priestly distortion 'which represents the divine being as withholding his mercy from the truly penitent, till a full satisfaction be made to his justice; and for that purpose, as substituting his own innocent son in the place of sinful man'. Typically the origins of this distortion were located by Priestley in a misreading of the figurative language of the Bible and, specifically, in what he saw as an attempt to describe the Crucifixion in terms familiar to converts from Judaism. Paine, unsurprisingly, was equally hostile to the doctrine of the Atonement. He claimed that the traditional understanding of the Crucifixion was based on pecuniary rather than moral justice, a product of the machinations of priestcraft which made 'God Almighty act like a passionate man who killed his son when he could not revenge himself'. Paine, of course, believed such doctrines to be part of the incubation of pagan mysteries which vitiated Christianity. Blake similarly represents Fuzon's fate as a druidic sacrifice, as I showed in Chapter 2, of the kind undertaken in Odin's secret groves. The Atonement is revealed to be one of the pagan doctrines Paine believed remained at the heart of Christian state religion.[53]

The Fuzon narrative is not all there is in *The Book of Ahania*. Equally important is Ahania's lament, which summons up the ideal of a pre-Urizenic liberty. Its vision of a world of unrestrained desire and reciprocal fulfilment is the equivalent of the Eternity described at the outset of *The Book of Urizen*. The same vision of a lost antinomian utopia opens *The Book of Los* in Eno's lament. What I want to concentrate on here, however, is the parodical relationship of these poems to the Bible. The Fuzon narrative of *The Book of Ahania* is a parodic version of Moses' exploits in Exodus and the rest of the Pentateuch, as

---

[53] See Priestley, *History*, ii. 152–3, and Paine, *CWP*, ii. 481 and 497.

well as part of the radical critique of the Christian doctrine of the Atonement. The narrative of *The Book of Los* moves the ironical treatment of the Old Testament on into the prophetic books of the Bible and also provides an ironic comment on the conventional reading of the Book of Revelation.

The Book of Los is perhaps the most opaque of all the work Blake produced in the 1790s. The narratives of *The Book of Urizen* and *The Book of Ahania* are partially reworked in the poem but elliptically reduced to the key struggle between Los and Urizen. Robert Lowth claimed that 'bold ellipsis' and 'studied brevity' were typical of biblical prophecy. Such a style elided history into a concentrated narrative which always kept in mind the promise of salvation: 'Prophecy frequently takes in at a single glance, a variety of events, distinct both in nature and time, and pursues the extreme and principal design through all its different gradations.' Prophetic elision is the basis of the narrative strategy of *The Book of Los*. There are two other aspects of the poem which encourage a reading of it as an extreme manifestation of prophetic discourse. First, the struggle between the prophet-bard and his rival the druid-priest is the primary if not the only narrative focus. Secondly, especially at its climax, the poem is crucially concerned with the language and paradigms of Revelation, the ultimate biblical prophecy.[54]

The prophetic nature of Los's endeavours is made explicit in the poem. Los is 'the Eternal Prophet' (E 91, Pl. 3, l. 31), 'the Prophet of Eternity' (E 94; Pl. 5, l. 25), and his 'Prophetic wrath' is described at length in Chapter II (E 92; Pl. 4, l. 18). The prophetic books of the Bible chronicle the attempts of the Hebrew prophets to bring back the children of Israel to a worship of the one, true God. Blake inverts the nature of this narrative. Instead of seeking to restore the authority of the transcendent Creator of Genesis, Los struggles against Urizen's aspiration to omnipotence. Blake's version of prophecy is a commitment to the Orcian principle of scattering religion abroad and recognizing the divine in the human. It is the passing of an age when human desire was recognized as a source

---

[54] See Lowth, *Lectures*, i. 98 and 102, and ii. 67.

of divine inspiration rather than as sinful appetite that Eno
laments in the first part of the poem:

> O Times remote!
> When Love & Joy were adoration:
> And none impure were deem'd.
> Not Eyeless Covet
> Nor Thin-lip'd Envy
> Nor Bristled Wrath
> Nor Curled Wantonness
>
> But Covet was poured full:
> Envy fed with fat of lambs:
> Wrath with lions gore:
> Wantonness lulld to sleep
> With the virgins lute,
> Or sated with her love.

(E 90; Pl. 3, ll. 7–9)

In this paradoxical account, the 'seven deadly Sins of the soul'
sired by Urizen in *The Book of Urizen* (E 72; Pl. 4, l. 30) become
positive energies. What the moral law has classified as sins are a
potentially positive set of desires. Once again Blake suggests
that conventional categories of morality often bring about the
deformations they claim to prevent.

The Los-centred narrative which makes up most of the poem
actually begins with a passage very reminiscent of the description of Urizen's creation of sin in *The Book of Urizen*. *The Book
of Los* has 'the Eternal Prophet' forced to watch over the vitiated
Creation of Urizen:

> Raging furious the flames of desire
> Ran thro' heaven & earth, living flames
> Intelligent, organiz'd: arm'd
> With destruction & plagues. In the midst
> The Eternal Prophet bound in a chain
> Compell'd to watch Urizen's shadow.

(E 91; Pl. 3, ll. 27–32)

The seven deadly sins emerge out of a similar maelstrom of
desire in *The Book of Urizen*:

> Rage, fury, intense indignation
> In cataracts of fire blood & gall
> In whirlwinds of sulphurous smoke:
> And enormous forms of energy;
> All the seven deadly sins of the soul.
>
> (E 72; Pl. 4, ll. 45–9)

Urizen's invention of the categories of sin from the fluxile community of Eternity is obviously the point at which the liberated desire celebrated by Eno ends. This detail from *The Book of Urizen* helps explain the narrative organization of *The Book of Los*; as Eno's vision of a liberated past fades, the narrative switches to the point when that state was lost.

Los in *The Book of Urizen* kept watch for Eternals on the fallen form of Urizen. He is introduced in the same situation in *The Book of Los*: 'bound in a chain | Compell'd to watch' (E 91; Pl. 3, ll. 31–2). His response is both as uncertain and violent as it is in *The Book of Urizen* where he is described 'cursing his lot' (E 73; Pl. 6, l. 44). Los's attempt to stamp out the flames of desire which surround him is also reminiscent of the Orcian attempt to stamp out the stony moral law in *America*, but the Eternal Prophet's energetic attempt to free himself threatens to extinguish all that is left of desire. Los's 'hot indignation' (E 91; Pl. 3, l. 48) is not restorative. It leaves desire 'wide apart' (l. 46) and 'bound up | Into fiery spheres from his fury' (E 91; Pl. 4, ll. 1–2) so that its flames give off neither light nor heat. As with Fuzon in *The Book of Ahania*, Los's indignation worsens the situation against which he strains. Just as Fuzon becomes identical with Urizen, so Los's struggles coalesce with the earlier description of Urizen's establishment of his universe in *The Book of Urizen*. Urizen 'fought with fire' in order to produce the solid obstruction of his world (E 72; Pl. 4, l. 14). He created a black globe and the vast rock of eternity which are parodic versions of the Heaven and Earth of the Bible. In Plate 4 of the book named after him, Los becomes similarly entrapped in a world of intractability and constriction:

> Coldness, darkness, obstruction, a Solid
> Without fluctuation, hard as adamant

> Black as marble of Egypt; impenetrable
> Bound in the fierce raging Immortal.
> And the seperated fires froze in
> A vast solid without fluctuation,
> Bound in his expanding clear senses.

(E 91; ll. 4–10)

The mention of Egypt, one of the few clear references to anything outside of the mythic world of the poem, suggests that Los has effectively passed into the Egyptian slavery suffered by Urizen's children at the end of *The Book of Urizen*. The displacement on to Los here is one of several minor variations of the narrative of the earlier poem in *The Book of Los*, though the implication that the potentially liberating energy of the prophet can degenerate into the priestly slavery associated with Egypt is typical of Blake's configuration of Los from his first appearance in the poems of 1794. In *Europe* Los's initial complacent acquiescence in Enitharmon's dominion is redeemed at the end of the poem. The situation in *The Book of Urizen* and *The Book of Los* is more complex. He struggles against Urizenic tyranny but his energy is constantly misplaced or thwarted. The reworking of *The Book of Urizen* in *The Four Zoas* manuscript reveals more explicitly the dangers of Los's energy coalescing with the cold obstruction against which it strives:

> The Prophet of Eternity beat on his iron links & links of brass
> And as he beat round the hurtling Demon. terrified at the
>   Shapes
> Enslav'd humanity put on he became what he beheld.

(E 336; p. 53, ll. 22–4)

The story of *The Book of Los*, and more diffusely of *The Four Zoas*, is one of the continual reapplication of prophetic energy to redeem itself from becoming what it struggles against.

Los's attempts to free himself from the stony law of Urizen stand in an ironic relation to the prophetic books of the Old Testament. The Hebrew prophets are continually chastising their people, and particularly their rulers, for falling away from the path of the true God. Their attempts to lead the people back

into the paths of righteousness only ever achieve precarious
success. They represent points of inspiration which are continually closed off. Los's struggles follow a similar pattern, though
Blake inverts their signification. Los represents a decentred
version of inspiration which does not emanate from a transcendent source but rather struggles against the will to transcendence
in Urizen. Such a conception of the corrupt nature of the
received version of the Deity was typical of radical critics of
Christian state religion in the 1790s. Enthusiasts saw the-God-
of-this-world as a force which sought to close off prophetic
inspiration in the present. For Dissenters like Price and Priestley, it was rational Christianity which was being obstructed.
Both traditions shared a sense of being part of a long, historical
struggle against the Antichrist of state religion. The Dissenting
minister James Bicheno interpreted the two witnesses of Revelation 11: 3 as 'all those who bear witness for civil liberty against
the tyrannies and oppressions of those princes and governors
whose passions have enslaved mankind and desolated the earth'.
More enthusiastic millenarians were equally clear that there had
been a continuous struggle against the Antichrist of state
religion not 'confined either to the Jews or any other particular
rank, age, sex, or condition of men'. Blake's attitude often
seems to be an extreme example of this tendency since he goes
a long way towards calling into question any notion of an extra-
human inspiration for prophecy. The emphasis on the immanence of the divine, typical of Christian enthusiasm, is taken to
an antinomian extreme by Blake in the 1790s.[55]

Blake's most concentrated statement of his conception of the
Old Testament prophets comes in Plates 12–13 of *The Marriage*,
where he describes the visionary dinner party with Isaiah and
Ezekiel. Isaiah makes it clear that his inspiration did not have its
sources in any transcendent deity: 'I saw no God. nor heard
any, in a finite organical perception; but my senses discover'd
the infinite in every thing, and as I was then perswaded. &
remain confirm'd; that the voice of honest indignation is the

[55] See Bicheno, *Signs of the Times*, 23–4. The other quotation, from Ritchie's
Wonderful Prophecies, and its context are discussed more fully in Ch. 1 above.

voice of God' (E 38). Ezekiel goes on to describe how the discovery came to be distorted into a state religion: 'all nations believe the jews code and worship the jews god, and what greater subjection can be' (E 39). The implication is that the biblical account, or at least its official interpretation, has distorted the history of prophecy. The 'voice of honest indignation', represented by Ezekiel's attack on 'the Priests and Philosophers of other countries', itself succumbed to a system of state relgion. Los's problem in *The Book of Los* is how to find a proper expression for that voice and to extricate himself from the process of reification described by Isaiah and Ezekiel.

He briefly manages to do this at the beginning of Chapter II when he breaks free from the 'hard bondage' (E 92; Pl. 4, l. 16) of the marble of Egypt. The association of Los with an escape from Egyptian slavery raises the spectre of Moses again. Blake's presentation of Los shares something of his ambivalent attitude to Moses as expressed in the representation of Fuzon in *The Book of Ahania*. The primary difference is Los's willingness to renew his struggle when he realizes he has fallen back into error. It is significant in this respect that the description of Los in the second chapter of *The Book of Los* contains much more definite echoes of the iconoclasm of Orc. The fires which are the objects of Los's hostility in the first chapter are replaced by the black marble which is much closer to the stony law Orc breaks up in *America* and, as in that poem, the stone is turned to 'dust' when destroyed. As the outlines of Urizen's solid obstruction become clearer, so Los gains a clearer idea of what he is fighting against even if his success is far from being confirmed in the poem. The echoes of *America* might be read as some sort of progress towards millenarian achievement. There is also a suggestion that Los is taking on some of the prophetic spirit of the reforming Christ celebrated by both Blake and Paine at different times in the 1790s.

Los's furious activities reveal a 'horrible vacuum' where the 'vast rock of eternity' he destroys had been (E 92; Pl. 4, ll. 25 and 12). He falls through the vacuum into 'our world' where he is 'like the babe I New born' (l. 38). At this point he takes on the prophetic potential manifested in the Christ-child at the

Nativity, but he is unable to live up to the promise of the Incarnation. As in *Europe*, the Nativity is a false dawn and Los's prophetic energy subsides into 'finite inflexible organs' (l. 45), the familiar Blakian trope of the diminution of the human faculties signifying the fall away from inspiration. The process culminates in a new creation which is akin to the dull and solid world of Urizen:

> The Lungs heave incessant, dull and heavy
> For as yet were all other parts formless
> Shiv'ring: clinging around like a cloud
> Dim & glutinous as the white Polypus
> Driv'n by waves & englob'd on the tide.
>
> (E 93; Pl. 4, ll. 54–8)

Although Los is involved in the generation of these lungs, he is not in any simple sense their author. They are produced as part of a struggle between a self-generating body and the conscious efforts of Los to control it. Los asserts himself as he rises 'on the waters' (l. 63), but his own multiplying organs cause him to fall back into the 'world of waters' (l. 66). The organic growth of 'the white Polypus', which is also Los's generating body, is reminiscent of the choking growth of the Tree of Mystery in *The Book of Ahania*. Los struggles against a reifying principle within himself, to bring the self-generating power in line with his prophetic inspiration.

At the close of the chapter Los does gain some measure of control over these processes:

> He rose on the floods: then he smote
> The wild deep with his terrible wrath,
> Seperating the heavy and thin.
>
> Down the heavy sunk; cleaving around
> To the fragments of solid: up rose
> The thin, flowing round the fierce fires
> That glow'd furious in the expanse.
>
> (E 93; Pl. 5, ll. 3–9)

Ironically the control Los gains only brings him once again into a position very similar to Urizen, who also arose on the waters in

The Book of Urizen. This proximity is confirmed when the light Los produces reveals Urizen's spine 'hurtling upon the wind' (l. 15). Once again Los threatens like Fuzon to fall back into the Urizenic condition. What Los achieves is the condition of the God of the Old Testament, who moves over the face of the water. Fuzon much more explicitly aspired to the role of 'God . . . eldest of things'. Both fall away from Blake's conception of prophetic inspiration as involved in scattering political and religious authority abroad. Both reproduce the form of Urizen, the patriarch of state religion. Fuzon's victory leads to the resurrection of Urizen and the defeat of his revolt. Los, 'the Eternal Prophet', has a deeper commitment, which means that when he sees his efforts have only given a renewed form to the Urizenic body of error he also renews his struggle against it.

His discovery of Urizen's spine leads Los, 'astonished and terrified' (E 94; Pl. 5, l. 20), to build his furnaces and renew his prophetic mission. The description of this process in the final chapter of *The Book of Los* is shot through with references to the Book of Revelation. Most obviously, Los's attempt to bind Urizen reworks the biblical description of the binding of Antichrist which obsessed millenarians in the 1790s. Radicals, such as Brothers's follower William Bryan, were in no doubt that the Antichrist was the-God-of-this-world promoted by state religion:

They are the Antichrist, the man of sin, which is to be revealed in this latter day, (that is) all the craft and serpentine subtilty with which they contrive to get to themselves all rule and authority, both civil and ecclesiastical, to enrich themselves by oppressing others, shall be discovered and abolished.

The binding of Urizen is represented as part of this process of discovery and abolition by Blake. Specific use is made of Revelation 20 (which J. L. Towers believed to be a description of the defeat of 'Monarchical Tyranny in general'). Urizen's spine, for instance, is 'Like a serpent' (E 93; Pl. 5, l. 16). Satan is described as 'the ancient serpent' in Revelation 20: 2, where he is bound for a thousand years. He is eventually released only to be disposed of once and for all in a lake of fire and brimstone in Revelation 20: 7–10. The process of binding the serpentine Urizen is never completed in *The Book of Los*. The other significant deviation from Revelation is the fact that Urizen is identified with the God of the Bible, a recurrent feature of Blake's portrayal of Urizen which is reinforced in the final chapter of the poem. The fiery sun, for instance, to which Los tries to bind Urizen becomes 'self-balanced' (l. 45) like the world created by the God of *Paradise Lost* (VII. 242). At his moment of triumph Urizen's heart becomes like the four rivers (l. 53) which flow through Eden in Genesis 2: 10. The implication is that the Urizenic religion founded in Genesis is dismally triumphant at the close of the poem. The promise of prophetic liberation in Revelation is revealed to be thwarted not promoted by the transcendent Creator of the Old Testament. As at the end of *The Book of Urizen*, the fraud of the providential plan promoted by Christian state religion stands revealed.[56]

Critics like Tannenbaum, ever eager to read political quietism in Blake's texts as early in the 1790s as possible, have represented the denouement of *The Book of Los* as a retreat from the version of the Apocalypse promised in poems like *America* and *Europe*: 'Blake's Bible of Hell lacks the all-important capstone, Blake's equivalent of the Book of Revelation, which would reiterate and bring to a period the cyclical pattern of illumination and obscurity, liberation and repression that exists both in the Bible and the Lambeth Books.' There are two separate points which I should like to make in response to Tannenbaum's conclusions. First, the apocalyptic close of *The Book of Los* does not invoke either the American or French Revolutions in the way, for example, *America* does. The primary referential ground of *The Book of Los* is to the Bible and its role in the maintenance of the received authority of state religion. The polemical trajectory of the poem is distinct from, though very much complementary to, the concerns of poems like *America*.

[56] See Bryan, *A Testimony*, 38, and Towers, *Illustrations of Prophecy*, i. 76, and ii. 737. The opposition between the sun created by Los and the serpent body of Urizen may be another detail based on Revelation, specifically the struggle between 'the woman clothed with the sun' and 'the ancient serpent' of Rev. 12.

The latter, together with 'The Song of Liberty', *Europe*, and *The Song of Los*, is effectively a bardic or prophetic song which celebrates the possibility of the liberation of humanity. These poems harness the Christian scheme of redemption to a narrative of history which puts human desire rather than the providential God of the received Bible at their centre. *The Book of Los* forms a distinct group with *The Book of Ahania* and *The Book of Urizen* which describes the establishment and continuing tenacity of state religion and reveals it to be a fraud. Their titles indicate that they are parodic versions of the sacred books which are formed out of the distortion of poetic tales. In *The Book of Urizen* it is principally the authority of Genesis which is undermined and its God revealed as the sponsor of a particular organization of reality which validates the hegemonic sociopolitical order. *The Book of Ahania* extends the critique of the Bible. The figures of both Moses and Christ are evoked in the narrative of Fuzon, who becomes a symbol of prophetic indignation corrupted into the authoritarianism of state religion. *The Book of Los* is a more generalized account of the tribulations of the prophetic impulse which overturns the notion that the prophets (including Christ) are to be thought of as the evangelists of state religion. Blake values the prophetic impulse but implies that its true expression is to be found in opposition to the principles of pious conformity being enforced with renewed vigour by supporters of Church and King in the 1790s.[57]

The parody of religious doctrine and forms evident in *The Book of Urizen*, *The Book of Ahania* and *The Book of Los* is typical of a strong current in radical writing in the Revolution controversy. Eaton's *Politics for the People*, for instance, was littered with hymns, creeds, prayers, and litanies attacking the complicity of Church and State. Other pieces published by Eaton appropriated religious forms to the celebration of the radical doctrine of liberty. Perhaps the millenarian focus and prophetic form of poems like *America* could be paralleled with the latter. What is clear is that both procedures are facets of the same radical determination to undermine the hegemony of

---

[57] See Tannenbaum, *Biblical Tradition*, 280–1.

received religious and political authority. It is a tendency in which Blake is deeply implicated.

A second point to be made in response to Tannenbaum's formulation is that its appeal to the notion of a narrative 'capstone' conflicts with the principle of rhetorical indeterminacy as adhered to in most of Blake's work. The determination to rouse the faculties to act implies that Blake wished the reader to continue the vision of liberation beyond the text. Heather Glen puts this well when she writes that the reader of Blake 'is not offered an authoritative and static text, but called upon to participate in a dynamic act of creation'. To close off the narrative with a capstone would reduce Blake's prophetic enterprise to the writing of scripture by precluding such participation. Even the more positive apocalyptic denouements of *America* and *Europe* do not represent such a closure. It is precisely the orthodox notion of a once and for all but endlessly deferred end of history which is contested in these poems. Apocalypse becomes a continuous process of transformation, available in the present and continuing in the future. Take the example of *The Song of Los*, where the resurrection of the grave is not the prelude to a moral Last Judgement but the beginning of an outpouring of human desire which shows no sign of abating. The more particular historical focus of *America* does not mean that the narrative of that poem reaches a definite conclusion when the description of the American Revolution is complete. The poem reaches a formal end on a note of suspense as the fires of liberty begin to corrode the *ancien régime* of Europe. The implication is that the American Revolution is part of a progressive continuum.[58]

Throughout the 1790s Blake's writing and designs return to two basic themes. One is the need to maintain and perpetually renew prophetic struggle, the second is the need to be aware of the dangers of this energy itself degenerating into the apostasy of state religion. To represent the possibility of the latter is not necessarily, as some critics seem to think, a loss of faith in politics. A powerful determinant on readings of Blake which

[58] See Glen, *Vision and Disenchantment*, 72.

wish to stress a retreat from politics is the notion that after 1795, in the face of repression at home and the Terror in France, radical commitment generally declined into disillusionment. Though there is undoubtedly some truth in this, it underestimates both the great variety of radical ideologies available in the 1790s and the continuing resistance put up against the forces of cultural conservatism in many quarters. Thomas Spence, for instance, was well aware of the intractable nature of the *ancien régime* but made his awareness the basis of a programme which called for its adherents to recognize the deeply ingrained nature of hegemonic principles: 'We must not leave even their stump in the earth, like Nebuchadnezzar though guarded by a band of iron. For ill destroyed royalty and aristocracy, will be sure to recover and o'er spread the earth again as before.' The situation described by Spence here is analogous to that at the end of *The Book of Los.* Nebuchadnezzar was a traditional symbol for Antichrist and it is as a kind of Antichrist that Blake describes Urizen as I showed above. Similarly, Spence's notion of the ruling hegemony as a pervasive, noxious growth parallels the organic expansion of Urizen's body in *The Book of Los* as well as the choking growth of the Tree of Mystery in *The Book of Ahania.* Both Spence and Blake drew on popular traditions of Christianity which were familiar with the idea of the stubborn and all-pervasive nature of evil and which often identified that evil in the structures and institutions of received authority. Both, like John Wright in his *A Revealed Knowledge,* celebrated the appearance of 'the GREAT LIGHT' but recognized that 'these perfidious enemies of the Name of GOD will keep themselves up for a Time in their obstinacy'. Although after 1795 Blake published nothing of his own work till *Milton* in 1804, there is little evidence in either his annotations or notebook that he renounced his political perspective on state religion. The culmination of the manuscript of *The Four Zoas,* a poem on which Blake probably worked from 1796 or 1797, still takes the form of a triumphal, apocalyptic transformation of the world:

> The Sun arises from his dewy bed & the fresh airs
> Play in his smiling beams giving the seeds of life to grow

And the fresh Earth beams forth ten thousand springs of life
Urthona is arisen in his strength no longer now
Divided from Enitharmon no longer the Spectre Los
Where is the Spectre of Prophecy where the delusive Phantom
Departed & Urthona rises from the ruinous walls
In all his ancient strength to form the golden armour of science
For intellectual War The war of swords departed now
The dark Religions are departed & sweet Science reigns.

(E 407; p. 139, ll. 1–10)

The 'dark religions' whose growth is chronicled and parodied in *The Book of Urizen, The Book of Ahania,* and *The Book of Los* have been swept away, but they have not been replaced by any capstone of history. Instead a new process, 'intellectual war', begins in place of the 'war of swords'.[59]

---

[59] See Spence, *The Restorer of Society* in *PWS*, 77, and Wright, *A Revealed Knowledge*, 25. Cf. Bicheno's claim that 'black and conflicting clouds will darken the hemisphere and obscure our prospect; but they will spend themselves and vanish': *Signs of the Times*, 36.

Conclusion: A Radical without an Audience?

THIS final chapter will be devoted to the discussion of a matter I raised at the close of my Introduction: the issue of the audience and reception of Blake's work. Paul Mann has suggested that 'the question of audience is the most egregiously underasked question in Blake studies'. The enquiry is particularly pressing for this book since I have sought to examine the continuities and disparities between Blake's rhetoric and that of a range of radicals, some of whom were for the first time discovering a popular political audience and instituting ways and means of reaching that audience in the 1790s. But the issue is not pressing only because of this context. The texts themselves, as Mann points out, are continually exhorting their readers in the public manner of prophetic discourse.[1]

There is an assumption in Blake studies that, having 'discovered' his copper-plate method of producing illuminated books, he intended to confine himself to this medium and simply renounce commercial publishing. This assumption has been given a rigorous theoretical form by Morris Eaves, who relates Blake's aesthetic to what he calls 'Romantic expressive theory'. For Eaves, Blake's ambitions were limited to 'generating a gratifying audience from the poet's deepest self'. The limitations of Eaves's theory have been adroitly discussed by Paul Mann and Jon Klancher amongst others. What I want to emphasize is the deeply teleological nature of Eaves's theory, its assumption that the 'invention' of the illuminated books and the limitation of their circulation to a very small number of individuals was Blake's desired goal merely because it was what he finally achieved.[2]

---

[1] See Paul Mann's 'Apocalypse and Recuperation', *ELH* 52 (1985), 5–10.

[2] I quote from Klancher's characterization of Eaves's argument in his *The Making of English Reading Audiences*, 5. See also Mann, 'Apocalypse and Recuperation', 4–5, and Barrell, *The Political Theory of Painting*, 224. Morris

It is more likely that Blake intended to make use of whatever means were available to reach a public. He continued, for instance, to produce his own paintings and prints while he was publishing the illuminated books. The visual aspects of the illuminated books did not preclude him from practising conventional painting and print-making. Why should we assume that he wanted his writing to be solely confined to illuminated poetry? Indeed Paul Mann and Robert Essick have suggested that Blake explored a variety of ways to publish the manuscript of *The Four Zoas* after he had been producing illuminated books for some years. The poem could have been brought out in a form combining designs etched on a plate with standard letter-press. This mode of production would have allowed publishing on a larger scale than the illuminated books and wider circulation if successful.[3]

All this is not to concede to Eaves that Blake conceived of the illuminated books themselves as a private development of aesthetic practice. Blake's 1793 *Prospectus* presents the illuminated printing method as an innovative advance in publishing which would allow him to reach an emergent public:

TO THE PUBLIC   October 10, 1793.

The Labours of the Artist, the Poet, the Musician, have been proverbially attended by poverty and obscurity; this was never the fault of the Public, but was owing to a neglect of means to propagate such works as have wholly absorbed the Man of Genius. Even Milton and Shakespeare could not publish their own works.

This difficulty has been obviated by the Author of the following

---

Eaves believes 'as the artist is the work, the artist is also the audience'. See his 'Romantic Expressive Theory and Blake's Idea of the Audience', *PMLA* 95 (1980), 794, and for a fuller exposition of his ideas, *William Blake's Theory of Art* (Princeton, NJ, 1982). Eaves's position does not only assume that Blake always intended his work to have a restricted audience, but also implies that he produced the illuminated books with particular purchasers in mind. This idea of Blake's mode of production has been disputed recently by J. Viscomi, whose 'The Myth of Commissioned Illuminated Books', *BIQ* 23 (1989), 48–74, suggests that Blake nearly always sold his work from stock.

[3] See Paul Mann, 'The Final State of *The Four Zoas*', *BIQ* 18 (1985), 204–9, and Essick's reply and development of his case in '*The Four Zoas*: Intention and Production', *BIQ* 18 (1985), 216–20.

productions now presented to the Public; who has invented a method of Printing both Letter-press and Engraving in a style more ornamental, uniform, and grand, than any before discovered, while it produces works at less than one fourth of the expense.

If a method of Printing which combines the Painter and the Poet is a phenomenon worthy of public attention, provided that it exceeds in elegance all former methods, the Author is sure of his reward.   (E 692)

Blake's experiments with copper-plate printing originated in the late 1780s, a time when others were formulating commercial projects to combine the skills of the poet and painter. These projects made the 1790s the great decade of the English illustrated book. Amongst the publishers active in these developments, John Boydell, Thomas Macklin, and Robert Bowyer are perhaps the best known. The various catalogues and related material issued by these publishers offer interesting parallels with Blake's 1793 *Prospectus*. They all share a tone of confident expansiveness and seek to define and attract a new audience for what they present as major innovations in book publishing.[4]

Thomas Macklin, for instance, in his 1791 catalogue of the pictures commissioned to illustrate his selection of English verse wrote, like Blake, of combining 'Engravings and the Letter-Press' in an innovative and necessary expansion of cultural production: 'The present state of the Arts in this country appeared particularly favourable to these undertakings. Genius at present wants only the stimulus of public favour to rival all that may be boasted of the ancient schools.' Ultimately Bowyer, Boydell, and Macklin foundered when their export market was cut off by the French Wars later in the 1790s, but early on in the decade it seemed that both their exhibitions and the illustrated books themselves would be fabulous successes in artistic and commercial terms. Blake, either as an engraver or

---

[4] For an excellent brief account of the illustrated book industry in the 1790s, see G. E. Bentley Jr.'s 'The Great Illustrated-Book Publishers of the 1790s and William Blake', in *Editing Illustrated Books*, ed. W. Blissett (New York and London, 1980), 57–96. Amongst the major publishers it is Boydell who has most interested modern scholars. See, for instance, S. H. A. Bruntjen, *John Boydell, 1719–1804* (London, 1985) and W. H. Friedman, 'Some Commercial Aspects of the Boydell Shakespeare Gallery', *Journal of the Warburg and Courtauld Institutes*, 10 (1947), 88–109.

as a painter, must have hoped to find employment in the initial prosperity generated by such ventures. In a rueful letter of 1805 he looked back on his exclusion from this period of expansion:

my Fate has been so uncommon that I expect Nothing—I was alive & in health & with the same Talents I now have all the time of Boydells Macklins Bowyers & other Great Works. I was known by them & was look'd upon by them as Incapable of Employment in those Works. (E 766–7)

By 1793 both Macklin and Boydell had their projects well under way. By that year it must have been apparent to Blake that he was going to be overlooked. His *Prospectus* suggests that Blake saw his illuminated books as the best means of overcoming this neglect and reaching what was still an expanding market.[5]

There was another commercial project which sought to combine the skills of painter, poet, and engraver in which Blake had a special interest. Joseph Johnson and Henry Fuseli put forward the idea of a Milton Gallery, in direct competition with Boydell, to be accompanied by a richly illustrated edition of the poetry:

PROPOSALS FOR ENGRAVING AND PUBLISHING BY SUBSCRIPTION THIRTY CAPITAL PLATES, FROM SUBJECTS IN MILTON; TO BE PAINTED PRINCI-PALLY, IF NOT ENTIRELY, BY HENRY FUSELI R. A. AND FOR COPYING THEM IN A REDUCED SIZE TO ACCOMPANY A CORRECT AND MAGNIFI-CENT EDITION, EMBELLISHED ALSO WITH FORTY-FIVE ELEGANT VIGNETTES, OF HIS POETICAL WORKS, . . . BY W. COWPER . . .

---

[5] See T. Macklin, *Catalogue of the Fourth Exhibition of Pictures* (London, 1791), 7. The only project which brought Blake any serious involvement in the expansion of the illustrated book-trade was Richard Edwards's illustrated edition of Young's *Night Thoughts*. From the beginning this was something of a financial disaster for Blake. Quite apart from the failure of the book to sell, Blake was paid only a derisory 20 guineas for producing over 200 water-colours and engraving over 40 of them. Blake had asked for 100 guineas, itself a fairly modest fee set against what Boydell and Macklin paid their painters and engravers. See Bentley, 'The Great Illustrated-Book Publishers', 77–90. Blake did engrave one plate after Opie for Boydell's 1799 edition of Shake-speare and this was only to improve upon earlier attempts by other engravers which proved unsatisfactory. See Bruntjen, *John Boydell*, 109. Blake was also among the engravers named in Bowyer's 1792 *Prospectus* for his illustrated edition of Hume's *History*, but he never actually contributed any plates. See *BRS*, 133.

Messieurs Bartolozzi, Sharp, Holloway, Blake, and other eminent Engravers have promised their Assistance in the Execution of the Plates.[6]

Marilyn Butler has noticed 'the manifestly radical connections' of the Milton Gallery. Milton was a great republican icon, revered by the Rational Dissenters and progressively minded readers who bought Joseph Johnson's books.[7] Johnson and Fuseli must have expected that this readership would have been attracted by a project focused on the great poet. Several critics have argued that it was specifically this audience which Blake also hoped to reach with the republican art of his illuminated books.[8]

---

[6] Blake evidently thought a lot of the idea of an illustrated Milton since he and Hayley returned to it in 1802–3, when Blake wrote to his brother that he had 'a head full of botheration about various projected works & particularly a work now proposed to the Public at the End of Cowper's Life, which will very likely be of great consequence; it is Cowper's Milton, the same that Fuseli's Milton Gallery was painted for, & if we succeed in our intentions the prints to this work will be very profitable to me & not only profitable, but honourable at any rate' (E 727). Fuseli himself persisted with the idea of a Milton gallery and opened an exhibition of paintings based on Milton's poetry in 1799 which proved to be a financial failure. See M. R. Pointon, *Milton and English Art* (Manchester, 1970), 106–8, and J. Knowles, *The Life and Writings of Henry Fuseli*, 3 vols. (London, 1831), i. 190–223.

[7] Johnson's *Analytical Review* praised William Hayley's 'Life of Milton' (1794), ironically published by Boydell in 1794, as a liberal retort to Samuel Johnson's Tory strictures in his *Lives of the Poets*. Hayley claimed that Johnson's *Life* was an example of 'how far the virulence of political hatred may pervert a very powerful mind'. See Hayley's 'Life' in *The Poetical Works of Milton*, 3 vols. (London, 1794–7), vol. i, p. lxi. For the praise of Hayley's 'Life', see *Analytical Review*, 23 (1796) 468–78. L. F. Chard II, 'Joseph Johnson: Father of the Book Trade', *Bulletin of the New York Public Library*, 79 (1975–6), 66, takes Johnson's publication of a long series of Milton's work from 1788 to indicate the publisher's republican inclinations. See also Tyson, *Joseph Johnson*, 115 and 152–4. For the ideological connotations of the Milton Gallery, see Butler, *Romantics Rebels and Reactionaries*, 45, and D. Bindman, *The Shadow of the Guillotine* (London, 1989), 166–9.

[8] John Howard traced an audience for the anti-Swedenborgianism of *The Marriage of Heaven and Hell* amongst Johnson's Dissenting constituency. More broadly, Marilyn Butler writes of Blake's 'quality of feeling' which she believes links him with associates of Johnson: 'the native tradition of Priestley and his fellow-Dissenter Richard Price, or even the ambivalent Anglo-American Paine'. Most recently Paul Mann has described Blake's 'very specific and accessible audience' as 'the left-liberal circle around the bookseller Joseph

It is reasonable to go further and suggest that Blake must have hoped that Johnson would help his work find a market. After all Johnson consistently employed Blake as an engraver in the 1790s, entrusting him with such important jobs as engraving the Portland Vase for the illustrations to Darwin's *The Botanic Garden*. Moreover, as the preceding chapters have indicated, much of Blake's rhetoric is bound up in language and themes which recur significantly in Johnson's publications. There is also more concrete evidence that Blake did make some headway in getting Johnson involved with selling and even publishing his work. Proofs of the poem *The French Revolution* are extant which bear Johnson's name as publisher. Though there is no evidence that the poem was ever published, this does indicate that Johnson was at some stage interested in supporting Blake's poetry. More significant in relation to the illuminated books is the title-page of the 1793 edition of the small book of designs called *For Children: The Gates of Paradise* which reads:

> Published by W. Blake No. 13 Hercules Buildings Lambeth
> and J. Johnson St. Pauls Church Yard.   (E 32)

The Gates is essentially a children's chapbook and as such was seeking to enter an expanding market of particular interest to Johnson. The publisher had already brought out, for instance, Mary Wollstonecraft's *Original Stories from Real Life* (1791), for which Blake designed and engraved the illustrations. *The Gates* is stylistically very similar to the plates Johnson commissioned from Blake for Wollstonecraft's book, a detail which suggests that it would have fitted neatly on to the bookseller's shelves. If Johnson did stock *The Gates*, Blake probably hoped that his shop would also be the retail outlet of the other illuminated books listed with *The Gates* in the 1793 *Prospectus*. Once again, however, there is no record that this hope was ever fulfilled.

Johnson'. See Howard, 'An Audience for *The Marriage of Heaven and Hell*', Butler, *Romantics, Rebels and Reactionaries*, 44–5, and Mann, 'Apocalypse and Recuperation', 7. Mann is over-specific in describing Johnson's left-liberal coterie as Blake's potential audience. It is not necessary to limit Blake to the Johnson circle as such in this way. It is quite possible he merely wished to sell them more impersonally through Johnson's shop.

Nor did Johnson's *Analytical Review* ever advertise *The French Revolution* or review any of Blake's illuminated books, though Johnson continued to employ Blake as an engraver right up until 1804.[9]

Why did Blake never gain the support from Johnson that he might have expected? I have no doubt that Mann is correct when he writes that any explanation of Johnson's failure either to publish *The French Revolution* or, so it appears, actually to stock any of the illuminated books 'must include the fact that the radical coterie which Blake targeted was still situated and defined within a distinctly bourgeois market place'. More precisely, Blake's writing and designs were caught up in a process in which a culture was defining itself as bourgeois, sorting itself out both from the patrician culture above and the unrespectability of those below. I believe Blake's vulgar enthusiasm functioned as the mark of an unrespectability which excluded him from this emergent public sphere.[10]

Blake's relationship to the Johnson circle is not easy to clarify. Nor can it be with so little information available. This paucity has led to fantasies about Blake's presence at the publisher's famous literary suppers. These suppers were attended by authors published by Johnson, influential Dissenters, and a variety of others of various political persuasions. The story of Blake's attendance at these suppers came from Gilchrist's Victorian biography, which enlarges on a hint in Tatham's manuscript 'Life of Blake'. Godwin's diary, the major source of information on those attending the suppers, contains only one clear reference to Blake in an entry for 4 April 1797. John Gabriel Stedman's *Journal* shows that Blake did at least dine once elsewhere with Johnson, if not actually at the famous supper parties. Erdman has concluded that 'we must suspect most of the circumstantial detail in the anecdotes of Blake's association' with Johnson. The real intimates of the publisher

---

[9] See Mann, 'Apocalypse and Recuperation', 7. On the continuities of style between Blake's engravings for Wollstonecraft and *The Gates*, see Essick, *William Blake Printmaker*, 68–9. Tyson discusses Johnson's particular interest in children's books: *Joseph Johnson*, 81–3.

[10] See Mann, 'Apocalypse and Recuperation', 7.

were those authors and others who defined themselves in terms of the respectable and rationalist discourse which Mann calls 'bourgeois'.[11]

Blake was known to Johnson as an engraver, a trade which had a complex professional status but which was clearly distinguished from the more respectable art of painting. While engravers could rise to public prominence and respectability (Blake's friend Sharp achieved at least the former), they tended to be treated as tradesmen rather than artists. Although the distinction was not always hard and fast, it was very much an operative one and institutionalized, for instance, in so far as the constitution of the Royal Academy stipulated that engravers could not become Fellows. It is likely that Johnson's circle would have regarded Blake as a peripheral figure, a copy-engraver who worked for Johnson rather than a writer or artist published by him. It is interesting to note in relation to this point how often in the relatively few references to Blake available to us from contemporary sources he is referred to as 'Blake the Engraver': defined by his trade in a way that painters and writers like Fuseli and Godwin were not.[12]

Fuseli's relation to the Johnson circle offers a useful contrast with Blake. Though Blake had known Johnson before the publisher knew Fuseli, the Swiss painter became much more intimate with Johnson. He was both published by Johnson and frequently attended the famous dinner parties. Fuseli supported Blake's efforts to make a living as an artist, but his attitude had the air of patronage about it. He put Blake's work forward while maintaining reservations about its completeness and propriety. The painter Farington, for instance, reported in his diary that Fuseli had told him that Blake was mad and that Catherine Blake had been a maidservant. Both Johnson and

[11] The best account of Blake's contacts with the Johnson circle is Erdman's in *Prophet Against Empire*: see pp. 152–62. See also *BR*, 40–1 and 530. Stedman's *Journal*, ed. S. Thompson (London, 1962), 383, records a dinner which both Johnson and Blake attended but it doesn't seem to have been at the publisher's house.

[12] For examples of references to 'Blake the Engraver', see *BR*, 45, 64, 74, 80, 91, 99, and 146. See also *The Diary of Joseph Farington*, vols. i–vi, ed. K. Garlick and A. Macintyre (New Haven, Conn., 1978–), ii 497 and 588–9.

Fuseli felt it fell to them to find a patron for Blake. It was they who arranged for him to enter the patronage of William Hayley from 1800 to 1803, a fact Blake reflected bitterly upon in 1803.

My unhappiness has arisen from a source which if explord too narrowly, might hurt my pecuniary circumstances. As my dependence is on Engraving at present, & particularly on the Engravings I have in hand for Mr H. & I find on all hands great objections to my doing anything but the meer drudgery of business, & intimations that if I do not confine myself to this, I shall not live. this has always pursud me. You will understand by this the source of all my uneasiness. This from Johnson & Fuseli brought me down here & this from Mr H will bring me back again.   (E 724)

Fuseli, Hayley, and Johnson are all indicted in this letter for trying to keep Blake at his trade of engraving. It is probable that the Johnson circle really regarded him as a tradesman, albeit an eccentric and gifted one, rather than an intellectual like themselves.[13]

Nor should we be too surprised that the radicals of Johnson's circle, who professed liberal and even democratic ideas, should have responded in such a way. There is plenty of evidence that the newly politicized lower classes were far from being regarded as equals by the more respectable radicals with which they were associated in debating clubs and publishing ventures. Iain McCalman, for instance, has shown that gentleman activists like Horne Tooke and Timothy Brown patronized 'a leavening of intellectual artisans and lower middle-class sorts' without ever taking them on as 'friends and equals'. Yet it is unlikely that Blake's social position in itself would have barred him from a fuller participation in the Johnson circle. The artisans McCalman discusses were often at least encouraged to publish by their wealthy associates and did move with intimacy in polite circles. London was a relatively fluid society. Those who rose from humble beginnings could participate in the public sphere if they were prepared to conform to a complex variety of social codes which confirmed their ascent. I have already argued that the rationalist discourse of the Johnson circle was essential to its self-

---

[13] Fuseli's comments on William and Catherine Blake are recorded in Farington's *Diary*, ii. 589.

definition as respectable and worthy of political representation. Blake eschewed the rationalist discourse essential to the self-image of the constituency of which Johnson's coterie was a part. The *Analytical Review* published by Johnson and for which most of his author friends wrote at some time, was very much the journal of Rational Dissent. Its attitude to artisan radicalism was ambivalent. Part of the same reflex was an unfailing antagonism to popular religious enthusiasm. Whether manifested in Swedenborgianism or the publications of Brothers and his followers, the *Analytical Review* was always aware of the dangerous nature of enthusiasm. The visionary dimensions of Blake's illuminated books would have functioned as the mark of an unrespectability which the Johnson circle was unlikely to appreciate.[14]

From a long perspective this response looks like a product of the emergence of the familiar middle-class values which became firmly enshrined in the bourgeoisie of the Victorian period. There is also a shorter perspective which offers other reasons to explain why the Johnson group would have been averse to the enthusiasm of Blake. The various answers to Burke published by Johnson in the early 1790s were vitally involved in refuting his claim that support for the French Revolution was a species of fanaticism related to the radical enthusiasm of the seventeenth century. Associates of Johnson's like Christie, Godwin, Priestley, and Wollstonecraft were keen to demonstrate the reasonableness of their radicalism. Blake would have been an ambiguous ally in such a cause. If this hypothetical argument is followed thus far, the non-publication of *The French Revolution* had less to do with any difference of political attitudes over events in France between Johnson and Blake than with a difference over the social politics of a style. There is too much enthusiasm in the poem for it to sit easily alongside the other answers to Burke published in 1791–2.[15]

[14] See McCalman, *Radical Underworld*, 84. On the *Analytical Review*'s attitude to artisan radicalism, see L. F. Chard II, 'Joseph Johnson', 67. For the *Analytical*'s views on enthusiasm, see pp. 50–1 above. Note also the discussion of the differences between Rational Dissent and enthusiastic millenarianism, pp. 38–46 above.

[15] On Johnson as a publisher of replies to Burke, see Tyson, *Joseph Johnson*, 122–4. Tyson numbers 13 such pamphlets or books.

This is not to say that Blake's rhetoric is absolutely different from the rationalism of the Johnson circle. Chapters 2, 3, and 4 above should have indicated how far Blake was involved with the issues and images which concerned writers and artists like Darwin, Fuseli, Geddes, and Priestley. His vulgar enthusiasm is only one component in a bricolage which contained elements of abiding interest to the progressive intellectuals associated with Johnson (though this eclecticism in itself may have functioned as a sign of unrespectability). What is more, Blake's own attitude to the aesthetic discourse, which ultimately excluded him in its distinction between the artist and the engraver, is not simple to describe. Like many of the aspiring literati described in McCalman's *Radical Underworld*, Blake evidently wanted to be included in the developing public sphere of the aesthetic. He aspired to the status of artist and wanted to establish a republican art rather than emulate those like Brothers and Spence who addressed themselves to the urban subclass. Blake's enthusiasm prevented his entry into the public culture of art, but his desire to enter (and transform) that culture directed him away from the audience which could have appreciated his enthusiasm. The latter is his distance from Brothers and Spence, the former his distance from Barry and Fuseli or Wordsworth and Coleridge. However much Blake wanted to reach an audience, the nature of his rhetorical and technical bricolage meant that an audience simply did not exist apart from the handful of individuals with antiquarian interests who bought his work.

That Blake believed otherwise may appear naïve to us, but any such judgement needs to be qualified. First, the unstable and emergent nature of new audiences in the late eighteenth century needs to be given due weight. The rapid rise and decline of the illustrated book-trade in the 1790s is one aspect of this instability, but it was more fundamentally a feature of broader structural changes in Britain's society and economy. There would also in the early 1790s have seemed to be more of a chance of Blake reaching an audience than later in the decade when the war against France was well under way and radical opinion was being squeezed by government repression. Secondly, an over-confidence in the power of truth to find its way irresistibly into the public consciousness was typical of many intellectuals in the period, perhaps not surprisingly given what Blake called the 'miracle' of the mass circulation of Paine's *Rights of Man*. Many radicals believed, as McNeil has said of Erasmus Darwin, 'that individuals had simply to think for themselves and the transformation of the world . . . would be automatic'. Perhaps this attitude is best exemplified in the writings of William Godwin, who believed that 'Sound reasoning, when adequately communicated, must always be victorious over error.' Blake echoes Godwin's confidence in *The Marriage of Heaven and Hell*: 'Truth can never be told so as to be understood, and not be believ'd' (E 38). Such a conviction is scarcely likely to have helped in the difficult search for an audience. Yet it should be remembered that Blake did explore new ways of reaching a broader public once the limitations of the illuminated books in this respect became apparent. Both the Essick–Mann thesis about Blake's publishing intentions for *The Four Zoas* and his 1809 exhibition of paintings show that he was never really content to find an audience in himself and a few admiring individuals.[16]

Late eighteenth-century Britain was a relatively fluid society in the process of creating for itself a bourgeois public sphere, but its fluidity was part of a process of self-definition which involved exclusion and repression. Blake's texts, while participating in much that was progressive about these developments, also substantiate a great deal of the language and perspectives of what was excluded as unrespectable. It is precisely a sense of Blake's relation to this alternative history which has attracted many of his modern readers, ironically providing inspiration for radical activists like E. P. Thompson and broader sections of the left long after his prospects of finding an audience in his lifetime had faded. Terry Eagleton has celebrated Blake as 'Britain's greatest revolutionary poet'. The judgement is historically inexact, even based on guesswork, but it is an appreciation stimulated by the very difference of Blake in the context of

[16] See McNeil, *Under the Banner of Science*, 71, and Godwin, *Enquiry concerning Political Justice*, i. 3 vols., ed. F. E. L. Priestley (London, 1946), i. 86.

what we know as the literature of his time. Concerted attempts to assimilate the poetry and designs to the paradigms of Romanticism have tended to play down this difference. I have put forward a less familiar context for understanding Blake, tracing his distinctiveness to a creative engagement with the Revolution controversy, many parts of which are excluded from our received cultural history. In this context, Blake's desire to rouse the faculties to act becomes something more than a reiteration of the Romantic emphasis on the power of the poetic Imagination. It is part of a dangerous enthusiasm for the 'rights of the living' to which radicals as different as Richard Brothers and Tom Paine also subscribed in the turbulent years of the 1790s.[17]

[17] See Eagleton, 'Editor's Preface' to E. Larrissy's *William Blake* (Oxford, 1985), p. ix. It is only necessary to consult the index to *The Making of the English Working Class* to see the importance of Blake to Edward Thompson.

Bibliography

A. UNPUBLISHED MATERIAL

1. Manuscripts

Bodleian Library, Oxford
    Douce, Francis, IV Commonplace Collection; MS Douce e. 29–37.
British Museum
    Dodd, Thomas, 'Memorials of Engravers in Gt. Britain, 1550–1800', Add. MSS 33394–33407.
    Huntington, William, 'Letters to his Family, Friends, and Congregation, 1778–1813', Add. MSS 46886, fos. 1–1166 *passim*.

2. Theses

Lineham, P. J., 'The English Swedenborgians 1770–1840: A Study in the Social Dimensions of Religious Sectarianism', Ph.d. thesis (Sussex, 1978).
Matheson, C. S., 'The Respective Functions of Text and Design in the Art of William Blake', D.Phil. thesis (Oxford, 1990).
Wood, M. M. G., 'Popular Satire in Early Nineteenth-Century Radicalism, with Special Reference to Hone and Cruikshank', D.Phil. thesis (Oxford, 1989).

B. PUBLISHED MATERIAL

The place of publication is London unless stated. The abbreviation *BIQ* indicates an article from the journal *Blake: An Illustrated Quarterly*.

1. Primary Texts

An Account of the Remains of the Worship of Priapus lately existing at

Isernia . . . in the Kingdom of Naples: in two letters: one from Sir William Hamilton, K. B., His Majesty's Minister at the Court of Naples, to Sir Joseph Banks, Bart., President of the Royal Society: and the other from a Person residing at Isernia: to which is added. A Discourse on the Worship of Priapus, and its connexion with the Mystic Philosophy of the Antients by R. P. Knight (1786).

The Age of Prophecy!: or, Further Testimony of the Mission of Richard Brothers, by A Convert (1795).

Analytical Review (1788–99).

Anti-Jacobin Review and Magazine (1799–1821).

Anti-Jacobin; or, Weekly Examiner, 4th edn., 2 vols. (1799).

The Anti-Levelling Songster (1793).

Association for Preserving Liberty and Property against Republicans and Levellers, *Liberty and Property Preserved against Republicans and Levellers: A Collection of Tracts (1792–3)*.

Barlow, Joel, *Works*, ed. with an introduction by William K. Bottorf and Arthur L. Ford, 2 vols. (Gainesville, Fla. 1970).

Bennett, James, and Bogue, David, *History of the Dissenters, from the Revolution in 1688 to the Year 1808*, 4 vols. (1808–12).

Bicheno, James, *The Signs of the Times; or, The Overthrow of Papal Tyranny in France, the Prelude of Destruction to Popery and Despotism: but of Peace to Mankind* (1793).

Binns, John, *Recollections of the Life of John Binns* (Philadelphia, 1854).

Blackwell, Thomas, *An Enquiry into the Life and Writings of Homer* (1735).

—— *Letters Concerning Mythology* (1748).

Blair, Hugh, *A Critical Dissertation on the Poems of Ossian, The Son of Fingal* (1763).

—— *Lectures on Rhetoric and Belles Lettres*, 2 vols. (1783).

Blake, William, *Complete Writings*, ed. Geoffrey Keynes (Oxford, 1966).

—— *The Complete Poems*, Longman Annotated English Poets, ed. W. H. Stevenson, text by David V. Erdman (1971).

—— *The Illuminated Blake*, annotated by David V. Erdman (Oxford, 1975).

—— *The Complete Graphic Works*, ed. David Bindman, assisted by D. Toomey (1978).

—— *William Blake's Writings*, ed. G. E. Bentley Jr., 2 vols. (Oxford, 1978).

—— *Europe: A Prophecy*, ed. with an introduction by G. E. Bentley Jr., Materials for the Study of William Blake, 2 (Memphis, 1978).

—— *The Paintings and Drawings of William Blake*, ed. Martin Butlin, 2 vols (1981).

—— *The Complete Poetry and Prose of William Blake*, ed. D. V. Erdman, rev. edn. (New York, 1982).

Blayney, Benjamin, *Jeremiah and Lamentations: A New Translation* (Oxford, 1784).

Boydell, John, *A Catalogue of Pictures in the Shakespeare Gallery Pall Mall* (1792).

British Critic (1793–1825).

Brothers, Richard, *A Revealed Knowledge of the Prophecies and Times*, 2 parts, 3rd edn. [?], (1794).

—— *The Writings of Mr. Richard Brothers, God's Anointed King and Shiloh of the Hebrews*, 6 parts (1798).

—— *Description of Jerusalem, its Houses and Streets, Squares, Colleges Markets, and Cathedrals, the Royal and Private Palaces, with the Garden of Eden in the Centre as laid down in the last Chapter of Ezekiel* (1801).

Bryan, William, *A Testimony of the Spirit of Truth, concerning Richard Brothers . . . in an Address to the People of Israel &c., to the Gentiles called Christians and all other Gentiles* (1795).

Bryant, Jacob, *A New System; or, An Analysis of Ancient Mythology wherein an Attempt is made to divest Tradition of Fable; and to reduce the Truth to its Original Purity*, 3 vols., 2nd edn. (1775).

Burke, Edmund, *The Works of Edmund Burke*, 7 vols. (1803).

Cadogan, W. B., *Liberty and Equality: Two Sermons* (Reading, 1792).

A Catalogue of an Extensive and Valuable Library of Books, sold by Phillips (1809).

Coleridge, Samuel Taylor, *Poems on Various Subjects* (1796).

—— *The Collected Works of Samuel Taylor Coleridge*, Gen. ed. K. Coburn, associate ed. B. Winer (1971–).

Cooke, John, *Monarchy no Creature of God's Making wherein is Proved by Scripture and Reason, that Monarchical Government is Against the Mind of God*, revised edn. with a preface by Daniel Isaac Eaton (1794).

Cooke, William, *An Enquiry into the Patriarchal and Druidical Religion, Temples &c* (1754).

Crease, J., *Prophecies Fulfilling; or, The Dawn of the Perfect Day* (1795).

Critical Review (1756–1817).

Darwin, Erasmus, *The Botanic Garden: A Poem in Two Parts* (1791).

—— *Zoonomia; or, The Laws of Organic Life*, 2 vols. (1794).

De Fleury, Maria, *Antinomianism Unmasked and Refuted and the Moral*

Law Proved from the Scriptures of the Old and New Testament to be Still in Full Force as the Rule of Christian Conduct (1791).

A Description of a Remarkable Vision, seen by Thomas Webster (1798).

Dutton, Thomas, *A Vindication of the Age of Reason by Thomas Paine in Answer to the Strictures of Mr Gilbert Wakefield and Dr. Priestley on this Celebrated Performance* (1795).

Erskine, J., *The Fatal Consequences and the General Sources of Anarchy: A Discourse on Isaiah. XXIV 1–5* (1793).

Evangelical Magazine (1793–1904).

Evans, John, *A Sketch of the Denominations of the Christian World*, 8th edn. (1803).

Farington, Joseph, *The Diary of Joseph Farington*, vols. i–vi, ed. K. Garlick and A. Macintyre; vols. vii–xvi, ed. K. Cave (New Haven, Conn., 1978–84).

Fisher, Samuel, *The Testimony of Truth Exalted* (1679).

Frend, William, *Peace and Union Recommended to the Associated Bodies of Republicans and Anti-Republicans* (St Ives, 1793).

A Friend, *Memoirs of the Life of the Rev. Thomas Wills, A. B.* (1804).

Geddes, Alexander, *Prospectus of a New Translation of the Holy Bible from Corrected Texts of the Originals, compared with the Ancient Versions with Variant Readings, Explanatory Notes, and Critical Observations* (Glasgow, 1786).

—— *A Letter to the Right Reverend the Lord Bishop of London, containing Queries, Doubts, and Difficulties, relative to a Vernacular Version of the Holy Scriptures* (1787).

—— *Dr. Geddes's General Answer to the Queries, Counsils, and Criticisms that have been Communicated to him since the Publication of his Proposals for Printing a New Translation of the Bible* (1790).

—— *The Holy Bible; or, The Books Accounted Sacred by Jews and Christians otherwise called the Old and New Covenants, Faithfully Translated from Corrected Texts of the Originals*, 2 vols. (1792–7).

—— *Dr. Geddes's Address to the Public on the Publication of the First Volume of the New Translation of the Bible* (1793).

—— *Critical Remarks on the Hebrew Scriptures Corresponding with a New Translation of the Bible* (1800).

Gentleman's Magazine (1731–1833).

Gerrald, Joseph, *A Convention the Only Means of Saving us from Ruin, in a Letter to the People of England* (1793).

Gibbon, Edward, *The History of the Decline and Fall of the Roman Empire*, 6 vols. (1776–88).

Gifford, William, *The Baviad and Maeviad*, 8th edn. (1811).

God's Awful Warning to a Giddy Careless Sinful World (1795).

Godwin, William, *Enquiry concerning Political Justice*, 3 vols., ed. F. E. L. Priestley (1946).

—— *Things as they are; or, the Adventures of Caleb Williams*, ed. with an introduction by David McCracken (Oxford, 1982).

Gray, Thomas, *Gray and Collins: Poetical Works*, ed. Roger Lonsdale (Oxford, 1977).

Green, Sarah, *A Letter to the Publishers of Brothers Prophesies, by Mrs. S. Green, in which she bears Testimony to the Sanity of Mr. Brothers* (1795).

Green, Thomas, *A Dissertation on Enthusiasm, shewing the Danger of its Late Increase, and the Great Mischiefs it has occasioned, both in Ancient and Modern Times* (1755).

Grose, Francis, *A Classical Dictionary of the Vulgar Tongue* (1785).

Harrington, James, *The Political Works of James Harrington*, ed. with an introduction by J. G. A. Pocock (Cambridge, 1977).

Hindmarsh, Robert, *Letters to Dr. Priestley* (1792).

—— *The Rise and Progress of the New Jerusalem Church, in England, America, and other Parts: Particularly in Reference to its External Manifestations by Public Worship, Preaching, and the Administration of the Sacraments, with other Ordinances of the Church*, ed. E. Madeley (1861).

How, Samuel, *The Sufficiency of the Spirit's Teaching without Human Learning: or, A Treatise tending to Prove Human Learning to be of no Help to the Spiritual Understanding of the Word of God*, 8th edn. (1792); first published 1651.

Howes, Thomas, *Critical Observations on Books Antient and Modern*, 2 vols. (1776–83).

[Huddesford, R.], *Topsy-Turvy, with Anecdotes and Observations illustrative of Leading Characters in the Present Government of France* (1793).

Huntington, William, *Advocates for Devils Refuted, and their Hope of the Damned Demolished: or, an Everlasting Task for Winchester and all his Confederates* (1794).

—— *The Utility of the Books and the Excellency of the Parchments*, 2nd edn. (1796).

—— *A Watchword and Warning from the Walls of Zion* (1798).

—— *Discoveries and Cautions from the Streets of Zion: by a Watchman of the night*, 2nd edn. (1802).

—— *Onesimus in the Balance; or, the Eternity of Hope Considered* (1806).

—— *Onesimus in the Balance and Obedience to the Civil Powers Proved* (1806).

—— *God the Guardian of the Poor and the Bank of Faith: or, A Display of the Providences of God which have at Sundry Times Attended the Author,* 2 parts, 10th edn. (1813).

—— *The Lying Prophet Examined and his False Predictions Discovered: being a Dissection of the Prophecies of Richard Brothers,* 2nd edn. (1813).

An Impartial Account of the Prophets, in the Beginning of this Century, recommended to be Seriously perused at this Time, when Prophecies and Revelations are too much disregarded and despised (1795).

Johnson, Samuel, *A Dictionary of the English Language in which the Words are deduced from their Originals and Illustrated in their Different Significations by Examples from the Best Writers,* 2 vols. (1755).

A Key to the Mystery of Revelation, whereby all its Dark Meanings, being reduced to one Regular System are easily accounted for and explained (1785).

King or no King; or, Thoughts on the Escape of Lewis XVI and on Kingly Office addressed to the Society of 1789 (1791).

Lackington, James, *Memoirs of the First Forty-Five Years of the Life of James Lackington,* 2nd edn. (1792).

Lilly, William, *Monarchy or no Monarchy in England: Grebner his Prophecy concerning Charles Son of Charles* (1651).

Lowth, Robert, *A Short Introduction to English Grammar with Critical Notes* (1762).

—— *Lectures on the Sacred Poetry of the Hebrews,* trans. G. Gregory, 2 vols. (1787).

M'Culla, Vigors, *The Bank Note; or, Engraver Carved in Answer to Onesimus, the Ecclesiastical State Tinker* (1806).

Macklin, Thomas, *A Catalogue of the Fourth Exhibition of Pictures, printed for T. Macklin, by the Artists of Great Britain: Illustrative of British Poets and the Bible* (1791).

Macpherson, James, 'A Dissertation Concerning the Aera of Ossian', in *Ossian,* ii. 213–31.

—— 'A Dissertation Concerning the Poems of Ossian', in *Ossian,* ii. 234–80.

Mallet, P. H., *Northern Antiquities; or, A Description of the Manners, Customs, Religions, and Laws of the Ancient Danes and other Northern Nations* [trans. T. Percy], 2 vols. (1770).

Mason, William, *Works,* 4 vols. (1811).

Mathias, T. J., *The Pursuits of Literature: A Satirical Poem in Dialogue,* 3 parts, 3rd edn. (1797).

The Measures of the Ministry to Prevent a Revolution are the Certain Means of bringing it on (1794).

Milton, John, *The Poetical Works of John Milton with a Life of the Author by William Hayley*, 3 vols. (1794–7).
—— *Milton: Poetical Works* ed. Douglas Bush (Oxford, 1966).
Monthly Review (1749–1845).
Moser, Joseph, *Anecdotes of Richard Brothers, in the Years 1791 and 1792, with some Thoughts on Credulity* (1795).
Munn, R., *The Loyal Subject; or, Monarchy Defended and Republican Principles Exploded by the Word of God* (n.d.).
New Annual Register (1780–1826).
Newton, Isaac, *The Chronology of the Ancient Kingdoms Amended* (1728).
—— *Observations on the Prophecies of Daniel and St. John* (1733).
Observations on the Life and Character of Alfred the Great (1794).
Ossian, *Fragments of Ancient Popular Poetry Collected in the Highlands of Scotland*, trans. James Macpherson (Edinburgh, 1760).
—— *Temora, An Ancient Epic Poem in Eight Books, together with other Poems, composed by Ossian, the Son of Fingal*, trans. James Macpherson (1763).
—— *The Poems of Ossian*, trans. James Macpherson, rev. edn. 2 vols. (1773).
[Oulton, W. C.] George Horne, *Sound Argument Dictated by Common Sense*, 3rd edn. (Oxford, 1795).
Paine, Thomas, *The Complete Writings of Thomas Paine*, ed. P. S. Foner, 2 vols. (New York, 1945).
Paley, William, *Reasons for Contentment addressed to the Labouring Part of the British Public* (1793).
—— *Works*, ed. E. Paley, 7 vols. (1825).
Percy, Thomas, ed., *Reliques of Ancient English Poetry, consisting of Old Heroic Ballads, Songs and other Pieces of our Earlier Poets*, 3 vols. (1765).
Pigott, Charles, *A Political Dictionary, explaining the True Meaning of Words* (1795).
Place, Francis, *The Autobiography of Francis Place*, ed. Mary Thale (Cambridge, 1972).
Politics for the People; or, A Salmagundy for Swine, 2 vols., the 1st in 2 parts (1793–5).
Preston, Thomas, *The Life and Opinions of Thomas Preston, Patriot and Shoemaker* (1817).
Pretyman-Tomline, G., *A Charge delivered to the Clergy of the Diocese of Lincoln at the Triennial Visitation of that Diocese* (1794).
Price, Richard, *A Discourse on the Love of our Country, delivered on Nov.*

4, 1789, at the Meeting-House in the Old Jewry, to the Society for Commemorating the Revolution in Great Britain, 2nd edn. (1789).

Priestley, Joseph, Institutes of Natural and Revealed Religion, 2 vols., 2nd edn. (Birmingham, 1782).

—— An History of the Corruptions of Christianity, 2 vols. (Birmingham, 1782).

—— Letters to the Right Honourable Edmund Burke, occasioned by his Reflections on the Revolution in France (Birmingham, 1791).

—— Letters to Members of the New Jerusalem Church (1791).

—— A Sermon Preached at the Gravel Pit Meeting in Hackney, April 19, 1793; being the day Appointed for a General Fast (1794).

—— The Present State of Europe Compared with Antient Prophecies: A Sermon Preached at the Gravel Pit Meeting in Hackney, February 28, 1794; being the Day Appointed for a General Fast (1794).

—— An Answer to Mr. Paine's 'Age of Reason', being a Continuation of Letters to the Philosophes and Politicians of France, on the Subject of Religion and of the Letters to a Philosophical Unbeliever (1795).

The Prodigal, Huntington Unmasked, and the Doors of his Face opened, his Challenge accepted, the Prophet exposed, his Abominations unfolded, Translations dissected, and his Doctrine discovered and condemned (n.d. [1802?]).

A Prophecy of the French Revolution and the Downfall of Antichrist: Being Two Sermons Preached many Years ago by the late Rev. John Willison, Minister of the Gospel at Dundee and now Reprinted from the Original which may be seen at the Publishers (1793).

Prophetic Conjectures on the French Revolution and other Recent and Shortly Expected Events (Philadelphia, 1794).

Prophetical Extracts (1795 [?]).

Prophetical Passages concerning the Present Times in which the Person, Character, Mission, &c. &c of Richard Brothers is clearly Pointed at as the Elijah of the Present Day, the Bright Star to Guide the Hebrews &c (1795).

Reid, William Hamilton, The Rise and Dissolution of the Infidel Societies in this Metropolis: including the Origin of Modern Deism and Atheism, the Genius and Conduct of those Associations, their Lecture-Rooms, Field Meetings, and Deputations from the Publication of Paine's Age of Reason till the Present Period (1800).

Relly, James, Antichrist Resisted in a Reply to a Pamphlet Wrote by W. Mason (1761).

—— The Sadducee Detected and Refuted, in Remarks on the Works of Richard Coppin (1764).

—— Christian Liberty; or, The Liberty wherewith Christ hath made us Free (1775).

Ritson, Joseph, ed., A Select Collection of English Songs, 3 vols. (1783).

—— ed., Pieces of Ancient Popular Poetry from Authentic Manuscript and old Printed Copies (1791).

—— ed., Ancient Songs, from the Time of King Henry the Third to the Revolution, 2 vols. (1792).

—— ed., Robin Hood: A Collection of all the Ancient Poems Songs, and Ballads now Extant relative to that English Outlaw, 2 vols. (1795).

—— The Letters of Joseph Ritson [ed. J. Franks], 2 vols. (1833).

Rousseau, Jean-Jacques, A Discourse upon the Origin and Foundation of the Inequality of Mankind, English trans. (1761).

Saltmarsh, John, Free Grace; or, The Flowings of Christ's Blood Freely to Sinners, 11th edn. (1792), first published 1645.

—— Holy Discoveries and Flames (1811), first published 1640.

—— Sparkles of Glory; or, Some Beams of the Morning Star (1811), first published 1647.

Shuckford, Samuel, The Sacred and Prophane History of the World Connected, 2 vols. (1728–30).

Southcott, Joanna, Letters &c to the rev. Stanhope Bruce (1801).

[Southey, Robert], Letters from England by don Manuel Alvarez Esprella, 3 vols. (1807).

Spence, Thomas, A Letter from Ralph Hodge, to his Cousin Thomas Bull (n.d. [1795]).

—— The Political Works of Thomas Spence, ed. H. T. Dickinson (Newcastle upon Tyne, 1982).

—— Pig's Meat: The Selected Writings of Thomas Spence, Radical and Pioneer Land Reformer, ed. with an introduction by G. I. Gallop, Socialist Classics, 2 (Nottingham, 1982).

Stedman, John Gabriel, The Journal of John Gabriel Stedman, 1744–1797 Soldier and Author, ed. Stanbury Thompson (1962).

Stone Henge: A Poem (1792).

Stukeley, W., Stonehenge, a Temple Restored to the British Druids (1740).

—— Abury, a Temple of the British Druids, with some others described, wherein is a more Particular Account of the First Patriarchal Religion; and of the Peopling of the British Isles (1743).

Swedenborg, Emmanuel, A Treatise concerning Heaven and Hell, trans. W. Cookworthy and T. Hartley (1778).

Terry, Garnet, A Description accompanying an Hieroglyphical Print of Daniel's Great Image or Mystical Man (1793).

—— Onesimus [psed.], *Letters on Godly and Religious Subjects*, 2 vols., 2nd edn. (1808).

Thomas, Thomas, *Virtues of Hazel; or, The Blessings of Government* (1794).

Toland, John, *Letters to Serena* (1704).

—— *Pantheisticon; or, The Form of Celebrating the Socratic Society*, English trans. (1751).

—— *A New Edition of Toland's History of the Druids with an Abstract of his Life and Writings*, ed. R. Huddleston (Montrose, 1814).

Towers, J. L., *Illustrations of Prophecy, in the Course of which are Elucidated many Predictions . . . And which are Thought to Foretell, among other Great Events, A Revolution in France, Favourable to the Interests of Mankind*, 2 vols. (1796).

Trenchard, John, *Christianity not Mysterious; or, A Treatise Showing that there is Nothing in the GOSPEL contrary to Reason, nor above it* (1702).

—— *The Natural History of Religion* (1709).

Volney, C. F., *The Ruins; or, A Survey of the Revolutions of Empire*, English trans. (1792).

Warburton, William, *The Alliance between Church and State; or The Necessity and Equity of an Established Religion and a Test Law Demonstrated* (1736).

—— *The Divine Legation of Moses Demonstrated, on the Principles of a Religious Deist, from the Omission of the Doctrine of a Future State of Rewards and Punishment in the Jewish Dispensation*, 2 vols., the 2nd in 2 parts (1738–41).

Wedderburn, Robert, *Truth Self-Supported: A Refutation of Certain Doctrinal Errors generally adopted in the Christian Church* [c. 1802].

—— *Trial of the Rev. Robert Wedderburn for Blasphemy* (1820).

Wesley, John, *The Journal of the Rev. John Wesley A.M.*, ed. N. Curnock, 8 vols. (1909–16).

Wetherell, William, *An Additional Testimony in Favour of Richard Brothers with an Address to the People of the World, both Jews and Gentiles, relative to the New Canaan* (1795).

Whitchurch, S., *Another Witness!; or, Further Testimony in Favour of Richard Brothers with a Few Modest Hints to Modern Pharisees and Unbelievers* (1795).

Williams, Edward [Iolo Morganwg], *Poems: Lyric and Pastoral*, 2 vols. (1794).

Williams, Eliza, *The Prophecies of Brothers Confuted from Divine Authority* (1795).

Wilson, Walter, *The History and Antiquities of Dissenting Churches and meeting Houses in London, Westminster, and Soulhwark, including the Lives of their Ministers, from the Rise of Nonconformity to the Present Time*, 4 vols. (London, 1808–14).

Winstanley, Gerrard, *Works*, ed. George H. Sabine (Ithaca, NY, 1941).

Wollstonecraft, Mary, *A Vindication of the Rights of Men* (1790) facsimile edn., ed. E. L. Nicholes (Gainesville, Fla. 1960).

—— *A Vindication of the Rights of Woman* (1792) ed. with an introduction by Miriam Bindy Kramnick (Harmondsworth, 1975).

Wonderful Prophecies, being a Dissertation on the Existence, Nature, and Extent of the Prophetic Powers in the Human Mind, 4th edn. (1795).

A Word of Admonition to the Right Hon. William Pitt, in an Epistle to that Gentleman occasioned by the Prophecies of Brothers, Fellows etc and the Notable Expositions of the Scripture Prophecies by Brassy Halhed, MP (1795).

Wright, John, *A Revealed Knowledge of some Things that will Speedily be Fulfilled in the World, Communicated to a Number of Christians Brought together at Avignon, by the Power of the Spirit of God from all Nations, now Published by his Divine Command for the Good of all Men* (1794).

2. *Secondary Texts: Critical, Historical, and Theoretical*

Adlard, John, *The Sports of Cruelty: Fairies, Folk-Songs, Charms, and other Country Matters in the Work of William Blake* (1972).

Aers, David, 'William Blake and the Dialectics of Sex', *ELH* 44 (1977), 500–14.

Altick, Richard D., *The English Common Reader: A Social History of the Mass Reading Public, 1800–1900* (Chicago, 1957).

Ashraf, P. M., *The Life and Times of Thomas Spence* (Newcastle upon Tyne, 1983).

Atherton, H. M., 'The British Defend their Constitution in Political Cartoons and Literature', *Studies in Eighteenth-Century Culture*, American Society for Eighteenth-Century Studies, ed. H. C. Payne, 11 (1982), 3–31.

Baker, W. S., *William Sharp Engraver with a Descriptive Catalogue of his Works* (Philadelphia, 1875).

Bakhtin, Mikhail Mikhailovich, *Rabelais and his World*, trans. H. Iswolsky (Cambridge, Mass., 1968).

—— *The Dialogic Imagination: Four Essays*, ed. Michael Holquist, trans. Karyl Emerson and Holquist (Austin, Tex., 1981).

Barrell, John, *English Literature in History 1730–1780: 'An Equal, Wide Survey'* (1983).
—— *The Political Theory of Painting from Reynolds to Hazlitt: 'The Body of the Public'* (1987).
Beer, John, *Blake's Humanism* (Manchester, 1968).
—— *Blake's Visionary Universe* (Manchester, 1969).
Bentley, G. E., Jr., *Blake Records* (Oxford, 1969).
—— *Blake's Books* (Oxford, 1977).
—— 'The Great Illustrated-Book Publishers of the 1790s and William Blake', in *Editing Illustrated Books: Papers given at the Fifteenth Annual Conference on Editorial Problems, University of Toronto, 2–3 November 1979*, ed. William Blissett (New York and London, 1980), 57–96.
—— '"The Triumph of Owen": William Owen Pughe and Blake's "Ancient Britons"', *National Library of Wales Journal*, 24 (1985), 248–61.
—— *Blake Records Supplement* (Oxford, 1988).
Bindman, David, 'Blake's "Gothicized Imagination" and the History of England', in *William Blake: Essays in Honour of Sir Geoffrey Keynes*, ed. Morton D. Paley and Michael Phillips (Oxford, 1973), 29–49.
—— *William Blake: His Art and Times* (1982).
—— 'William Blake and Popular Religious Imagery', *Burlington Magazine*, 128 (Oct. 1986), 712–18.
—— *The Shadow of the Guillotine: Britain and the French Revolution*, with contributions by Aileen Dawson and Mark Jones (1989).
Bloom, Harold, *Blake's Apocalypse: A Study in Poetic Argument* (1963).
Boase, T. R., 'Illustrations of Shakespeare's Plays in the Seventeenth and Eighteenth Centuries', *Journal of the Warburg and Courtauld Institute*, 10 (1947), 83–108.
Bodleian Library, *Catalogue of the Printed Books and Manuscripts Bequeathed by Francis Douce, esq., to the Bodleian Library* (Oxford, 1840).
—— *The Douce Legacy: An Exhibition to Commemorate the 150th Anniversary of Francis Douce (1757–1834)* (Oxford, 1984).
Boulton, J. T., *The Language of Politics in the Age of Wilkes and Burke*, Studies in Political History (1963).
Bronowski, J., *William Blake and the Age of Revolution* (1972).
Bronson, B. H., *Joseph Ritson: Scholar at Arms*, 2 vols. (Berkeley, Calif., 1938).
Bruntjen, Sven H. A., *John Boydell, 1719–1804: A Study of Art Patronage and Publishing in Georgian London* (1985).

Burke, Peter, *Popular Culture in Early Modern Europe* (1978).

Butler, Marilyn, *Jane Austen and the War of Ideas* (Oxford, 1975)
—— *Romantics, Rebels and Reactionaries: English Literature and its Background 1760–1830* (Oxford, 1981).

—— ed., *Burke, Paine, Godwin, and the Revolution Controversy*, Cambridge English Prose Texts (Cambridge, 1984).

Cannon, Garland, 'The Construction of the European Image of the Orient: A Bicentenary Reappraisal of Sir William Jones as Poet and Translator', *Comparative Criticism*, 8 (1986), 167–88.

Cantor, P. A., *Creature and Creator: Myth-making and English Romanticism* (Cambridge, 1984).

Carr, Stephen Leo, 'Illuminated Printing: Toward a Logic of Difference', in *Unnam'd Forms: Blake and Textuality*, ed. Nelson Hilton and Thomas A. Vogler (Berkeley, Calif., 1986), 177–96.

Chard, Leslie F. II, 'Joseph Johnson: Father of the Book Trade', *Bulletin of the New York Public Library*, 79 (1975–6), 51–82.

Chase, Malcolm, *The People's Farm: English Radical Agrarianism 1775–1840* (Oxford, 1988).

Clarke, Michael, and Penny, Nicholas, eds., *The Arrogant Connoisseur: Richard Payne Knight 1751–1824* (Manchester, 1982).

Curtis, F. B., 'Blake and the Booksellers', *Blake Studies*, 6 (1975), 167–78.

Damon, S. Foster, *A Blake Dictionary: The Ideas and Symbols of William Blake* (Boston, 1965).

Derrida, Jacques, *Writing and Difference*, trans. Alan Bass (1978).

Dorson, R. M., *The British Folklorists: A History* (1968).

Dozier, R. R., *For King, Constitution, and Country: The English Loyalists and the French Revolution* (Lexington, Ky., 1983).

Eaves, Morris, 'Romantic Expressive Theory and Blake's Idea of the Audience', *PMLA* 95 (1980), 784–801.

—— *William Blake's Theory of Art* (Princeton, NJ, 1982).

Eliot, T. S., *The Sacred Wood: Essays on Poetry and Criticism*, 7th edn. (1980 reprint).

Erdman, David V., 'William Blake's Debt to Gillray', *Art Quarterly*, 12 (1949), 165–7.

—— 'Blake's Early Swedenborgianism: A Twentieth Century Legend', *Comparative Literature*, 5 (1953), 247–57.

—— 'William Blake's Debt to Joel Barlow', *American Literature*, 26 (1954–5), 94–8.

—— *Blake: Prophet Against Empire. A Poet's Interpretation of the History of his own Times*, 3rd rev. edn. (Princeton, NJ, 1977).

Essick, Robert N., 'Blake and the Traditions of Reproductive Engraving', *Blake Studies*, 5 (1972), 59–103.

—— *William Blake, Printmaker* (Princeton, NJ, 1980).

—— 'The Four Zoas: Intention and Production', *BIQ* 18 (1985), 216–20.

—— and Pearce, Donald, eds., *Blake in his Time* (Bloomington, Ind., and London, 1978).

Feldman, Burton, and Richardson, Robert D., *The Rise of Modern Mythology 1680–1860* (Bloomington, Ind., and London, 1972).

Ferber, Michael, *The Social Vision of William Blake* (Princeton, NJ, 1985).

Fisher, P. F., 'Blake and the Druids', *Journal of English and German Philology*, 58 (1959), 589–612.

—— *The Valley of Vision: Blake as Prophet and Revolutionary*, ed. Northrop Frye (Toronto, 1961).

Fox, Susan, 'The Female as Metaphor in William Blake's Poetry', *Critical Enquiry*, 3 (1977), 507–19.

Friedman, W. H., 'Some Commercial Aspects of the Boydell Shakespeare Gallery', *Journal of the Warburg and Courtauld Institutes*, 10 (1947), 88–109.

Frosch, T. R., *The Awakening of Albion: The Renovation of the Body in the Poetry of William Blake* (Ithaca, NY, 1974).

Frye, Northrop, *Fearful Symmetry: A Study of William Blake* (Princeton, NJ, 1947).

Garfinkle, N., 'Science and Religion in England, 1790–1800: The Critical Response to the Work of Erasmus Darwin', *Journal of the History of Ideas*, 16 (1955), 376–88.

Garrett, Clarke, *Respectable Folly: Millenarians and the French Revolution in France and England* (Baltimore and London, 1975).

Gaskill, Howard, '"Ossian" Macpherson: Towards a Rehabilitation', *Comparative Criticism*, 8 (1986), 113–46.

Glen, Heather, *Vision and Disenchantment: Blake's 'Songs' and Wordsworth's 'Lyrical Ballads'* (Cambridge, 1983).

Good, J. M., *Memoirs of the Life and Writings of the Reverend Alexander Geddes, Ll.d.* (1823).

Goodwin, Albert, *The Friends of Liberty: The English Democratic Movement in the Age of the French Revolution* (1979).

Harrison, J. F. C., *The Second Coming: Popular Millenarianism 1780–1850* (1979).

Haslewood, J., *Some Account of the Life and Publications of the late Joseph Ritson* (1824).

Hempton, David, *Methodism and Politics in British Society, 1750–1830* (1984).

Hill, Christopher, *The World Turned Upside Down: Radical Ideas during the English Revolution*, 2nd edn. (Harmondsworth, 1975).

Hilton, N., 'The Spectre of Darwin', Review of the Garland Facsimiles of the Poetry of Erasmus Darwin, *BIQ* 15 (1981), 37–48.

Hole, Robert, *Pulpits, Politics, and Public Order in England 1760–1832* (Cambridge, 1989).

Hone, J. Ann, *For the Cause of Truth: Radicalism in London, 1796–1821* (Oxford, 1982).

Hooper, Ebeneezer, *The Celebrated Coalheaver; or, Reminiscences of the Reverend William Huntington, S.S.* (1871).

—— *Facts, Letters, and Documents (Chiefly Unpublished) Concerning William Huntington, his Family and Friends* (1872).

Hopkins, James K., *A Woman to Deliver Her People: Joanna Southcott and English Millenarianism in an Era of Revolution* (Austin, Tex., 1982).

Howard, John, 'An Audience for *The Marriage of Heaven and Hell*', *Blake Studies*, 3 (1970), 19–52.

Huehns, Gertrude, *Antinomianism in English History, with Special Reference to the Period 1640–60* (1951).

Johnston, Arthur, 'William Blake and "the Ancient Britons"', *National Library of Wales Journal*, 22 (1981–2), 304–20.

Jones, Gareth Stedman, *Languages of Class: Studies in English Working Class History 1832–1982* (Cambridge, 1983).

King-Hele, Desmond, *Erasmus Darwin* (1963).

—— *Doctor of Revolution: The Life and Genius of Erasmus Darwin* (1977).

—— *Erasmus Darwin and the Romantic Poets* (1986).

Klancher, Jon P., *The Making of English Reading Audiences, 1790–1832* (Madison, Wis., 1987).

Knowles, John, *The Life and Writings of Henry Fuseli*, 3 vols. (1831).

Kowle, C. P., 'Plate iii and the Meaning of *Europe*', *Blake Studies*, 8 (1978), 89–99.

Kumbier, William, 'Blake's Epic Meter', *Studies in Romanticism*, 17 (1978), 163–92.

Larrissy, Edward, *William Blake*, Rereading Literature (Oxford, 1985).

Leonard, D. C., 'Erasmus Darwin and William Blake', *Eighteenth-Century Life*, 4 (1978), 79–81.

Lévi-Strauss, Claude, *The Savage Mind*, The Nature of Human Society, 2nd edn. (1972).

Liu, Alan, *Wordsworth: The Sense of History* (Stanford, Calif., 1989).

Locke, Don, *A Fantasy of Reason, the Life and Thought of William Godwin* (1980).

McCalman, Iain, *Radical Underworld: Prophets, Revolutionaries and Pornographers in London, 1795–1840* (Cambridge, 1988).

McGann, Jerome, J., *The Beauty of Inflections: Literary Investigations in Historical Method and Theory* (Oxford, 1985).

—— *Social Values and Poetic Acts: The Historical Judgement of Literary Work* (Cambridge, Mass., 1988).

McNeil, Maureen, *Under the Banner of Science: Erasmus Darwin and his Age* (Manchester, 1987).

Mann, Paul, 'Apocalypse and Recuperation: Blake and the Maw of Commerce', *ELH* 52 (1985), 1–32.

—— 'The Final State of *The Four Zoas*', *BIQ* 18 (1985), 204–9.

Manuel, F. E., *The Eighteenth Century Confronts the Gods* (Cambridge, Mass., 1959).

Marks, Mollyanne, 'Structure and Irony in Blake's *The Book of Urizen*', *Studies in English Literature 1500–1900*, 15 (1975), 579–91.

Matthews, R., *English Messiahs: Studies of Six English Religious Pretenders 1656–1927* (1936).

Mee, Jon, 'The Radical Enthusiasm of Blake's *The Marriage of Heaven and Hell*', *British Journal for Eighteenth-Century Studies*, 14 (1991), 51–60.

Messman, Frank J., *Richard Payne Knight: The Twilight of Virtuosity*, Studies in English Literature, 89 (The Hague, 1974).

Mitchell, W. J. T., *Blake's Composite Art: A Study of the Illuminated Poetry* (Princeton, NJ, 1978).

Morgan, Prys, *Iolo Morganwg*, Writers of Wales (Cardiff, 1975).

—— 'From a View to a Death: The Hunt for the Welsh Past in the Romantic Period', in *The Invention of Tradition*, Past and Present Publications, ed. E. Hobsbawm and T. Ranger (Cambridge, 1983), 43–100.

Morton, A. L., *The English Utopia* (1952).

—— *The Everlasting Gospel: A Study in the Sources of William Blake* (1958).

—— *The Matter of Britain: Essays in a Living Culture* (1966).

—— *The World of the Ranters: Religious Radicalism in the English Revolution* (1970).

Oliver, W. H., *Prophets and Millennialists: The Uses of Biblical Prophecy in England from the 1790s to the 1840s* (Oxford and Auckland, 1978).

Ostriker, Alicia, *Vision and Verse in William Blake* (Madison, Wis., 1965).

Owen, A. L., *The Famous Druids: A Survey of Three Centuries of English Literature on the Druids* (Oxford, 1962).

Paley, Morton D., *Energy and Imagination: A Study of the Development of Blake's Thought* (Oxford, 1970).

—— 'William Blake, the Prince of the Hebrews, and the Woman Clothed with the Sun', in *William Blake: Essays in Honour of Sir Geoffrey Keynes*, ed. Paley and Michael Phillips (Oxford, 1973), 260–93.

—— '"Wonderful Originals"—Blake and Ancient Sculpture', in *Blake in his Time*, ed. Essick and Pearce, 170–97.

—— '"A New Heaven is Begun": William Blake and Swedenborgianism', *BIQ* 13 (1979), 64–90.

Paulson, Ronald, *Representations of Revolution (1789–1820)* (New Haven, Conn., and London, 1983).

Philp, Mark, *Godwin's Political Justice* (1986).

—— *Paine*, Past Masters (Oxford, 1989).

Pocock, J. G. A., *The Machiavellian Moment: Florentine Political Thought and the Atlantic Republican Tradition* (Princeton, NJ, 1975).

—— *Virtue, Commerce, and History: Essays on Political Thought and History, chiefly in the Eighteenth Century*, Ideas in Context (Cambridge, 1985).

Pointon, M. R., *Milton and English Art* (Manchester, 1970).

Punter, David, 'Blake: Social Relations of Poetic Form', *Literature and History*, 8 (1982), 182–205.

Reventlow, H. G., *The Authority of the Bible and the Rise of the Modern World*, trans. J. Bowden (1984).

Rigby, Brian, 'Volney's Rationalist Apocalypse: "Les Ruines ou Meditations sur les Revolutions des Empires"', in *1789 Reading Writing Revolution: Proceedings of the Essex Conference on the Sociology of Literature July 1981*, ed. F. Barker *et al.* (Colchester, 1982).

Robbins, Caroline, *The Eighteenth-Century Commonwealthman: Studies in the Development and Circumstances of English Liberal Thought from the Restoration of Charles II until the War of the Thirteen Colonies* (Cambridge, Mass., 1959).

Robinson, J. W., 'Regency Radicalism and Antiquarianism: William Hone's *Ancient Mysteries Described* (1823)', *Leeds Studies in English*, NS 10 (1978), 121–44.

Roe, Albert S., '"The Thunder of Egypt": Israel deliver'd from Egypt is Art deliver'd from Nature & Imitation', in *Essays for S. Foster Damon*, ed. A. H. Rosenfeld (Providence, 1969), 158–95.

Roe, Nicholas, *Wordsworth and Coleridge: The Radical Years* (Oxford, 1988).

Roper, Derek, *Reviewing Before the 'Edinburgh' 1788–1802* (1978).

Roston, Murray, *Poet and Prophet: The Bible and the Growth of Romanticism* (1965).

Rubel, M. M., *Savage and Barbarian: Historical Attitudes in the Criticism of Homer and Ossian in Britain, 1760–1800* (Amsterdam, New York, Oxford, 1978).

St Clair, William, *The Godwins and the Shelleys: The Biography of a Family* (1989).

Schorer, Mark, *William Blake: The Politics of Vision* (New York, 1946).

Scrivener, Michael, 'A Swedenborgian Visionary and *The Marriage of Heaven and Hell*', *BIQ* 21 (1987–8), 102–4.

Shaffer, E. S., *'Kubla Khan' and 'The Fall of Jerusalem': The Mythological School in Bible Criticism and Secular Literature 1770–1880* (Cambridge, 1975).

Smith, Olivia, *The Politics of Language 1791–1819* (Oxford, 1984).

Stafford, Fiona, *The Sublime Savage: James Macpherson and the Poems of Ossian* (Edinburgh, 1988).

Stafford, William, *Socialism, Radicalism, and Nostalgia: Social Criticism in Britain, 1775–1830* (Cambridge, 1987).

Tannenbaum, Leslie, *Biblical Tradition in Blake's Early Prophecies: The Great Code of Art* (Princeton, NJ, 1984).

Tayler, Irene, *Blake's Illustrations to the Poems of Gray* (Princeton, NJ, 1971).

Taylor, R., *The Political Prophecy in England* (New York, 1911).

Thomas, Keith, *Religion and the Decline of Magic: Studies in Popular Beliefs in Sixteenth and Seventeenth-Century England* (1971).

Thompson, E. P., 'History from Below', *TLS* (1966), 279–80.

—— *The Making of the English Working Class*, 2nd rev. edn. (Harmondsworth, 1968).

—— 'Anthropology and the Discipline of the Historical Context', *Midland History*, 1 (1972), 41–55.

—— 'Patrician Society, Plebian Culture', *Journal of Social History*, 7 (1974), 382–405.

—— 'The Crime of Anonymity', in *Albion's Fatal Tree: Crime and Society in Eighteenth-Century England*, ed. Douglas Hay and others (1975), 255–344.

Tolley, M., '*Europe*: "To those ychain'd in sleep"', in *Blake's Visionary Forms Dramatic*, ed. David V. Erdman and John E. Grant (Princeton, NJ, 1970) 115–45.

Tucker, S., *Enthusiasm: A Study in Semantic Change* (Cambridge, 1972).

—— 'Biblical Translation in the Eighteenth Century', *Essays and Studies* (1972), 106–20.

Tyson, G. P., *Joseph Johnson: A Liberal Publisher* (Iowa City, Iowa, 1979).

Vincent, David, *Literacy and Popular Culture: England 1750–1914* (Cambridge, 1989).

Viscomi, Joseph, 'The Myth of Commissioned Illuminated Books: George Romney, Isaac D'Israeli, and "ONE HUNDRED AND SIXTY designs . . . of Blake's" ', *BIQ* 23 (1989), 48–74.

Watkins, Owen C., *The Puritan Experience* (1972).

Whitley, W. T., *The Baptists of London 1612–1928: Their Fellowship, their Expansion with Notes on their 850 Churches* (1928).

Williams, Raymond, *Culture and Society 1780–1950* (1958).

Wilson, Mona, *The Life of William Blake*, ed. Geoffrey Keynes (Oxford, 1971).

Wittreich, Joseph Antony, Jr., 'Painted Prophecies: The Tradition of Blake's Illuminated Books', in *Blake in his Time*, ed. Essick and Pearce, pp. 101–15.

Worrall, David, 'William Blake and Erasmus Darwin's *Botanic Garden*', *Bulletin of the New York Public Library*, 78 (1974–5), 397–417.

Wright, Thomas, *The Life of William Huntington, S.S.* (1909).

Index